teens stress life
violence
school
anxiety
change

The Age of

OUTRAGE:

Strategies for Parents and Educators

Lisa Wright, MA, MEd
High School Counselor

Parents and fellow educators--

It's time to talk, to have an open, honest discussion about what's going on in your teen's world and in our world, and it's time for real change.

We cannot wait.

We cannot let outrage, aggression, or violence define our world and your teen's future. Nor can we take the path of least resistance.

Educators need your help, and you need our help, too.

Together we have the power to create real change in teens' lives and in the world around us. Together. A team.

I urge you to set aside any preconceived beliefs or memories about "the way it used to be" and to read this book fully, with open hearts and clear minds.

We are at a crossroads, and we are better together.

Let's do this.

It all starts with an open, honest conversation.

Table of Contents

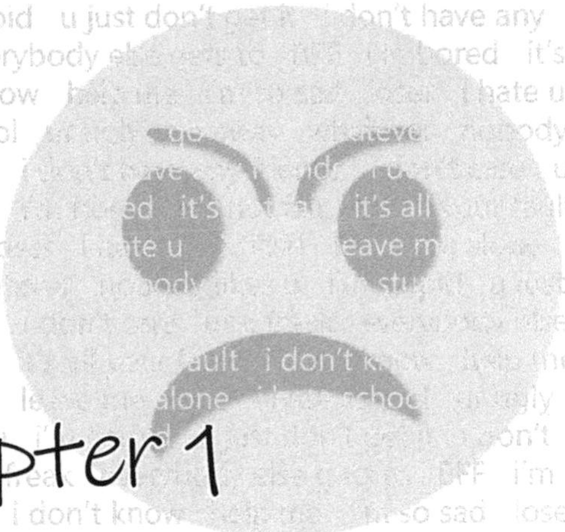

Chapter 1

Introduction

Chapter 1

Introduction

Columbine. Sandy Hook. Parkland. Aurora. Sutherland Springs. Santa Fe. Schools. Movie theaters. Workplaces. Parades. Concerts. Churches. Synagogues. Mosques. Social media. Apps. 24-hour news. Movie violence. Video game violence. Internet. Streaming live. Crime. Apathy. Hate. Indifference. Outrage. Intolerance. Disrespect. He said. She said. Suicide. Depression. Hopelessness. Fear of missing out. Self-hate. Self-medication. Peer pressure. Perfection. Bullying. Self-respect. Self-doubt. Hazing. Grades. GPA. No child left behind. Disengagement. I'm right. No, I'm right. Me. Now.

Parents and fellow educators, this is life today. We can't hide from it, and instead of wringing our hands and shaking our heads over how terrible everything is, it's time for us to do something about it. Our world today is filled with serious stressors at every turn, and while it is true that there have always been stressors in the lives of humans, it seems that today's world is different. Today's world can be such a brash, chaotic, "noisy" place filled with so much in-your-face information, activity, and 24-7 frenetic energy that as adults (never mind kids) we struggle to stop down, take a moment, and just be. In the past, moving "away from the city" might have slowed life down and helped solve the issue of being exposed to the 24-7 lifestyle, but with the advent of first the internet and then social media, we all became instantly exposed to stress at all hours of the day, no matter where we live. For today's teens, this is all they know.

Today's kids only know this world, and the average kid does not recognize that the 24-hour "on" lifestyle can have a pretty serious downside. While kids of yesterday (well, yesteryear) whiled away the summers riding bikes barefooted from dawn to dusk and came home at night to watch *Little House on the Prairie* or *Love Boat* with their families, kids today have endless options of how to spend their time, many of which are electronic and, compared to previous generations, hidden away from the watchful eyes of parents. (In fact, as a side note to give us a frame of reference, according to Merriam-Webster, the term "24-7" was first used in print in 1985. Think of how much life has changed, and sped up, since that year.)

We all know too much of a good thing can be bad, and the loss of some of life's simplicity is evident in malls and restaurants everywhere as kids and adults sit engrossed in their phones. Together but alone. Televisions and the internet blare the latest outrage, and we are all exposed. Some modern kids may never even get on a bike, and for most, the days of roaming free all summer long are long gone from a safety standpoint (real or perceived). Life's stressors wear on adults who have had more time to develop the skills to weather life's challenges, but life's stressors can have a profound impact on youth whose minds are still developing. Who or what will be next? Why is there so much hate and anger everywhere? Why are people so aggressive towards each other? Why are so many people turning to violence as the answer? What happened to simple kindness?

Some will say that things really haven't changed all that much. Yes— there were "bad things" that kids were exposed to in earlier generations. The 60s, for example, were defined, in part, by drugs, shootings, and violence, yet people persisted. From an educator's point of view, however, today's generation of kids are exposed to so much more at earlier ages than previous generations, and it shows in the schools of today. Adults in today's world get overwhelmed by all that we see, hear, and experience, and our kids are not immune to it. No matter how hard adults might try to shield kids from modern day stressors, the truth is that our kids are on the front line of it all, and it is their "normal." The very act of adults shielding kids from stress can make things worse for kids in the long run (more on that in a later chapter), so what can a parent do?

While this book will address many areas of a teen's life, one goal of this book is to address school shootings and what we can all do to help prevent them. School (and other similar) shootings are the ultimate senseless act, and educators, parents, and society want nothing more than for them to stop. A goal of this book and of this educator is to begin a serious, personal conversation about what parents, educators, and society can proactively do to help prevent future school shootings. We will discuss school shootings in depth in this book, but in its simplest form, there is no simple fix for school shootings. School shootings and other school violence will not stop because "someone else" does something about it. Parents and people who touch the lives of kids are at the very root of what it will take to stop future school shootings. Think of it as the quintessential drop in the water/ripple effect. Each parent's single drop of change and influence will eventually create

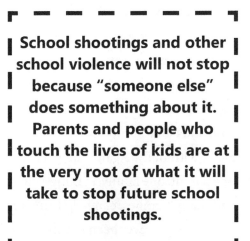

School shootings and other school violence will not stop because "someone else" does something about it. Parents and people who touch the lives of kids are at the very root of what it will take to stop future school shootings.

a much larger, much-needed change in the complex landscape of school shootings and other violence. Change can, and must, happen, and educators are right there with you.

While we will talk about school shootings, this book is also about the ugly side of modern life—specifically, stressors and habits that can contribute to hateful or violent behavior as an outcome. School shootings are among the most visible violent acts, but modern humans are acting out towards other humans and even themselves in many hateful, violent ways, and we have to the power to make a change. One thing I know for sure is that doing nothing will change nothing, and something must change. We cannot be ok with taking the path of least resistance, of not getting involved, and we cannot sit passively hoping for change or hoping someone else will do "it," whatever "it" is. Change must be actively initiated, and there must be follow-through. While it is very difficult, to put it mildly, to predict the next school shooting or other senseless act of violence, all hope is not lost. It cannot be. Part of reality is that no one can predict what is next no matter how hard they work and how much they monitor. But it is time for change. Real change made by real people who love their kids. We cannot passively sit back and hope that things will change on their own. Rather, we must all take action to create our own change.

You may be wondering what you as an individual can do to take action in a world filled with such BIG issues that you seemingly have no control over and create positive change that impacts your family directly. This book aims to focus on real-world issues affecting the daily lives of kids on which you can have a direct, immediate, positive impact and, as a result, can help your kids and family navigate the even bigger real-world issues we are all faced with daily. Again, the goal is a ripple effect—the ripple effect of just one parent, one family, making a change, that, when applied to many parents and many families, can help bring real, positive, change to our world.

Have you ever been to a meeting—work meeting, neighborhood HOA, PTA or booster club—any type of meeting in which the discussion was aimed at bringing about some type of change—and when you left the meeting, you knew in your heart that no real change was going to come about? Not because the people in the meeting didn't want the change or didn't truly care—they really, genuinely want the change. Rather, no change would come because the meeting skimmed over or ignored the real, underlying issues that need to be addressed in order for real change to occur. This concept can be applied to "small" issues (compared to solving world hunger or achieving world peace) or "big" issues (solving world hunger or achieving world peace). Typically, this lack of real action occurs because in reality, the issues people are earnestly trying to solve are so big, overwhelming, and riddled with elements we cannot control, that people just do the best they can do, which leads to a surface level "fixing" of the issue at hand. This book does not promise to immediately solve all of the modern world's problems, but it does aim to take a "real talk" look at a range of issues facing our kids today from an educator's perspective and give parents and fellow educators strategies they can use to work with their kids to improve their own worlds. If we all work together on this, anything is possible.

So why write this book? I am a long-time educator who sees the effect of stressors on kids and their parents on a daily basis, but I have also witnessed how the stressors and kids themselves have evolved over the years. My perspective is unique in that I am a GenXer, and my career in education began in 1991 right out of college just before cell phones and the internet came into common use (and before teachers had a computer in their classroom) and has spanned to the current IGen generation, or those students who, according to psychologist Jean Twenge, were born in 1995 and later, grew up with cell phones, had an Instagram page before they started high school, and do not remember a time before the internet (Twenge, 2017, p. 59). I have personally witnessed the change in students over the generations between Gen X and the current IGens, and I am concerned, like everyone else, about the current state of education and students' coping skills when it comes to dealing with life.

I wrote this book because I am a "doer" who prefers taking action. I am by nature impatient and cannot, will not, wait for someone else to step up and take a stand. When I myself am faced with the overwhelming stress that is part of all of our lives in the modern world, I prefer to be able to take action and DO SOMETHING. I strongly believe that while we may not be able to stop all of the violent, horrible events happening in the world around us, we can and must be proactive with kids to help them navigate our frenetic world. Too much of what is currently happening in response to violent events is reactive and hand-wringing. All hope is not lost, but it is time for active change, and that change begins with you and your family.

This book is not meant to be a perfect, step-by-step how-to guide about parenting, educating, and working with teens in the modern world. Life is complicated, people are complicated, and the state of our modern world is very complicated. But we must try to make a change, and that change starts within you, the parent, and within your kids, as well as within the educational system and society. While most of this book will seem aimed at parents of teenagers and educators or other people who work with teenagers, the information in this book is useful for parents of and those who work with pre-teens and younger children who will, eventually, become teens themselves and who may already struggle with some of the issues we will discuss in the following chapters.

A central goal of this book is to take an honest look at real issues teens face and begin an open discussion between parents and educators about what we can do to help our teens and each other. By working together, we can begin to reverse the current trend (in schools and in the real world) that violence, aggression, anger, and murder are the answers to solving problems. This book takes a close look at how people make decisions when faced with stress, failure, anger, disappointment and other problems/difficult emotions

> **By working together, we can begin to change the current trend (in schools and in the real world) that violence, aggression, anger, and murder are the answers to solving problems.**

in order to "deal with the problem." This book is about acknowledging that we have more control and power to help than we may realize, and by addressing the areas we can control and where we can help, we can create change that starts right now.

Before we begin, I want to acknowledge that this is not a book based solely on academic research, although academic research exists for many of the topics I am going to cover (pro and con, I am certain) and has been included throughout the book. Rather than write purely based on research studies, I have written from my heart and from my own experiences, which means I likely have my own biases based on these experiences. I want to acknowledge that from the beginning. I do not claim to have all the answers; I do not think anyone can claim that, with or without research. But I do believe that from my extensive experience in education and working with people, I have information and observations that could help someone, somewhere navigate this complicated world in which we, and our kids, live today.

Many chapters in this book do contain research, and I have included a bibliography of materials including research and other articles, blog posts, videos, and other sources that tie into the topics we cover in this book (some that I have referenced in this book, as well as additional sources). While my bibliography is extensive, there is certainly more research out there than the list I have provided, and I am also certain that one can find research to support or discredit any thought or belief one might have. To keep it simple, I write from the heart and interject research, and you, the parent, must decide what works for you, your kids, and your family. The language in this book is intentionally conversational, because I want it to feel the same as if we were sitting in my office at school having a conversation over what we should do to help address the problem.

To help the reader understand the context from which I am writing, I want to tell you about my background, which may be very similar to or very different from yours. I am currently a public high school counselor in Texas who has worked in education for the past 27 years. Almost everything I will write in this book is based on my personal experiences and observations during my 20 years of teaching through my current eighth year as an urban high school counselor. To provide further context on my background (because virtually everything I say in this book is based on this specific experience), my background includes the following, all of which is from public schools (not private):

Counseling Experience

*Currently in my 8th year of high school counseling.

*Of those 8 years of high school counseling, one was in a suburban high school; currently in my 7th year in a large urban high school.

*Completed counseling internships at middle school and high school level.

*Completed both a state alternative certification program and a regular certification program through a college master's degree program. Both culminated in the same state counseling certification test.

Teaching Experience

*10 years of high school teaching (4 different high schools and districts).

*10 years of middle school teaching (3 different middle schools and districts).

*Teaching experience is from a variety of schools and districts; most at large schools (defined as having more than one high school in the district).

*Teaching experience is from districts that were suburban, semi-urban, and urban.

*Teaching experience is from both "core" and elective classes. I mention this because some educators who have taught only one area or the other may believe a teacher's experience is "different" in the other area. For example, core classes such as English, science, math, or social studies may be required for students to take to graduate and/or may have state testing mandates and expectations that go with the class. Electives may or may not be required to graduate depending on the state graduation plan and may be classes that students choose to take, which may impact a student's motivation in the class.

Specific Teaching Experience

*High school English I and II (on level and honors).

*High school journalism, yearbook, newspaper, psychology, and sociology.

*7th and 8th grade English language arts.

*7th and 8th grade journalism, yearbook, newspaper.

*High school and middle school cheer coach for the first 10 years of my career; high school student council sponsor; middle school UIL (University Interscholastic League) academic contest coach.

Other Education Notes and Background Information

I have worked at Title I schools for much of my educational career. Title I is defined by the U.S. Department of Education as:

> Title I, Part A (Title I) of the Elementary and Secondary Education Act, as amended (ESEA) provides financial assistance to local educational agencies (LEAs) and schools with high numbers or high percentages of children from low-income families to help ensure that all children meet challenging state academic standards. Federal funds are currently allocated through four statutory formulas that are based primarily on census poverty estimates and the cost of education in each state (Program Description).

I have a master's degree in counseling and a master's degree in political science and criminal justice, but I have not been a very political person over the course of my life. It is important that I mention my lack of political vigor (political apathy) as we will briefly discuss politics to a minimal extent later in this book, and it is important to state that this book is not written from a political stance, but rather from an educator's stance. Full disclosure—I wanted to attend law school but could not afford to have no job and attend law school full time, so a master's degree in political science and criminal justice was an attainable goal in a similar area that I could achieve while still working full-time as an educator.

I have a bachelor's degree in English and psychology. I have always been interested in why people do what they do, say what they say, and choose the actions they choose, so psychology was a natural choice for a major.

I am not a licensed professional counselor (LPC), which means my credentials are limited to school counseling vs running my own professional counseling business.

On a side note, I am married to a high school band director (part of the reason we have worked in a variety of schools and have moved around), and we do not have kids of our own (not by choice, but that's another book). I mention being childless because I acknowledge that my perspective may be different from those who do have kids of their own in that my experience is purely based on working with and educating kids, not parenting them at home.

To provide one final point of context, I am a first-generation high school graduate and a first-generation college attendee/graduate. I was born and grew up in a small town in Texas in which I knew almost all my friends/peers for my entire life. I attended and graduated from my small-town public school in Texas. At the time, it was (and still is) a one-high-school town, and when I grew up, it had one elementary school, one intermediate school, and one junior high school. My years in school were very different from modern kids' experiences in school, and your kids' school experiences are likely very different from your own school experiences.

Now that you have a general picture of who I am and where my perspective is coming from, let's begin.

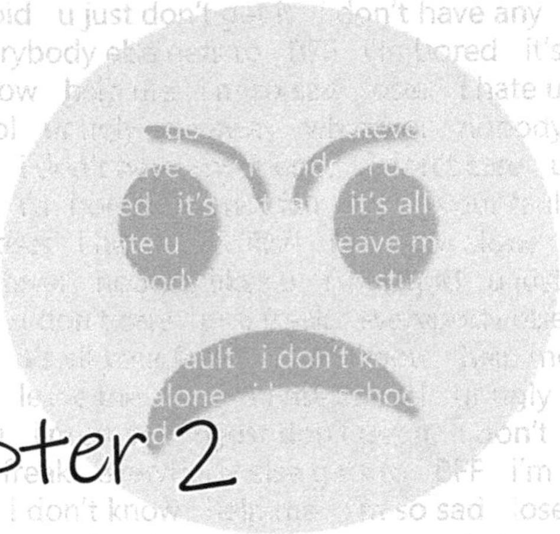

Chapter 2

Brain Development

Chapter 2

Brain Development

To give parents and educators background for this book, it is helpful to have a brief discussion about how children's brains develop. It is well-documented that children's brains are not fully developed until they reach their mid-20s. The Facts for Families information below from the American Academy of Child & Adolescent Psychiatry (2016) gives an excellent explanation of teen brain development and decision-making:

> Many parents do not understand why their teenagers occasionally behave in an impulsive, irrational, or dangerous way. At times, it seems like teens don't think things through or fully consider the consequences of their actions. Adolescents differ from adults in the way they behave, solve problems, and make decisions. There is a biological explanation for this difference. Studies have shown that brains continue to mature and develop throughout childhood and adolescence and well into early adulthood (para. 1).
>
> Scientists have identified a specific region of the brain called the **amygdala** that is responsible for immediate reactions including fear and aggressive behavior. This region develops early. However,

*the **frontal cortex**, the area of the brain that controls reasoning and helps us think before we act, develops later. This part of the brain is still changing and maturing well into adulthood (para. 2).*

Other changes in the brain during adolescence include a rapid increase in the connections between the brain cells and making the brain pathways more effective. Nerve cells develop myelin, an insulating layer that helps cells communicate. All these changes are essential for the development of coordinated thought, action, and behavior (para. 3).

So what does this mean? It means that teens are impulsive and don't think things through the same way adults do. When you are thinking to yourself (as an adult) "what were you thinking?!" when your teen makes a seemingly illogical choice or decision, the answer is that he/she wasn't really thinking. At least not the way you might make a decision as an adult with a fully formed brain. According to Facts for Families (2016):

Teens' actions are guided more by the emotional and reactive amygdala and less by the thoughtful, logical frontal cortex. Research has also shown that exposure to drugs and alcohol during the teen years can change or delay these developments (para. 4).

*...based on the stage of their brain development, adolescents are **more likely to** act on impulse, misread or misinterpret social cues and emotions, get into accidents of all kinds, get involved in fights, and engage in dangerous or risky behavior. Adolescents are **less likely to** think before they act, pause to consider the consequences of their actions, or change their dangerous or inappropriate behaviors (Changing Brains Mean that Adolescents Act Differently From Adults section).*

Facts for Families (2016) confirms that all is not lost when it comes to the teen brain, however:

These brain differences don't mean that young people can't make good decisions or tell the difference between right and wrong. It also doesn't mean that they shouldn't be held responsible for their actions. However, an awareness of these differences can help parents, teachers, advocates, and policy makers understand, anticipate, and manage the behavior of adolescents (para. 5).

Other experts agree. According to Arain, Haque, Johal, Mathur, Nel, Rais, Sandhu and Sharma (2013):

...evidence suggests that the brain remains in its active state of maturation during adolescence. Such evidence supports the hypothesis that the adolescent brain is structurally and functionally vulnerable to environmental stress, risky behavior, drug addiction, impaired driving, and unprotected sex. Computed tomography and MRI studies also provide evidence in support of this hypothesis. Brain maturation occurs during adolescence due to a surge in the synthesis of sex hormones implicated in puberty including estrogen, progesterone, and testosterone.

...Sex hormones also significantly influence food intake and sleep requirements during puberty. In addition to dramatic changes in secondary sex characteristics, sex hormones may also influence the learning, intelligence, memory, and behavior of adolescents.

...The development and maturation of the prefrontal cortex occurs primarily during adolescence and is fully accomplished at the age of 25 years. The development of the prefrontal cortex is very important for complex behavioral performance, as this region of the brain helps accomplish executive brain functions (pp. 458-459).

25: The age by which most brains are fully developed. Just think of the major life decisions people make well before the age of 25—marriages, choosing college majors and/or careers—the list goes on. By the way, Arain, et al. (2013) include in their work a diagram of examples of "executive brain function" (as mentioned above), which do not effectively happen until the brain fully matures at the age of 25: inhibiting inappropriate behavior and initiating appropriate behavior, foreseeing and weighing possible consequences of behavior, modulation of intense emotions, and impulse control and delaying gratification, among other very significant brain functions (Fig. 3, p. 453). Think back to your own middle/high school/early post high school years, and I'll bet every one of you can think of at least one very bad (or at least very impulsive) decision you made before the age of 25. I definitely know I can!

When parents come to my office to discuss any variety of concerns about their child, I very often try to remind them that their children do not make decisions the same way as we do as adults, not to excuse their behavior, but to provide context to parents so they know that no matter how egregious the student's actions or decisions have been, they are teens, and they are making decisions like a teen with a teen brain. It only seems obvious to us as seasoned adults what the better decision would have been because we are adults whose brains have fully developed, and we are old enough to have developed some level of wisdom through our own lives and experiences. And together we try to navigate that child through high school.

> ...children do not make decisions the same way as we do as adults... no matter how egregious the student's actions or decisions have been, they are teens, and they are making decisions like a teen with a teen brain.

As we continue throughout this book, it will be important to keep children's brain development in mind as we look at the issues they face and that we all face when it comes to school violence and other types of aggressive and/or risky behaviors that teens engage in. Now that we have had a basic discussion of brain development, let's move on.

Chapter 3

Control, Worldview & Self-Responsibility: How Our Beliefs Impact Our Actions

Chapter 3

Control, Worldview & Self-Responsibility: How Our Beliefs Impact Our Actions

Before we can discuss what to do to help our kids (and even ourselves), we must look at how our brains work in relation to how we see the world. If you have been on social media or even watched television in the last few years, you have seen the viral stories that are passed around because of their entertainment value, but they tell a bigger story that relates to this book. February 2015—The Dress. Was it black and blue or white and gold? May 2018—Yanny or Laurel. Did you hear Yanny in the audio clip? Laurel? Both? March 2015—an audio clip with high-pitched frequencies that only "young people" (emphasis added for effect) can hear. These are simple, entertaining examples, but we could go further and list any number of controversial stories from the news and know that we do not all see events in the world the same. Even something as simple as a conversation at work can be construed as many ways as there are people involved in the conversation. Life is complicated, and today's world seems, according to my life experiences and worldview, more complicated than ever, and it is these complications that lead to many of the stressors that we all live with every day.

Each individual's point of view is like a fingerprint—we all have them, but they are all slightly different, which is what makes us unique. The same is true with how people view life and their experiences in life, which is what can lead to complications in relationships and interactions with other people. Many people do not consider that their view of reality is actually their *perception of reality*, and that the next person has an equally strong yet very different perception of reality about the same issue or situation. These varying perceptions of reality are why people can vehemently disagree on so many things in life that, to each individual person, seem so obvious (and right). Given any situation in life, people will have their own unique "take" on it based on their own **worldview**, or the individual way we all view our own "worlds," or situations.

According to a *Psychology Today* blog post, DeGraff (2017) says "Your worldview is your greatest strength, but also your greatest weakness" (title section). DeGraff continues:

A worldview is more than a type or a style. It's a collection of deeply held beliefs about how we interpret and experience the world. A dominant worldview is a comprehensive conception of the world from a specific standpoint. We derive these views from our personal experiences as well as the cultures in which we are socialized, for we are neither self-contained nor self-created. We exist as part of a larger community and system. Our dominant worldview may change over time as we experience new situations and become more self-aware of our own inclinations (para. 1).

In revealing your greatest strength, your dominant world-view also reveals your greatest weakness. Furthermore, it considers how each kind of thinker and leader interacts with others, so you can determine the other people you need to surround yourself with most (para. 2).

Just as kids' brain function is developing and evolving, so is their worldview. As kids are growing up, their worldviews are growing with them and are dependent on the individual life experiences they have had. In the bigger picture, when we combine all people together with their individual worldviews, such as students in a high school, it is easy to see where the stresses and stressors come from based solely on each student's individual worldview. Just as each adult does in the "real world," each individual student genuinely believes his/her perception is the accurate, correct one, and for each individual person, it *is* accurate (for him/her). But the student standing next to him/her may have a completely different opinion of the exact same scenario depending on his/her own worldview that he/she genuinely believes. Our individual worldviews are essentially "filters" or "lenses" through which we view, evaluate, and interpret everything we see and experience. It is these differing worldviews, different *perceptions* of reality, that lead to conflict in the real world among adults and in high schools among teens. That conflict can mean hateful words via text or social media, or in-person arguments or fights, or worse.

Differing worldviews have been around since the dawn of time, but in our current age of instant outrage and the actions humans are taking when they are outraged or feel "wronged" in some way, it is critical that we work together as educators, parents, and a society to help our kids navigate and understand the limitations of all of our opinions, especially in terms of being "right." Often,

> **...we must find ways to meet in the middle, agree to disagree, respect others' opinions even if we don't agree with them, and to find a way to get along.**

everyone is "right," even if the opinions are polar opposites. It is easy to see that for mass chaos to not break out (in a high school or in our world in general), we must find ways to meet in the middle, agree to disagree, respect others' opinions even if we don't agree with them, and to find a way to get along.

In terms of violence in schools and in the world, some might argue that mass chaos has already broken out. Going on a shooting rampage cannot be the "ultimate answer" to solving our problems, nor can any other act of violence or hate such as road rage, "jumping" a kid in the hall or behind the school, adults brawling at a little league football game, or spouting hateful rhetoric online when we "disagree" with someone or something, to give just a few examples. We are ALL responsible for our own behavior and for helping adults and kids realize that each person's opinion, to that person, is the correct opinion, and we can all still get along even if we do not see things the same way. School safety in the modern world in many ways depends on adults teaching kids tolerance of and respect for other people's opinions, and safety in the "real world" depends on all of us reigning in our emotions and prioritizing respect for human life above being "right" or "getting revenge" for a perceived wrong that has been done to us. We have reached (passed?) a tipping point, and we must band together in a universal fight against violence, hate and intolerance of opinion.

In addition to people's perceptions and worldviews, the concept of **control** is another area that has a major impact on how people interact with other people, whether kids or adults. Control of ourselves and/or of others, or the perceived lack of it, is a common point of frustration in people, whether they actively realize it or not. In its simplest form, we can only control ourselves and our own reactions to others' behaviors, but many humans spend a lot of time and energy trying to control others, pinning their own emotions on what others do, and experiencing the stress and turmoil in their own worlds when the other person or persons refuse to cooperate (if they even know what the other person's expectation was in the first place!). When people are confronted with conflicting worldviews, many may fully believe they have no control over what happens or what they do next, whether it is their emotional or even a physical reaction.

In reality, people *choose* what happens next—how they react and even feel about the conflict, but for many people, what happens next may not *feel* like a choice to them because of their worldview, which (in their minds) absolves them of their responsibility for their actions. For many, the resulting belief is one of *look what you made me do...*, which puts the blame and responsibility for their own actions on another person.

A simple illustration of this is people watching a football game on television. We yell at the television for the coaches and players to do this and that, and when it doesn't happen, we are frustrated, and our hopes are dashed. With social media at our finger tips, we are able to immediately express our view online and find others who agree with us as well as those who vehemently oppose us. This sports example becomes far more serious when it becomes a real-world parent brawl at a kids' sporting event when, again, people have differing worldviews and try through shouting matches or fist fights (or worse) to control what other people around them are doing so that they fall into the aggressor's own perception of "how things should be." These real-world brawls and other forms of "outrage" are occurring too frequently in today's world, thus the importance of people taking a moment to consider other people's views in order to control their own reactions to a situation. We cannot reach a point in our world in which we become so desensitized to violence that brawls become the "new normal."

Another example is any type of teen friendship or (perceived) romantic relationship in which one friend has one expectation of the friendship/ relationship and the other friend does not share that expectation. Teen A wants Teen B to act a certain way (essentially control that person's behavior, even if Teen A doesn't realize that is what he/she wants) and gets stressed out, angry, upset, depressed, etc., when Teen B does not do what Teen A wants him/her to do. I see this situation a lot in talking to teens about their frustrations with their friends, their parents or other family members, their teachers, etc. Very often the teen is upset about and talks about what he/she wants the other person to do and is upset that the other person isn't doing it, when the other person doesn't know anything about it. At that point we have the discussion that we can only control our own behavior and how we react to the other person's behavior as well as about good communication skills (more on that later). When we add the element of social media to the mix for teens (and adults, for that matter), stress often ensues because now Teen A not only wants the other person to do something specific (that Teen B may not even know about) but also has a front-row view via social media of when Teen B is doing something else entirely, such as hanging out with or showing romantic feelings for Teen C when Teen A wants to be the recipient of those feelings and actions.

Ultimately, while we cannot as humans control what other people think, do, or say, **we do have control over ourselves and how we react to what other people think, do, or say.** The challenge lies in how we *choose* to react when we are faced with things that upset us in some way. We are all human, complete with human emotions. Life's events make us happy, sad, angry, sentimental—all of the feelings that make us feel alive. We are not robots void of emotion, and we act like it, but our worldview about our emotions and how we deal with conflict can and does affect what we do and how we are able to cope with life's stressors. Some people operate under the belief system that our emotions and thus actions happen "to" us, leaving us with little or no control over our own situation and behaviors. Under this mindset, people can fall into a pattern of life that is a constant state of reaction, a roller coaster of emotions that are perceived to be direct results of actions that happen "to us" as we passively live our lives and wait for the next event to happen to us. In its simplest form, waiting for the next event to happen to us and spinning out of control when it happens is a much more stressful state of mind to be in compared to recognizing that while we cannot control all of life's events, we do have control over how we react in the face of life's events, which does give us a sense of control over our lives.

Life events that we have no control over definitely happen to us—day in and day out. That is part of being alive and human. Accidents happen; misunderstandings and disagreements occur; shocking, tragic, heartbreaking events happen out of the blue. In discussing control over our emotions, the message I am sending is not that we should never get upset, hurt, or angry. Sometimes an event is so tragic and shocking that we react in extreme ways with extreme emotions. Even in these situations, however, we cannot "take the law into our own hands" to try to right a wrong. What I am mostly talking about is what happens when and after we experience reactionary emotions, including what actions we take, particularly with day-to-day problems and conflicts we all face. To make our world a more peaceful and a safer place, we can choose how we react to negative events, and we need to recognize that sometimes we actually had a hand in creating the negative event when it comes to dealing with other people.

According to a *Psychology Today* blog post, Brandt (2014) points out that people can be "reactive" with their emotions and reactions in response to conflict in relationships:

When you feel threatened, your body's fight-or-flight response is triggered. You become flooded with stress hormones and the reasoning part of your brain, the neocortex, shuts down. Your partner says something critical and instead of responding rationally or thoughtfully, you attack. By responding to conflict reactively, you leap to an emotional conclusion. You let the other person determine your response and behavior. Being triggered can stop your ability to regulate yourself and being unable to regulate yourself is the end of communication and intimacy. When you're reactive, you enter "automatic pilot" mode. You stop being conscious of your words, tone of voice, or body language... You want to win (para. 3-7).

In other words, emotional control goes out the window when people operate in this "reactionary" state of mind. While the above example is about relationships specifically, the same reactionary concept can be applied to humans' reactions to any type of stressful event (road rage is a good example most of us have experienced on some level). When people consistently and habitually deal with stress and conflict using this method, it is easy to see how relationships become fractured and broken.

One's perception of control often mirrors one's perception of **self-**

responsibility. My experience working in education has been that very often, people (kids and adults) feel that life and life's events happen "to" them, as if they are watching a movie in which they play a completely passive role and have no control over their circumstances. And while yes, many people (kids and adults) have only so much control over their life circumstances because we inherit our living situations, we do have, to some extent, control over our lives and actions we take within those circumstances. I will talk more about grades in a separate chapter, but one simple example of this involves some high school students' perceptions of how student grades happen. It goes something like this: student gets report card with failing grade on it. Student's angry reaction: the teacher failed me. By saying that the teacher failed the student, the student illustrates a belief system that they had little or nothing to do with the grade, and that it happened to them as they stood passively by with zero control. When I meet with the student to discuss what's going on and we dig deeper and begin to look at what led up to the failing grade, inevitably we find many actions that the student has direct control over, namely negative student habits including but not limited to: student did not turn in all work and had grades of 0 on many assignments; student does not maintain an effective (or any) study routine and, as a result, failed each test for the grading period; student was frequently absent from class due to skipping; etc.

Another teen example of this that comes up frequently is teens getting mad at a coach when the teen is not selected for a team or some other similar situation in which the teen wanted things to go a certain way, and they didn't. The teen (and very often, the parent) reacts very angrily and lashes out at the adult or adults in charge (or perceived to be in charge) and personally attacks those people for a sometimes laundry list of reasons not related to the actual tryout, etc. Life is full of disappointments, and it is human to feel let down or even angry when things do not work out. Not making a team or otherwise getting what someone wants is a very powerful life lesson in which adults can teach kids to monitor their own emotions and reactions and build strength and resilience as a result. More on this in another chapter.

As adults, it is easy for us to see that with a few minor changes in behavior and habit (self-responsibility), the student could have had a much better grade than he/she *earned* (as opposed to *received* or *was given* by the teacher). This belief system can be applied to just about everything people do, say, and believe, and the best part is that the belief system can be changed for the better (in both kids and adults). An important role for you as the parent is to help foster a more productive belief system at home so that your child sees that very often his behavior (and the earned results) is a choice, and when he/she makes better (more productive) choices, the stress level that comes from making less responsible decisions (in this example— the stress that came from the events that led up to the "bad" grades) can be alleviated.

So now what? We know that teens are growing and changing. Their emotions and perceptions of how to handle their emotions are evolving. Their worldviews are developing daily. They are interacting with other teens every day and as a result are continually learning to navigate the sometimes rough waters of a wide range of young relationships—from friendships to teammates to classmates walking the halls of a high school to the seemingly boundless online/electronic world as well as to interacting and communicating with adults both in school and in the "real world." We will talk more about the online/electronic world in another chapter, but the concept of "perception is reality" based on the online world applies heavily to teens and their relationships in that teens are exposed to what they believe relationships (and their whole lives, for that matter) are *supposed* to be like via images (mirages) they see on the internet, television, and social media, and they sometimes struggle to live up to an unrealistic perception, which they then perceive to be a failure on their part. While teens will become better at controlling and reacting to their emotions and at navigating relationships with others as they mature, there are things you, the parent, can do to help your child foster better relationships with you, your family, and your child's peers that can make navigating life as a teen much more tolerable. Much of what we discuss in this book will help you with this challenging part of parenting.

Ultimately, to make all of our worlds a better, safer place, we all—adults and kids—must work together to recognize and take ownership of our personal role in promoting hate, discord, intolerance, or violence. As adults, we must model a better way of "doing life" for our young people and for our adult peers. We must find a way to overcome our differences and instead promote positivity and productive actions. The tragic events that we are all so weary of and want changed are directly connected to the human emotions and opinions that we all experience and how we react to them, as well as to

> **Ultimately, to make all of our worlds a better, safer place, we all—adults and kids— must work together to recognize and take ownership of our personal role in promoting hate, discord, intolerance, or violence.**

our perceptions of our own worlds and how we believe they "should be." We cannot look at these events in isolation from the human element that goes into the decision-making of the human who commits the act of hate, whether it is a school (or any) shooting, a fight in the hall, or cursing out a teacher or school administrator for asking for order in the school so that students can receive an education. The time is now.

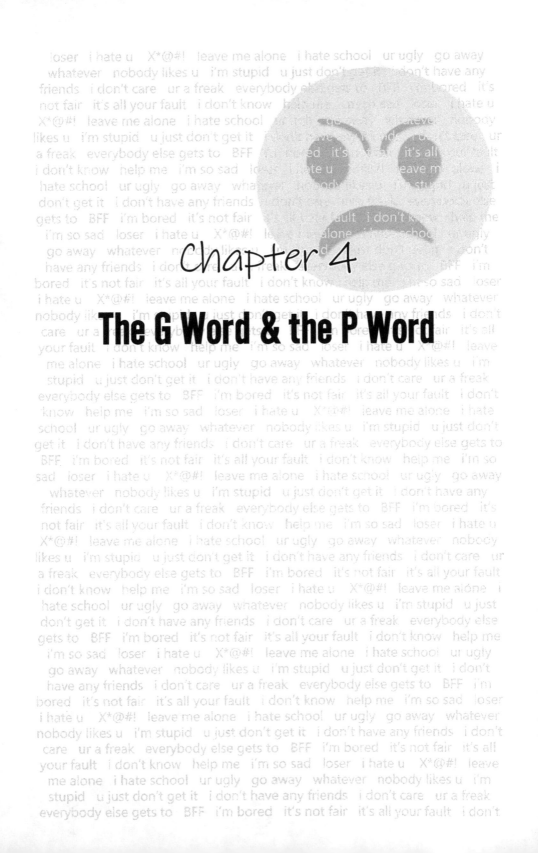

Chapter 4

The G Word & the P Word

Chapter 4

The G Word & the P Word

Warning—before you dive into this chapter, please note that this chapter (and this book as a whole) is NOT a statement on specific politics, but a book that includes any discussion about school violence cannot be written without a discussion about guns and politics and their relationship to school violence. I implore you as a reader to set aside your political beliefs about guns as you continue to read. I assure you, my motivation in writing this book has **ZERO** to do with politics and **EVERYTHING** to do with the safety of educators and students across our nation who are risk of violence **EVERY DAY**. If you have read this far, hopefully you are beginning to see that the current state of school shootings is about far more than guns and laws, but because guns are a key weapon of choice in school violence, we must be able to openly discuss the issue (without the conversation devolving into hate or anger) to be able to address it. Ultimately, this book is not about guns or laws. It is about people, and it is about the power we each have in ourselves to create change in people in an effort to stop school shootings and other violence.

I began this book when the Santa Fe High School (Texas) shooting happened in May 2018, and as I have worked to complete this book, more and more violence has occurred. In the time since I began writing this book, the stats on gun violence alone have continued to rise at alarming rates. As an educator I recognize that there are more types of violence than gun violence, but as a person who has worked in a variety of schools for the past 27 years, I must acknowledge that modern-day students and educators are at risk for violence toward them every single day, and guns are one of the most dangerous and accessible methods for committing multiple murders in a short amount of time. When this method is combined with the natural impulsivity of teens as well as the copycat phenomenon that we will discuss later in this book, it is obvious that educators and students are in a grave, precarious reality that demands action.

When the Santa Fe shooting happened, I went through the same emotions I believe most everyone did: shock, disbelief, anger, sadness, frustration, and so on. Like others, my mind screamed "enough!" As an educator, I am weary of it, which I know is an obvious understatement for all of us—educators or not. I do not know if educators see the problem differently from the public (non-educators) or parents, but this book may shed some light on that question. In my 27 years of being an educator in public schools, this is the first school year I have EVER been concerned for my own safety. Through the years, others have asked me if I worry about someone bringing a gun to school or acting violently towards me or others, and I was always able to honestly answer "no" for every other year before this current school year. My worldview tells me that things are different now, and what we are all faced with is whether things are permanently different (a "new normal") or if we can work together and make a change. As I have said before, the time is now. **We are at a crossroads, defined by Merriam-Webster as a "crucial point especially where a decision must be made."** We must act now, and we must do more than **react** as each event continues to happen. We cannot become desensitized to the violence that is plaguing our schools and our nation.

I titled this chapter the G Word and the P Word because in order to address school safety, we must discuss two hot topics—guns and politics. I have mentioned that I have not been a political person in my adult life. I have not been for or against guns and gun control, and over the years I hadn't had the need to take a stand one way or another. In order to discuss the current state of education and violence in this book, I believe it is important that I address my own worldview when it comes to politics in general. One key reason I have been apolitical over the years (despite having a master's degree in political science—remember, I wanted to go to law school) is that since the beginning of my career in education, politicians have repeatedly used "education" as a platform to get elected. Political promises of improving the state of education have been made for the past three decades (my time in education), but what many of us in education have actually experienced is this:

an increase in expectations/mandates (by both the state and by parents— more on that later) and

a decrease in funding and support (financial and otherwise) in meeting the increased expectations/mandates and an overall system of doing more with less (larger class sizes, etc.).

This book is not an exposé on or even a criticism of education, so we will not go into great detail about the perceived woes of American public school education as there is still much that occurs every day in public school classrooms that is excellent despite the daily stress on educators to do more with less. The wealth of personal comments from educators out there in social media tell a vivid story, however, about the inner workings of public education—specifically life in a modern-day real-world classroom overfilled with students who are living often chaotic lives in a stress-filled world, and those of us who have been at it for a long time can tell you *things have changed.* I say this not as a political statement, but as a reality that those of us in education live with every day.

Again, I bring up politicians/politics and education not to make a political statement about anything but rather to make a statement about where to go from here. If I am writing a book that includes discussion about violence in schools, then I must acknowledge that much of that violence is gun violence and school shootings, and it might seem that my next step would be to discuss whether gun control would "fix" the problem or not. This book is not about gun control at all, but I do have to address the topics of politics and politicians and parents. As I mentioned earlier in this book, I bring all of this up to point out that we (the public, educators, parents, students) CANNOT wait for politicians to "fix" it. Because you are reading this book, I assume you want to improve the life and relationships of your child and yourself, so like the meetings that mean well but accomplish little that I mentioned in a previous chapter, by reading this book, you (the reader) and I (the writer) are in a meeting to try to make something better, and we do not want to waste our time talking about the surface issues without addressing the much bigger, can't-do-much-about-it-alone-but-we-are-still-going-to-try issues, which is, in this case, school shootings and guns. Again, these are NOT political statements—these are only statements about my reality working in schools for almost three decades.

As I began this book, the talk in the news to address school shootings was to arm teachers and add more guards. As a long-time educator, I can firmly say that violence in schools is so much more complicated than adding more guards, or limiting the number of school doors, or arming teachers, or school safety drills and plans, or even metal detectors. Your memories will depend on your age, but think back to the pre-Columbine days, before school shootings became a "thing." (Yes—I know there were shootings before this, but Columbine really is the big one that changed the landscape for many educators.) Columbine happened in April 1999. I entered education in December 1991/January 1992. I had scant few years as an educator before things irreversibly changed. What we thought was a one-time event with Columbine grew into shooting after shooting after shooting that has continued almost 20 years with no end in sight—my entire educational career. Kids in schools today do not know anything other than a world in which they go to school each day not knowing if they will get shot.

Think back to the mid-90s and before. Your memories may differ from mine depending on where you grew up (rural, city, etc.) and your age, but guns were very accessible in my small town, and it was not uncommon for people (adults and teen drivers) to have a gun hanging on a gun rack in their truck's back window. Most did not lock their trucks with these guns inside, readily accessible. We all

> **Kids in schools today do not know anything other than a world in which they go to school each day not knowing if they will get shot.**

had access to guns, and no one dreamed of using a gun to shoot someone anywhere—never mind a public place such as a school, church, concert, or movie theater. There has been a clear and dangerous shift since that time (for me, 1980s), and unfortunately, it is ultimately not about the laws. PLEASE KEEP READING. I WANT CHANGE, TOO. To acknowledge—yes, if there were no guns, there would be no school shootings (no guns anywhere owned by anyone), but teens who want to hurt someone (or adults for that matter) would find another way to hurt someone. As just one example, more than one person has used a vehicle to purposely injure and kill multiple people.

The fact remains, however, that guns are among the deadliest of methods chosen by those who want to commit violence, particularly mass violence, in schools (and all the other public places in which mass violence has occurred in our country). Most unfortunately, it is people who have changed and society that has changed, and we need to work on that as a society while acknowledging all parts of the problem, even if it is politically distasteful for some. Just as people didn't change overnight to get us to the state of where we are today, they are as unlikely to change back overnight, so we must address the issue of access to guns as we work to bring our society back to one that is less prone to outrage and violence as the answer.

As a side note on the heated topic of guns and schools, some who are opposed to discussing any form of gun control might not have been in a school in some time. The point I want to drive home on that is that schools today are not the same as they were when many, many Americans were in school. We cannot make modern day decisions about school safety based on an image of schools from thirty, or even ten, years ago. I implore those of you who are unwilling to acquiesce when it comes to finding a solution about guns but who have not physically been in a school in some time to go volunteer for one week or even one day in a public school in America. (Again, I am only speaking about my own experience, all of which has been in public schools.) Try many of them—urban, suburban, and any in between. See for yourself how much life and schools have changed.

To be perfectly clear, it is not the changed *schools* that cause school shootings. It is the change in people, in society, in the ways people deal with "problems." The hate, aggression, anger and motivation to commit violent acts comes from within the individual based on his/her own views of the world, and because of this, things are different in schools today compared to most adults' own school experiences. The opportunity to bring a gun to school (or anywhere) and commit a shooting has always been there.

> **I implore every adult to set aside his/her own worldview when it comes to schools, politics, and guns, and see the modern world for what it is so we can work together to make it safer for all of us.**

What is different is the individual today choosing to act on and carry out that decision. I implore every adult to set aside his/her own worldview when it comes to schools, politics, and guns, and see the modern world for what it is so we can work together to make it safer for all of us. (And no, I am not saying all modern day students are filled with hate.)

Again, I bring this up simply to make the point that we cannot wait for politicians and the rhetoric about gun control and school safety to "fix" anything because the issues are separate from and deeper than guns. The visible and catastrophic outcome that occurs when a teen chooses to take a gun to school and use it, however, *is* a school shooting with irreversible consequences. The situation with school shootings is far more complicated than the rhetoric, and it isn't really being discussed by politicians. I do not fault politicians for not having all the answers. Like the meetings I mentioned earlier in this book, politicians meet and are simply doing the best they can given what their expertise is and what they have control over. Most politicians, even those who make the "Big Decisions" about education, have never been educators themselves, which is among the most common complaints educators have about the government mandates that are handed down to be fulfilled by educators, but that is for another book.

Educators and kids are on the front line when it comes to school shootings, and when the Santa Fe shooting happened, I knew I had to write this book to at least put some other ideas out there—to try to scratch the surface of what is happening so we can do something to actively address the situation before it happens again. So much of what is focused on publicly and by politicians is how to react to school shootings and violence—adding more rules and more guns in the form of security (arming teachers/adding more armed guards), changing the number of doors on schools, improving school security plans, etc. The pressure is on politicians to do something in response to school violence. **Very little has been publicly focused, however, on getting to the root of the problem—the human side of the problem, which is a prime goal of this book.**

In defense of politicians and the decisions they make, it is difficult to expect politicians, most of whom have likely never worked in a school setting—the very setting they are charged with "fixing"—to begin to understand what happens in schools and the daily lives of students. If we are all honest, we can agree that we are all armchair quarterbacks with things we know very little about but have strong opinions about, and politicians are doing the best they can based on their impression from the outside looking in when it comes to schools and students. Just as we educators shake our heads at the decisions that politicians make that impact our daily lives as educators (billions spent on high stakes testing while continually cutting the budget for schools is just one example), we also shake our heads about politicians' reactions or perceived lack of reaction to school violence and what needs to be done.

"Mental health" as a cause of school shootings and other acts of violence is a central topic that has been discussed nationally, but it is such a broad topic and reality that I think it is easy to become overwhelmed with what any of us can really do to help, even school counselors and administrators who are professionally equipped to help. Ultimately, there is no mental health safety "matrix" we can all follow that will precisely pinpoint the next school shooter or person planning to commit any act of violence anywhere, but we must continue to try. We will discuss school shooters and mental health specifically in other chapters as well as ways we can all help identify those who are at risk of committing acts of violence.

While this book will be useful to parents and educators of all teens, it must be mentioned that most parents of school shooters say they never saw it coming when it was their child who was the shooter. We all hope that each school shooting will be the last. I urge parents, however, to have their eyes wide open and to be brutally honest about their own children so that if there is anything that can be prevented, parents will have had the chance to do just that. The information in this book will also apply to bullying, which is another big issue of today's world that parents and educators are grappling with that is often mentioned in the same breath as school shootings. We are all faced with today's issues, and as with any complex issue there is likely no simple answer to "fix" it, but there are many things parents and educators can do to positively impact kids, and if we all work together, we can effect some type of positive change (politicians included).

Chapter 5

Grit & Resilience

Chapter 5

Grit & Resilience

So, we know that teens' brains continue to develop and don't fully mature until around the age of 25 (25!). We also know that we do not all view the same situation in the same way because of our highly individualized worldview, or lens through which we view everything in our worlds. And we know that we all live in a complicated, frenetic, 24-hour world in which we are exposed to, well, *everything* all the time, especially when exposed to the online world. And we also know that in America we live in a world in which school shootings and violence have become an all too common go-to for resolving emotional issues. When we really stop and try to take it all in, it can be very overwhelming for the most positive and determined of us. But we also know we have a choice of how to react. We have a choice to individually and/or collectively give up, shrug our shoulders, and tell ourselves our world is irretrievably broken as we shake our heads and go back to our social media feeds (myself included). ***What a tragedy. Unbelievable. So thankful that is wasn't our school/kids/lives. So thankful it wasn't me.*** All the types of words we all utter when faced with the latest shooting or act of violence, school or otherwise.

Or we can try to make a change. **Real. Positive. Individual.** Things we can all do. Things that go beyond the news stories and the magazine articles reporting the aftermath. **Proactive.** Real, positive, individual change that we have control over that, when combined with other individuals, can create a wave of positive influence and change. **That's where we go from here.** But first, we need to address the concepts of grit, resilience, and growth mindset along with self-efficacy—four powerful keys to helping kids become the best versions of themselves who, in turn, are more capable of handling life's stresses.

Why do some kids who seem to have it "all" struggle emotionally or otherwise (as stereotypically defined: stable home life, growing up with both parents—even better if parents are educated, enough money to live comfortably, etc.), while others who seem to have so much "less" excel emotionally or otherwise (as stereotypically defined: single-parent home, low income, unstable home life, parents never home/always working, etc.)? You are probably getting the picture from previous chapters: it's complicated. *Real life is not a stereotype.*

We are at a critical point in this book, and I ask that you take what have discussed so far about emotions, control, worldviews, etc. and app to your own emotions and actions as we continue. The goal of this b real talk, not glossing over. The issues that have led to this moment i have been glossed over far too long. There is a saying about doing t thing over and over and expecting different results... We must do s different in order to achieve different results. If we want chang make change.

Moving forward in this book, I ask you—parents and fellow educators who are reading this book—above all else and receptive to the information in the book. Some of th this book will help you. A lot. Some of the information make you angry and defensive, which, if you read the e find is part of the issue in today's easily outraged world the philosophy of this book is based on the idea that we live in a world filled with outrage, a world in which the desire to be "right" invokes in some an anger that is so strong when presented an opposing view that the opposing view is never truly heard, whether it is right or wrong. Anyone who has watched the news or been on social media recently knows this to be true.

With this in mind I urge you to proceed reading with a clear, open mind so that the information can be received and digested, and then you can decide how best to move forward with the information based on your own parenting style and beliefs. Some information may apply to you directly, some just a little, and some not at all. Please know that this book is NOT a personal attack on anyone or any parenting style, and there is no one way to best raise a child. We in education love your child and want what's best for him or her, just as you do.

This book, however, may rip some bandages off issues that have evolved during my years as an educator, and the ripping may hurt, but can ultimately help. At any rate, that is the goal of this book. We have a saying in education that the pendulum swings this way and that way to indicate when something we have already experienced in education years earlier (a concept or "big idea," usually) has swung back into favor, usually under a different name. As much as things change, things stay the same, and we know that no matter what the current state of the world, parents and guardians still love their kids and want what's best for them. We are just taking a temperature check at this state of the game. Let's dive in.

> **Please know that this book is NOT a personal attack on anyone or any parenting style, and there is no one way to best raise a child. We in education love your child and want what's best for him or her, just as you do.**

First let me say that while kids are individuals with differing personalities, strengths, backgrounds and worldviews, there are some qualities that all humans possess that can have a powerful impact on how they view and manage life and life's continual stressors (this is true for adults and kids). If we could create a stress-free world for all of us, we would certainly do it, but as adults we know that there will always be stress in life, and the key is to learn skills to manage the stress so our lives are not derailed when something "bad" happens. One of the most significant concepts I will cover in this book is the concept of **resilience**. As educators we have noticed that many modern-day students lack the same level of resilience that previous generations of students had, or that we ourselves had when faced with hardships when we were growing up. *Psychology Today* describes resilience:

> *Resilience is that ineffable quality that allows some people to be knocked down by life and come back stronger than ever. Rather than letting failure overcome them and drain their resolve, they find a way to rise from the ashes. Psychologists have identified some of the factors that make someone resilient, among them a positive attitude, optimism, the ability to regulate emotions, and the ability to see failure as a form of helpful feedback. Even after misfortune, resilient people are blessed with such an outlook that they are able to change course and soldier on (para. 1).*

Self-efficacy is another quality of humans that impacts what humans believe they can do. The *American Psychological Association* describes self-efficacy:

> *Self-efficacy refers to an individual's belief in his or her capacity to execute behaviors necessary to produce specific performance attainments (Bandura, 1977, 1986, 1997). Self-efficacy reflects confidence in the ability to exert control over one's own motivation, behavior, and social environment. These cognitive self-evaluations influence all manner of human experience, including the goals for which people strive, the amount of energy expended toward goal achievement, and likelihood of attaining particular levels of behavioral performance (para. 1).*

Cassidy (2015) explains self-efficacy:

Self-efficacy relates to an individual's perception of their capabilities. It has a clear self-evaluative dimension leading to high or low perceived self-efficacy. Individual differences in perceived self-efficacy have been shown to be better predictors of performance than previous achievement or ability and seem particularly important when individuals face adversity (p. 1).

What this ultimately means is that some people have a better self-perception or self-belief about themselves and do "better" than others—in academics, in life, bouncing back from setbacks, dealing with stress, etc. Kids who are more resilient bounce back from struggles more easily than those who lack resilience. Notice I did not say "without effort" or "without pain." Bouncing back takes effort, but those who are more resilient are better at it. In its simplest form, self-efficacy is the concept in our minds of "I think I can…" (or "I think I can't" so I won't even try).

For example, Student A makes a 79 on a test in AP World History and comes home to you in despair, desperate to "get" the teacher to allow the student to do something, anything, to raise the grade. Student B makes a 79 on the same test, accepts the outcome, and plans a way to increase his/her performance on the next tests so that the 79 doesn't happen again, or in other words, learns from his/her mistake. For one student, perceived "failure" is seen as a defining, unacceptable event that MUST be changed. For the other student, perceived "failure" is seen as a moment in time or life experience to learn from and, as a result, grow. Another example is Student C who, when faced with the first "hard" class in which achieving a high grade (as defined by the student—for one student that might mean an A and for another student that might mean a 70), wants to immediately drop the higher level class (quit the task that he/she is finding difficult) and go to a perceived "easier" lower level class in order to achieve the higher grade without a higher level of effort, which is what is likely actually needed to achieve a higher grade in the higher level class in the first place.

Another important concept that impacts how people view and manage difficulty is known as a **growth mindset**, coined by Stanford psychologist Dr. Carol Dweck. Dweck coined the terms fixed and growth mindsets to describe the attitudes and beliefs people have about learning and intelligence. Students with a **fixed mindset** believe they are born with their abilities and that they are unchangeable. In contrast, students with a growth mindset believe that their abilities can be developed and improved over time with practice (Robinson, 2017, p. 18).

Yet another important concept to commit to memory is the concept of **grit**. Merriam-Webster Dictionary defines grit as "firmness of mind or spirit: unyielding courage in the face of hardship or danger." In other words, the wherewithal to keep at it; to keep going when the going gets tough, and believing that success is possible.

Duckworth (2016) describes grit:

Grit is passion and perseverance for long-term goals. One way to think about grit is to consider what grit isn't. Grit isn't talent. Grit isn't luck. Grit isn't how intensely, for the moment, you want something. Instead, grit is about having what some researchers call an "ultimate concern"—a goal you care about so much that it organizes and gives meaning to almost everything you do. And grit is holding steadfast to that goal. Even when you fall down. Even when you screw up. Even when progress toward that goal is halting or slow (Angela Duckworth Grit website).

Resilience, self-efficacy, growth mindset, grit. Four terms that essentially mean that your kids can be trained to believe in themselves, to not panic in the face of failure, to keep pushing forward, even in the face of adversity, which for some modern teens can be defined as losing their phone privileges. These traits and belief systems can be reinforced and built-up in your kids from a young age so that by the time they are teens, it is a natural part of their belief system and learning style, and facing problems becomes less dramatic and more a part of daily life.

According to Dweck, Walton, & Cohen (2014):

Although no definitive answer is available yet, certain mindsets and goals may contribute to grit. Students who have a growth mindset about intelligence, learning goals, a higher-order purpose, and a sense that they belong in school may well show more grit in their academic work. Academic success requires more than ability. It requires the application of ability and the growth of ability through sustained hard work. Mindsets, goals, and self-regulatory skills— non-cognitive factors that contribute to academic tenacity—play key roles in this enterprise (p. 13).

What can parents do (or refrain from doing) to build resilience in their kids? To foster a growth mindset? To promote grit? To foster a strong self-efficacy, or belief in one's own self? We will explore a wide array of areas that can be affected by possessing or lacking these qualities. We all know people are born with certain personalities, strengths, and weaknesses. We are imperfect humans. But the beauty of resilience, self-efficacy, grit and growth mindset is that these concepts can be taught to and/or fostered in your kids, and in an effort to help your child you may be chipping away at these qualities in your child without even realizing it, regardless of your education level, income level, background, or love for your child. Self-awareness is the first step. As you read this book and self-reflect, you may be surprised at your own worldview, or the lens through which you view everything that happens to you and that you are, and how much it colors your view on, well, everything.

Chapter 6
Communication Skills

Chapter 6

Communication Skills

As we know, teens are filled with changing hormones, worldviews, and emotions. They also have little basic life experience and often lack effective communication abilities and, as a result, struggle to communicate well with others (parents and family members included). The lack of good communication skills alone can make the stress in their worlds seem, at times, insurmountable. This is true for adults as well in that our communication skills are tied to our personalities, our worldviews, and our own life experiences.

Before I became a school counselor, I believed to some extent that when I became a counselor I would be able to help people solve their problems. Anyone with life experience knows that solving all problems is an impossible task, otherwise someone would have done it by now. Now that I am a counselor, when I am talking to my students, I sometimes tell them this story as we begin to discuss where to go from here with the student's current situation we are discussing so that we can highlight the fact that in life we are faced with challenges that we cannot necessarily change but must still "deal with." Most students at the high school level understand that in life, the problem usually doesn't just go away, especially if it involves wanting other people to do something (which it very often does). Very often, the problem the student is discussing has nothing to do with school and everything to do with home and relationships. The student and I use this story as a jumping off point and context for looking at their problems objectively.

Another key observation I made once I became a school counselor is the lack of real communication many people have with one another. I believe that I became a fairly good communicator as a result of the course my life has taken working in education, not necessarily because of what my home life was like growing up. So, my worldview includes a strong belief that communication is good, that it comes fairly easily to me, that it helps people navigate the toughest of situations, and that all people can work on being better communicators. The ability to communicate well with others is not a "fixed" skill that we have, but rather, with some work and stepping out of our comfort zones, a skill that can be improved on and that can make an immediate positive difference in people's lives. As a teacher for twenty years, I (obviously) talked to students all day and honed those communication skills, but I spent considerably less time talking to parents. When I became a counselor, as I began talking to students and parents on a deeper level than I was able to in the classroom, I immediately saw that the root to helping (if not solving?) many situations that were presented to me was in communication. Because of this, talking to my students and parents about basic communication skills has become commonplace in my daily life.

We discussed in an earlier chapter that kids sometimes perceive their lives to be like a movie, and they try to live up to and emulate what they see on screen or online. Perception is reality. Many movies or televisions shows are scripted off a central problem in which there is bad communication. In the movies and on television, poor communication leads to drama and humorous situations, and everything magically works out in the end.

For example, on a recent long-running popular television show, an entire story arch centered around a female character and a male character who obviously had feelings for each other based on their behaviors as well as their conversations with other people, but the series went on and on with episodes where they did not communicate with each other. Comedy and shenanigans ensued. They ended up together in the end during a dramatic finale. Most often, in real life, there is no dramatic finale where everything works out. People just struggle to communicate, and real problems ensue.

A quick internet search reveals a wealth of information on improving communication skills. According to a *Psychology Today* blog post, Goldsmith (2011) says communication is the most important thing in all our relationships (title section). Goldsmith includes fighting fairly as a key element to good communication. Specifically, Goldsmith recommends:

Avoiding verbal attacks, bad language, and criticizing. He recommends staying on topic to avoid having a conversation disintegrate into an uncomfortable argument.

Focusing on the current issue and avoiding bringing up past arguments. Stay in the present.

Being clear about your feelings and encouraging the person you are talking to to also be clear about his/her feelings.

Having patience and avoiding interrupting the person you are communicating with.

Recognizing that differences of opinion are a way of life that make life more interesting than if everyone agreed on everything.

Taking a time-out if you are not in a proper state of mind to have a conversation, but having the conversation in a reasonable amount of time. Don't ignore or stuff the emotions away as a way to not have the conversation.

Using "I" statements which frame the issue as something you are feeling and is less accusatory than using words that make the other person defensive (para. 2-11).

As Goldsmith says, "I" statements are where you talk about how you feel and give a corrective action rather than just telling (the other person) what you think they are doing wrong (para. 11). An easy example to understand "I" statements goes something like this: Instead of saying to your teen: "You never listen to me or help me clean up" say "It bugs me when I have to ask you three times to help me clear the table after dinner."

Like many other areas of life and human qualities and skills, communication skills can be worked on and improved. The first step is to take note of our own communication habits that we find we continually fall into. Then we can practice positive communication skills as we interact with other people. As adults, we can model strong communication skills and work with our teens to teach them these skills as well as help them practice these skills when dealing with their own interactions with others.

According to the website *Habits for Wellbeing*, other good communication skills include:

Active listening—listening with your whole body and self.

Non-verbal communication—eye contact, facial expressions, etc.

Asking questions—open (what do you think about…) or closed (what did you say when he told you to leave?

Being clear and succinct.

Clarifying and summarizing—what the other person has said to ensure you are on the same page.

Being empathetic—showing the ability to understand where the other person is coming from.

Providing feedback—feedback is a two-way street.

Developing trust and rapport—harmony with the other person.

Being present—in the moment and conversation (Taylor, N.D.).

The list of good communication skills goes on, and if you know this is a weak spot for your kids or yourself/your own adult relationships, I encourage you to read more about it. There are numerous free resources out there that can help immensely. What good communication ultimately boils down to is being able to clearly express yourself honestly without having the conversation devolve into a personal attack or argument. Too often, this is the path people take which in turns leads to an avoidance of communication with that person, and as we know, ongoing lack of communication can often be worse than an argument.

One way to help your child build his or her own communication skills, particularly at the high school level, goes back to not doing for your child, but rather teaching your child to do for him/herself. For example, if your child is struggling in a class or feels he/she received an "unfair" (another perception-is-reality term) grade, rather than immediately reaching out to the teacher for the child, talk through a plan with your child to have him or her talk to the teacher directly. The best time for the child to do this is during the teacher's tutorial times. Although I agree that most kids know how to use email (but need work on content, format, and composing an email—but that is another book), I am a big supporter of in-person conversations, so I recommend teaching your child how to talk to his/her teacher and helping your child practice it beforehand. As the student continues to go in and talk to his/her teachers about any class/academic concerns or tutoring, the student's confidence level will improve along with his/her abilities to communicate and advocate for himself/herself. If, after your child has tried this route and no outcome or improvement has been reached, do reach out to the teacher, but include your child in the conversation so that you are not swooping in and doing everything for him/her. More on this in another chapter.

> **What good communication ultimately boils down to is being able to clearly express yourself honestly without having the conversation devolve into a personal attack or argument.**

Good communication skills are honed by practice. We will talk about phone usage and other electronics in another chapter, but having your child put down his/her phone and have conversations with you is the perfect place to start. For example, have a family movie night either at home or out, and require the family to put all electronic devices away so that after the movie, the entire family can engage in a family discussion about the movie. This simple act will help your child's conversational and communication skills in a stress-free setting, and it will also help improve your child's analysis skills needed in school when he/she is required to read, analyze and provide evidence. Simple, but too often not done. When a more difficult situation comes up at home that requires communication/discussion, use the same techniques that you did while discussing the movie (tone of voice, body language, questioning techniques, etc.), and teach your child to do the same. Strong communication skills and style can help people (kids and adults) navigate the most difficult of conversations.

As a high school counselor, I am continually reminded as I work with students and their parents that many people, many families, struggle with communication skills, and as a result, struggle with resolving conflict within their families. So, it is not a surprise that people in general struggle in the "real world" with resolving conflict through effective communication and choose instead to react in anger, outrage or violence. Working with your own family to notice and genuinely improve on your family's own communication skills will go a long way towards helping your family resolve conflict, and it will certainly carry over and affect how your child chooses to communicate and interact with other students at school when trying to resolve conflict there.

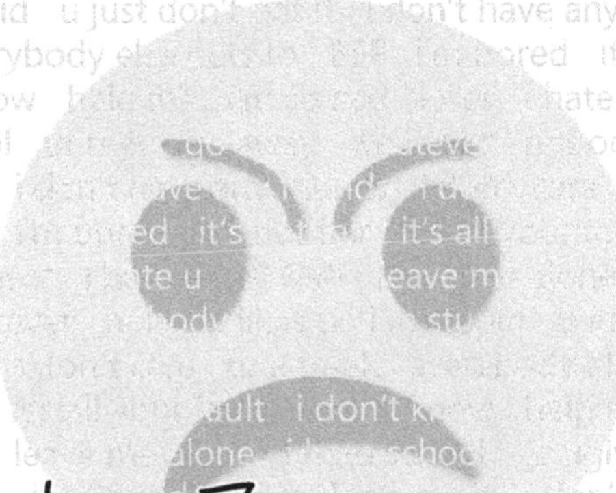

Chapter 7

Consequences & Motivation

Chapter 7

Consequences & Motivation

J ust as resilience, self-efficacy, grit and a growth mindset are important qualities to cultivate in raising a strong, resilient child, we must also focus on motivation and consequences in shaping as well as relating to a child. We can all remember our own childhoods and how we learned to make better decisions as a result of previous decisions we made and the outcomes that came along with those decisions. Obviously, our own parents' parenting styles had an impact on us individually, but learning to deal with consequences is a fairly universal human experience that shapes all of us regardless of the specifics of our upbringing.

Dictionary.com defines **consequence** as "a result or effect of an action or condition." Riebling (N.D.) breaks down consequences into "natural consequences" and "logical consequences." Natural consequences are those that happen naturally as a result of a decision one makes, such as the child who refuses to wear a jacket on a cold day and ends up being cold (para. 3). In this example, the child will (hopefully) learn from that experience of being cold and not argue about wearing a jacket the next time. Riebling says logical consequences require more adult involvement, but they are also connected to the misbehavior: if a child runs out into the middle of the street, he must hold his parent's hand for the rest of the walk and learn from the repercussions of his actions (para. 3).

To the adult thinker, it seems pretty obvious that when one action is taken, something else happens as a result. The examples are endless:

*Child touches hot stove, child gets burned;

*Child talks about friend behind friend's back, friend finds out, friend gets mad at child;

*Child doesn't do homework or study for tests, child gets 0 on grade and fails tests, child fails class for the grading period;

*Child *does* do homework and *does* study for tests, child gets improved grades, child very likely passes the class for the grading period (all of which impacts the child's self-efficacy, or belief about him/herself).

Adults are not mind readers, but in many cases adults can absolutely predict the future in terms of their child's behavior and the consequences that can possibly follow that behavior. High school counselors do it all day long when meeting with students about grades, attendance, and the many actions that students take when earning or losing their high school credits. If I had a dollar for every time I said "Are you turning in all your work?" or something similar (and the student's answer is "no") when meeting with a student about grades…

According to a *Psychology Today* blog post, Baron (2014) breaks down natural and logical consequences as applied to teens:

There are two types of consequences: natural and logical. Natural consequences…happen as a result of behavior that are not planned or controlled. Nature, society, or another person, without parental involvement, imposes natural consequences. Parents neither determine nor deliver natural consequences. Instead, you allow nature or society to impose the consequence on your child by not interfering. Logical consequences do not occur "naturally" as a result of behavior, they are determined and delivered by the parent (para.

4).

Baron points out that today's parents, in an effort to be helpful and involved, seek to minimize natural negative consequences so that their teen can avoid the subsequent discomfort, pain and shame of his actions (para. 5). According to Baron:

Our culture holds a faulty belief that effective parenting means protecting your child from uncomfortable emotions and experiences. As parents, we often feel emotionally depleted because we do too much in the wrong areas (over-parenting, rushing in to "fix" things, micromanaging) and too little in the right areas (role-modeling, allowing your child to have his own struggles and feelings, stepping back and breathing).

Many parents believe that if their child is uncomfortable or suffering the normal pains of life, they are failing as a parent. Parents ask themselves, "What more can I do?" instead of asking, "What more can my child do?" Rather than provide support for the child as he moves through his issue, the parent attempts to rush in and fix whatever is troubling him so both the parent and their child can be happy again and the parent can feel like a good parent (para. 6-7).

Baron goes on to point out in working so hard to help their kids, parents are actually sending some powerful messages to them that are not actually helping mold a strong, resilient child:

You are special so normal rules don't apply to you.
You are weak and incapable of dealing with this; so let me fix it for you.
Failure is bad and must be avoided at all costs.
You are incapable of coming up with a solution yourself (para. 9).

As a high school counselor, I can assure you that I deal with these exact scenarios on a daily basis, and they have gotten more exaggerated the longer I have been an educator. As parents and educators have worked increasingly feverishly to help students be more successful in school, student work ethic and concern about deadlines has dramatically decreased, which in turn motivates parents to work harder on their end to force their child to "do better." As I have told many parents when meeting with them about this phenomenon, the adults are usually the only ones alarmed by the student's low grades, lackadaisical approach to deadlines and studying, and increasing apparent disregard for any consequences of these actions. Meanwhile, the kid sits by wondering "what's the big deal?" More on that in another chapter.

After hundreds and hundreds of student meetings about all things school, I can tell you with absolute certainty that student motivation is the key to everything, and it has become increasingly difficult to encourage and foster student motivation in an alarmingly high number of students. The truism of "you can lead a horse to water, but you can't make him drink" is completely spot-on when it comes to educating students. When I tell people that, whether it is a parent or a teacher who has come in pulling her hair out over a particular student who won't work in her class, however, I sometimes get the feeling that the parent or teacher thinks I've become jaded or just don't care, when the exact opposite is true. The field of education has become filled with hand-wringing anxiety over "What are we going to do?!" and "We have to do something!" while the teens are seemingly more relaxed about academics than ever. I have met with hundreds of students over the years about "what's going on" with them trying to convince them the errors of their ways, and I know for sure that without an individual's motivation to do something, we are all (adult) talk and no action.

To put it into context based on my own experiences: In the beginning of my career in education in the 1990s, most kids "did what they were supposed to" in school with little or no cajoling by myself as an educator or by their parents. The school counselor had to intervene academically very little in those years, based on my own experiences. I should note that in the 1980s, no one I knew, and I mean no one, talked to the school counselor ever. Not once. Not about scheduling, and definitely not about "issues" they were having in their lives. Any life issues were handled at home and/or by the student on his/her own or were not handled at all. As the 1990s progressed into the 2000s, a higher percentage of my students struggled with getting their work done and with exhibiting study skills (and thus motivation for all things academic), and there was an increase in the activities of school counselors in actively working with students to be successful at school and outside of school. In today's world, as a high school counselor, I am inundated with meetings with students about grades, attendance, and other very serious issues that students are coping with both in and out of school, including serious mental health concerns for which they are often getting ongoing professional treatment outside of school. It is a completely different world today from the one I worked in beginning in the very early 1990s, never mind the one I graduated from high school in in the 1980s.

One concept I have taken particular note of as a high school counselor is that of **motivation**. In the current state of modern education, very often those who are the most concerned and the most motivated for a student to "do better in school" (or life) are the educators (teachers, counselors, administrators) and the parents—AKA the adults in the student's life. As with other scenarios I have described in this book, the student very often sits by nonchalantly waiting for the adults to "chill out" because "it's not that big of a deal" ("it" can apply to many different things, but "poor" grades are a top contender). I very quickly learned through working with hundreds of teens (and their exasperated parents) that it really doesn't matter what I as a school counselor want or what the parents want for the kid. We can want it for them all day, but if the kid is not motivated to want it too, a struggle will ensue (academic struggle, struggle for parents to get kid to do what they

> **In the current state of modern education, very often those who are the most concerned and the most motivated for a student to "do better in school" (or life) are the educators (teachers, counselors, administrators) and the parents—AKA the adults in the student's life.**

want him/her to do, etc.).

Does that mean we as adults should throw up our hands and give up? No, absolutely not. That is the very definition of taking the path of least resistance, and it just doesn't work. We have, however, seemingly lost our way in some ways when it comes to student accountability, so there is ample room for improvement in that area. We must as adults continue to stay the course and instruct and guide our kids while holding them accountable for their actions, but a working knowledge of motivation, particularly when working with a teen mind that is not fully developed, can help adults in the process. Sometimes, in order to help the teen be successful, we have to redraw the picture of success and accept it as adults, even if it looks different from the adults' original idea of success. As just one example, let's say that the parents' goal and dream for their child was for the child to graduate high school and attend a specific prestigious (personal perception) college, but through a series of choices the student made throughout high school, getting into that specific college (at least right out of high school) is no longer an option. The reality is that that student can still turn things around by making different decisions and go on to a different college to earn a college degree often in the exact same field. Different dream, same (essential) result.

In researching the concept of motivation for this book, I ran across an excellent analysis of teen motivation by licensed social worker and behavior coach Dennis Bumgarner, which I will excerpt here. Parents (and educators), take note. As I have asked in other chapters, as you read, I urge you to remain open-minded about Bumgarner's ideas, which are based off his own extensive experiences working with seemingly unmotivated teens and adults. His ideas may at first seem counter to what you instinctively want and think you should do as a parent. I can confirm that his three decades of experiences working with teens mirror my own and are worth reviewing and applying in your life with your own teen.

In his e-book *Motivating Your Intelligent but Unmotivated Teenager*,

Bumgarner points out that there are two basic methods parents take when trying to motivate an unmotivated teen:

the application of external consequences (incentives and punishments)

words, words, and more words, delivered with increasing emotion (introduction, para. 6).

Raised eyebrow? This must sound familiar to you. I myself have used the talking method again and again and again as a school counselor/teacher tasked with "getting kids to pass their classes." As I read Bumgarner's work, I could not help but smile, shake my head, and see truth in his words (even though counselors do not dole out punishment at school):

> *When one punishment hasn't worked, you've tried another and perhaps another, hoping that you'll find just the right punishment delivered with just the right amount of adversity that the motivational light will go on. And you've talked, Lord knows you've talked: lectured, sermonized, prodded, cajoled, exhorted, pleaded, explained, threatened, scolded, reprimanded, badgered, painted pictures of dire futures, spoke of flipping burgers—all to no avail (introduction, para. 6).*

Bumgarner points out that parents (and I am certain educators everywhere) mistakenly interchange their own motivation with the motivation of the teens they are working with, one-size-fits-all, while at the same time using an appeal to common sense in an effort to get their children to "see the light," all the while being positive and encouraging (p. 1). After all, if punishment doesn't work, then positivity and encouragement have to work, right? See the previously-mentioned truism about the horse and the water. As a high school counselor, I can tell you that at times this works, but with your truly unmotivated student, nope.

Bumgarner points out six fundamental facts about motivation that we all need to take note of, educators included:

Motivation is not a matter of "rah-rah" or a good, old pep talk.

Bumgarner says motivation is not about what we naturally try to do—motivate and say "you can do this!" The reason, according to Bumgarner, is actually very simple—the teen you are trying to motivate does not actually believe what you are saying. The teen now feels like you don't "get" him/her (p. 1).

Carrots and sticks are rarely motivational. Bumgarner says that there are people who respond to rewards and consequences, but for the very unmotivated teen, the problem might be that the teen is demoralized, disheartened or depressed, and rewards and consequences generally do not work in these situations (p. 3). With the uptick in students suffering from depression (more on that in another chapter), it makes sense why there are more teens who do not respond to typical rewards and consequences.

Our understanding of the relationship between motivation and performance is backwards. Bumgarner says that most of us see the process of motivation as motivation, then action. He says that motivation actually comes after the action, whatever that action is. It is by doing the act that we actually build motivation to complete the act. Bumgarner gives examples of doing household chores as adults, like cleaning the garage. We put it off until we finally get in there and start doing it, and by doing it, we basically pick up steam (motivation) to finish the task. Bumgarner suggests we focus on changing the teen's behavior, which in turn can lead to an increase the teen's motivation to continue to behavior (p. 5).

Motivation is not an individual characteristic. Bumgarner says describing teens as "highly motivated" or "not very motivated" implies that motivation comes from within the individual. This belief is what drives parents and educators to try to talk the teen into being motivated (with the rah-rah or by "getting in the teen's head") (p. 9).

Motivation is a function of relationship. So here is the biggy. Bumgarner says that motivation is actually a function of the teen's relationship with his/her parents (and I would add educators as a secondary relationship). Bumgarner says:

> *Truly motivational relationships are not those in which one of the members is in a one-up position, as when an authority directs the behavior of a subordinate. Relationships which are motivational are genuine partnerships, where neither member lords power over the other (p. 10).*

This is likely a hard one to wrap your head around because it flies in the face of the traditional parenting style of parents setting expectations and teens falling in line with those expectations. Anyone with an unmotivated teen (educators included), however, will reach a point of being willing to try anything to get the teen to do something other than being unmotivated, and Bumgarner's assertions make a lot of sense in the context that what we have all been trying has fallen on seemingly "deaf ears." (Remember the leading the horse to water thing…no amount of talking to the horse will get it to drink, so we walk off frustratedly saying "suit yourself!" while shaking our heads.)

One person does not motivate another. Bumgarner says he has worked for almost thirty years helping teens and adults find their own motivation, but in doing so, he asserts that he himself has not been the motivator of his clients. Bumgarner explains:

> *When successful, I believe that what I did was help them discover their own motivation. I was able to help them tap into what was truly meaningful to them. I was instrumental in eliciting their intrinsic inspiration for change. I helped them clarify what they wanted. I assisted them in assessing, in a straightforward, honest, yet respectful fashion, whether what they were doing was actually in service of their stated goals or whether they were merely deluding*

themselves. But I did not motivate them (p. 12).

Bumgarner says durable motivation is intrinsic, and people connect with something that is internally important to them, which is why punishments and rewards seldom work. It is also why parents' (and educators') efforts to inspire their kids doesn't work (p. 12).

OK. As a long-time educator, I know that parents and educators everywhere are thinking that while some of this makes sense, you know in your hearts that you have motivated another person to "do better," "be better," etc. It was something that you knew in your gut as it was happening. You are not wrong here, but it is likely because of the relationship you have/had with your teens/students, not because you did or said something that directly caused the teen to do something in return. We will discuss the concept of adults taking notice of teen (or adult) behaviors when it comes to identifying potential school/mass shooter behavior (and stepping in to stop it) in another chapter, and I think the concept is similar here.

There is a difference between a student/teen being truly (completely) unmotivated and a teen who *appears* unmotivated but who is actually "falling through the cracks" because he/she is choosing to take the path of least resistance and doing nothing (or very little). A teen might actually be motivated deep down but hasn't run into the adult who will take a "not on my watch" leadership stance with the teen (remember--they are still teens thinking with a not-fully-formed teen brain, and they still need adult guidance). In this scenario, the adult takes notice and elicits that motivation from that teen via a strong working relationship with that student. Again, the value and power of relationships and their potential to elicit positive change in so many scenarios in this book cannot be emphasized enough. It should be noted that negative relationships can also impact our behaviors, but again, we on some level can choose how we act and react in both positive and negative relationships. Digging in our heals in a negative relationship isn't productive, thus the obvious value of a positive relationship. After all, we all, as humans, have an innate need for positive relationships and thrive from the interaction those relationships give us. An example that works here is one of an athlete/coach relationship. In its simplest form, if the student perceives the relationship to be positive, the student will "work for" the coach more so than when the student perceives that he/she "can't work for that coach" (likely related to the relationship that student has wiith that coach). The key in this example (and all other relationships) is that there is always a way to turn that relationship around by putting in a little work (on both sides).

I should also point out that we as educators are (for the most part) already motivated, so when we listen to a guest motivational speaker, for example, we do feel inspired and motivated by that speaker (even though we do not have a relationship with that speaker), and this is true for many teens as well. When we are working with extremely (per our adult standards) unmotivated teens (ex. Two high school years have gone by and no high school credits have yet been earned), however, the traditional "motivators" may not work, but adults can invest their efforts in their relationship with the teen in order to keep guiding them to make "better" decisions for themselves and to help get to the "root" of the problem. This is true for classroom teachers as well. More on that in a moment. Bumgarner explains:

So while the relationship component is crucial in the motivation process, one person does not motivate another. Rather, one can... evoke another's personal motivation. I don't motivate you or you me, but it is in the synergy developed within the relationship that motivation can be found (p. 13).

Again, while this book is not an analysis of what makes a teacher a "good" teacher, it is worth discussing the connection between student motivation and the classroom setting because it is the very place that most seemingly unmotivated teens display their willful lack of motivation that, in turn, parents are tasked with working on with their teens at home when the student is doing poorly in school and/or when the teacher or counselor calls home to enlist the help of the parents. (I have mentioned that we must all be a team here, right?) Any educators who are reading this book can tell you that the "secret" to being a strong, effective educator with good classroom management skills is forging a strong, authentic relationship with the students in the teacher's classroom. It won't surprise anyone to know that this does not always happen for a variety of reasons.

In its simplest form, students can easily see through someone who is just going through the motions and does not genuinely care about the student or the education the student is getting in that teacher's classroom. As an example, when teachers learn their students' names quickly at the beginning of the year and make a point of learning something individual about each student (which, in teachers' defense, is a challenge with large class sizes), it begins establishing that teacher's relationship with those students and can go a long way toward establishing effective classroom management. Establishing those relationships is not a guarantee that all students in that classroom will work for and with that teacher, but it certainly increases the number of students who will buy into the teacher and the teacher's class, upping the overall odds that the student will be productive in that class. Not learning students' names in the first days and weeks of school is a missed opportunity for a teacher, either by choice or as a result of the large classes sizes or perhaps a combination of both, to form genuine relationships with students and, as a result, create some semblance of order in the classroom.

Some teachers struggle to find their footing in the classroom and make the attempt to manage their classrooms by sheer force, which puts all parties involved in a constant adversarial battle of wills. No amount of discipline referrals will change some students' behaviors, and with the very large classroom sizes that teachers are saddled with in today's educational landscape, there is not enough time in the day to use this educational method exclusively. (No, I am not saying teachers should never write a discipline referral. It just cannot be the only method of "working with kids" or "managing behavior." Kids should definitely be held accountable for their behaviors.)

Other teachers may take the opposite approach of the path of least resistance in which anything goes (which I have addressed in other chapters). Want a hall pass every day? Sure. Want to have your ear buds in all period and not hear a word I say? Fine. Work not turned in? You let me know when you're ready to get it to me. Let's just get through the day. Good grades for everyone! In defense of teachers who take this path, I believe some of it comes from the intimidation of working with very large classes of willful, aggressive teens who are seemingly not motivated to seek an education for themselves. It is also a coping skill that teachers develop from experiencing circumstances beyond the teachers' control with no relief in sight, such as large class loads, a perceived lack of disciplinary support from administrators, and a perceived lack of support from parents who attack them when the teacher reaches out for help. Teachers often feel beaten down by an educational system that loads on the expectations and numbers of students but offers little in the way of relief. It is a recipe for illiteracy.

We all know that smaller class sizes could go very far in helping teachers provide a better, more individualized education for students as well as helping teachers to be able to forge better relationships with their students, but the money never seems to be there, and class sizes are larger than ever (the ever-evolving philosophy and expectation in education to do more with less). The struggle is real for teachers in large classrooms. An analysis of the state of education is for another book, though. The point here is that teachers can make their lives easier and provide a more sound education for their students, even in large classrooms, by refocusing their efforts on forming real relationships with the kids in their classrooms, which in turn can create a setting in which students intrinsically want to work for (and with) the teacher, which is a very different setting as compared to one in which the teacher feels he/she must force the students to work and to care, which is usually a losing battle. Ultimately, teachers should always remind themselves that they are the adult in the room and proceed accordingly.

A natural human reaction when other humans refuse to try is to throw

71

up our hands and let the other human suffer the consequences. When teachers do this with unmotivated teens, though, they may momentarily feel like they are "winning" by allowing the student to "get what he deserves," but this is actually the perfect time to have a one-on-one with the student to try to forge a relationship with the student and get down to what the "real" problem is. As a high school counselor, I look at class size numbers all day long and completely recognize that in the over-filled classrooms of modern education, these relationships are suffering (i.e. not happening at all at times), and I hope that at some point the educational pendulum will swing back to recognizing the value in smaller class sizes. Smaller class sizes combined with a purposeful goal in education of forging relationships with students just might achieve the "big picture" goals of education (lowered discipline rates, higher graduation rates, students with better quantifiable educational skills, etc.--never mind reducing violence in schools). But I digress.

Whew. So what in the world can we do to help unmotivated teens if what we have been doing seemingly doesn't work? Bumgarner defines motivation as *Motivation=Change-Oriented Movement*. Bumgarner explains:

...motivation is a matter of change and that the change is directed toward behavior rather than thinking...When behavior changes, changes in thinking often follow in their wake (p. 14).

Bumgarner says that the traditional belief is that teens change to avoid discomfort, but he says that is not the case. He adds that "bad feelings and unpleasant experiences tend to immobilize teenagers...this is particularly true if the teenager is discouraged, overwhelmed, or otherwise in a negative state of mind" (p. 14). Bumgarner says research shows that teens are more likely to change when three conditions are in place:

*The teenager associates the change with something of intrinsic value (p. 15). The motivation to change must come from within the teen himself.

*The teenager is able, willing, and ready to change (p. 16). This simply means that the teen will not be forced to change by way of yelling, arguments, etc.

*The teenager is in an environment that is marked by safety, acceptance, and empowerment (p. 17). Some parents may scoff at this one as being a mark of teens being "soft" compared to previous generations. Bumgarner points out that the single most important component to a relationship is that the teen can express his thoughts and feelings without evaluation or criticism. Bumgarner points out that these thoughts and feelings must be presented civilly and emphasizes that parents do not have to tolerate any (negative/unacceptable) behavior from their kids, but rather are encouraged to listen without judgment. What is desired is communication between the parent and the teen (p. 17).

So if the key to motivation is action, then how do we as adults work to spark action in teens in order to help them find their own motivation? As we discuss in other chapters of this book, Bumgarner goes on to explain that the key to motivation, which is actually change-oriented movement, is to work with your teen to form goals, which are formed initially through questions. When it comes to improving a teen's performance at school, Bumgarner says it is important to frame those questions in terms of helping the teen figure out what he/she wants for him/herself. Examples Bumgarner gives include questions like "Do you want to graduate?", "Do you want to go to college?", "Do you want to make passing grades?" (p. 35). As a school counselor I would add "Do you want to take these classes again when you lose the credit for them?" I ask this question all the time, and teens almost 100% of the time answer no. The key, Bumgarner says, is that the teen (not the parent—and I would add not the school counselor or teacher) needs to come up with the goal. I would add that parental and educator guidance is useful in helping the teen form effective goals—remember, the main goal is for the teen to take ownership of his/her actions, but adults still need to help kids in that process.

There are many resources available for parents and educators to help teens in forming goals. **SMART goals** refer to well-known characteristics of goals that we use in the field of education and that are universally used in human resources, business, and other areas. A quick internet search shows how universal the use of SMART goals is. According to classroom.synonym. com, SMART goals in education help students and educators develop clear plans and follow the acronym: **specific, measurable, achievable, relevant and time-bound (para. 1-5).**

Specific goals are just that—specific and not broad. They focus on specific activities, such as turning in all work in each class each week (a positive way to word a goal of avoiding earning any 0s for work not turned in during the week). While "becoming a pediatrician" is a wonderful, broad goal for a teen to have, breaking it down into smaller, specific goals to help reach that broader goal is the goal here (no pun intended).

Measurable goals follow the same thought process in that they are specific and can be measured. Earning an 80 or higher on all tests the first time they are taken is a measurable goal. "Doing better in school" is broad and not measurable.

Achievable goals are reachable and attainable. Losing 20 pounds by next weekend is not a (healthily) reachable and (realistically) achievable goal. Spending 30 minutes per night studying for an exam is an achievable goal that can help teens reach a different goal, such as the one of earning an 80 or higher on all tests.

Relevant goals are those that are relevant, or important to, the teen trying to achieve the goal (*not to the parent or educator*). If the teen, for example, wants to be able to get his/her driver's license and the parents' expectation for that to happen is that the teen must pass all of his/her classes with an 80 or higher for the 6-weeks grading period, then the goals a teen sets for him/herself would be relevant to the larger goal of getting the driver's license and ultimately getting to drive. A relevant goal might be that the teen records all homework (including studying for tests/quizzes) in a planner that he/she uses each night to remind the teen what to do to help him/her achieve the 80 or higher on tests goal that is tied to the bigger goal of getting the driver's license.

Time-bound goals have time limits. A time-bound goal would be for the teen to complete all homework each night before 11:00 p.m. Another time-bound goal would be for the teen to make an 80 or higher on every test taken the first time it is taken during the month of October.

Helping teens learn to effectively set and meet goals not only helps reinforce the teen's intrinsic levels of motivation, but it also reinforces the reality that teens DO have control over what happens to them in many ways, particularly with grades. As we have discussed in other chapters, grades do not happen to teens. Teens are active (and sometimes passive) participants in earning the grades they eventually receive. It is critical for parents to reinforce at home that just as grades do not happen to teens, neither does an education. Education is an active process in which teens must actively pursue getting "educated." It will not happen magically, and it certainly will not happen if the teen has earbuds in and is actively disengaged from his/her education.

> Helping teens learn to effectively set and meet goals not only helps reinforce the teen's intrinsic levels of motivation, but it also reinforces the reality that teens DO have control over what happens to them in many ways, particularly with grades.

Bumgarner, when presenting to parents, asks parents if they have argumentative kids who are resistant to what the parents want their kids to do. He points out that resistance is not a characteristic of a person but that a person can be resistant to a relationship (p. 49). (There's that relationship word again.) One easy way to understand this concept is to think about your child behaving and acting one way for one person (you) and behaving and acting an entirely different way for another person. For example, your teen is "Johnny on the spot" for his basketball coach, arriving for 5:00 a.m.

practices with little or no cajoling, eating healthily and working out on his own, but when you ask him to pick up his dirty laundry off the floor and put away his clean laundry, he waits and waits and waits until an argument erupts. Same kid. Different reasons for choosing the behavior he chose. In this example, the teen wants to please the coach and ultimately wants playing time on the team, and the teen is willing to work for it because it is internally important to him. As far as pleasing you, meh. Not so much. Resistance.

Bumgarner points out some **key elements that promote resistance: advice, arguing, and convincing.** Rather, Bumgarner says:

> *To have a motivating relationship with your teenager, you will no longer attempt to advise, persuade, convince, or argue with her. You will decline to be the source of all wisdom regarding academic success. You will abandon efforts aimed at enticing or encouraging different school-related behaviors by offering rewards or threatening punishments. Instead, you will help your child be clear about her goals. You will listen empathically to her concerns, withholding judgment. You will pursue the discrepancies you hear and see between her stated goals and her performance. In doing this, you will make all resistance vanish. And you may just transform your relationship with your teenager (p. 56).*

For some parents of resistant teens, despite the best efforts of the parents, their teens continue to make bad decisions. In that case, Bumgarner suggests parents make a clear change of direction that begins with a speech (shortened and excerpted here) similar to this (which may seem, at first glance, like throwing the white flag of giving up):

> ...My love for you has led me to do whatever I could to assure your academic success, because I know how important it is to your future. I have nagged, lectured, yelled, pleaded, punished, and nagged some more because I have so much wanted you to be

successful.

I've come to realize that, not only have my well-intentioned efforts not worked, they have gotten in your way. And they have certainly contaminated our relationship.

...It's not that I believe that school is no longer important, or that I no longer care. It's just that I've finally come to realize that it's your decision and your life, and that I can do nothing to change things.

So...I will no longer bother you about school. I will not ask about homework, or what tests you have coming up, or whether you're studying, or what your grades are.

If you continue to fail, I will be heartsick and beside myself with worry. But I've decided not to make a bad situation even worse by adding a lousy relationship between us on top of your poor academics.

...If I slip back into old habits, I expect you to remind me of the promise I'm making to you today. But this is my pledge to you: I love you too much to allow what has been happening between us to continue to happen (pp. 57-58).

Insert wide-eyed emojis here. Taken at face value, it would be quite scary for many parents to say anything like this to their kids and actually mean it and still feel like good, effective parents. Bumgarner goes on to say that after making a statement such as this, parents must follow through and do and say nothing when it comes to academics. Essentially, parents are putting the proverbial ball in the teen's court. Bumgarner says parents should then focus instead on the relationship with the teen while observing what happens next. It is very likely that for the first several days, the teen will continue as is making bad academic decisions, waiting for you to do as you have always done and step in, argue with him/her, yell at him/her, etc. Bumgarner says that when the teen does start putting forth effort, even if it is minimal at first, the parent must resist the urge to go back to rah-rah cheerleader mode and praise the teen, and instead wait it out. Bumgarner proposes that your child's behavior will change as a reaction to you and your own changes (p. 60).

I would add here that in this "phase" parents should not be expected to adopt an "anything goes" stance in all other areas of your teen's life. The conversation above and resulting stance is about academics and could eventually be about other areas that need improved motivation, but this does not mean you as parents should allow your teen to "run amok." If your teen drives, for example, that is a privilege that you can choose to allow or not allow. If the grades cannot be handled, then it probably goes without saying that teen driving cannot be handled, or that it should at least be a package deal in which driving is a privilege that must be earned, even if it is inconvenient for you and your family.

> Using convenience as a reason to condone behavior you do not approve of is a form of going down the path of least resistance. The teen needs to see that his actions affect other people and that the universe does not revolve around him/her.

Using convenience as a reason to condone behavior you do not approve of is a form of going down the path of least resistance. The teen needs to see that his/her actions affect other people and that the universe does not revolve around him/her. This is likely true with phone usage and other beloved electronic media. After all, if most of us stop working, we also stop getting paid. Taking a more hands-off approach to your teen's academics does not mean you are allowing him/her to party and sleep 24-7, living the life of (an uneducated) prince/princess (no offense to any real princes/princesses out there—this is clearly an exaggerated-for-effect example of my worldview of real princes/princesses). This conversation simply means you are putting the teen in the driver's seat of his/her education by ceasing to micromanage him/her and argue with him/her about his/her academic choices and are instead waiting for the teen to "fix it" himself/herself. This also means that you are using all of that saved mental energy that you would have spent nagging to instead focus on building a solid relationship with your teen in the meantime and beyond.

In another chapter we discuss the effects of parents swooping in to "save"' their kids, and Bumgarner's work echoes what can happen when parents ensure that their teen avoids any type of failure. In this example, it is the teen's experience and internal motivation that will ultimately change his/her behavior. By making decisions, good or bad, the teen will experience the natural consequences of his decisions, such as losing a high school credit and having to retake the class. It is these life lessons that have taught all of us "how we should be" in order to achieve what we want to achieve and avoid future negative consequences. Essentially, parents sometimes need to step back and let their kids experience the consequences of their decisions in order to help them see for themselves why it is important for them to make better decisions the first time around. It is important to note that Bumgarner's work is focused mainly on teen academics. Parents should still be parents and should not disengage from parenting when they see their teens putting themselves in life-altering dangerous situations. When it comes to the art of being successful at school, however, less is very often more when it comes to parents feeling they must micromanage their kids in that this creates a vicious cycle of the parent being the active participant and the teen being the passive bystander.

In closing this chapter, I am reminded of instances in which I am interacting with parents and teens in the school setting. Very often, this interaction comes when I am meeting new students and their parents, usually when the student is enrolling at my school for the first time. It is very easy to see the parent/child dynamic based on how the enrollment conversation goes. As a high school counselor, my goal is to talk mainly to the student because, after all, the high school education is the student's, not the parent's, and I am working to establish a relationship with the student from this very first meeting. Some well-intentioned parents can essentially steam-roll the conversation by trying to talk over their kids, talk for their kids, or otherwise not let their kids get a word in or express their own opinion about something, even if my question is directed at the student.

I mention this to drive home the point that teens must practice the skills that they will need as they get out of high school, and that practice can only occur if the parents step back and let their kids take the wheel. Notice that I did not say anything along the lines of "do nothing" and "let whatever happens happen." I am pointing out, though, that often kids are far more capable than their parents believe, and when parents let go and let them fly, all will not automatically end in academic doom. What will very likely happen is that kids will learn to be responsible for their own behavior and take ownership of their decisions and their educations as they learn to become productive, successful adults. Isn't that what we all really want, anyway?

Chapter 8

Failure & Swooping

Chapter 8

Failure & Swooping

This hurts me more than it hurts you is a phrase that has been uttered by many parents at some point in their parenting career, but it seems it is a path chosen less frequently by today's modern parents for their kids despite the parents' obvious love for their kids. Some of life's best lessons (or ones that create the most growth) are painful, and when parents and the educational system prevent that pain, kids are not able to practice being resilient.

What can parents do to foster the building of resilience in their kids? One of the best but seemingly most difficult ways for modern parents to promote resilience in their kids is allowing their kids to "fail," or more specifically to experience the consequences of their actions. Yes, you read it correctly. It is no secret that sometimes modern parents go out of their way to ensure that their children do not fail, or experience a situation that is stressful, negative, or less than perfect. To quote Marie Barone from *Everybody Loves Raymond* —"It comes from love." It may come from love, but it also chips away at kids' ability to do something themselves without an adult swooping in to "fix" it for them. And this inability to function through stress continues well into adulthood for today's kids who have never learned to face a stressful situation and fail and get through it to see that life goes on. We all know or have heard of situations in which kids reach their twenties but struggle to deal with stress or problems without their parents continuing to step in. In the defense of parents everywhere, however, schools are equally responsible for creating a world in which kids do not learn to fail and move on. More on that later.

It all began innocently enough (based on my general memory of how things changed and evolved): During the 1990s, education and parenting entered into a time during which the goal became finding a way for everyone to "win." It seemed that overnight we went from individuals legitimately "winning" or earning something (anything) to everyone on the team getting a trophy in the spirit of not hurting anyone's feelings. In elementary school, for example, when a student had a personal birthday party or other gathering outside of school, the trend went from inviting only the classmates/friends the student liked or was friends with to inviting the entire class so that no one's feelings were hurt. It was the beginning of the path to our current uber political correctness and a simultaneous cultural avoidance of conflict in schools. The line of thinking in schools changed to the belief that everyone wins, then no parent will come to the school the following day complain. In another example, in the cheerleading world in some sc during that time, the trend went from traditional cheerleading try which the best candidates earned a limited number of spots on t squad based on skill and ability to a system of cheerleading "si which anyone interested could cheer. Everyone wins; no one one complains.

Around that same time, in the classroom, the trend i districts mandated policies in which teachers had to acc work and were forced to give minimum allowable grad A minimum average of 60 for the 6-weeks) began so bounce back grade-wise and hopefully earn a passin

Again, the intention of these educational policies was good—supporting the student to be successful and to better learn the material. Eventually test corrections and retesting on failed major tests to earn a higher grade also became district-mandated policies, which were justified by the educational system because the goal of education was for children to learn, and a one-time test grade was not a final goal of education. Again, all of this began innocently enough and with good intentions.

All of this "help" being provided by educators and the educational system, however, proved to have a very real down-side. Since the early 1990s these district-mandated practices have reinforced negative habits in students that have steadily worsened over time:

increased late work

increased numbers of 0s for grades

higher levels of procrastination

a lack of true study skills

higher levels of apathy towards school and education

higher levels of disciplinary issues tied to apathy towards school

I have spoken with hundreds of students and parents over the years about these student habits that cut across all students regardless of socioeconomic status/race/parent education status/etc., and most parents see it in their kids but are baffled about it, saying their child has "always" been like this. I remind them that this current state of education is the only reality these students (in my case, teenagers) have known their entire educational career. It only seems strange to older people who grew up under different educational and parental expectations—usually a different generation.

It should be noted that the level of apathy towards school that an increasing number of students display is an alarming trait in that kids who do not care have nothing to lose, and when it comes to committing acts of violence, the most apathetic kids can be among the most dangerous. I am not saying that every apathetic student will be a school shooter, but I am concerned about the high level of apathy towards education and towards other people that I have seen develop over the years and its implications when it comes to acts of school violence or aggression toward teachers, administrators and other students, as well as toward the students' parents. Many of the students who display apathy towards the academic side of school also show apathy when it comes to discipline efforts and following basic school policies including respect for authority.

Ultimately, the apathetic student will not be well-educated when he/she leaves high school, and all of us in society need to be very concerned about that. Students do not become magically educated once they are out of high school (without actively seeking an education), and these students eventually become adults who need to be productive citizens, so it should behoove all of us to make a concerted change when it comes to working on the roots of problems that are contributing to student apathy.

Although this book is not a criticism or analysis of education, in the defense of kids everywhere, I should add that for some kids, the level of apathy towards education is likely also tied to the state graduation plan as well as No Child Left Behind (NCLB). NCLB is a 2001/2002 federal law that essentially sought to ensure that all students were educated but that tied students' progress to money meant to help school districts educate disadvantaged students, and all schools' progress was monitored by the government and by the public through reports of the schools' data. Buzzwords like Adequate Yearly Progress, Proficiency, Highly Qualified Teachers, Standardized Testing, Teaching to the Test, School Report Cards, Underfunded, and Subgroups hit schools and eventually newspapers, and school districts earnestly sprang into action but over time struggled to meet the new mandates. Like most ideas in education, the intention was good: educate all kids with the best teachers so all kids have a better shot at life when they got out of school. Like many other well-intentioned moves in education, this one also had a downside.

What all this educational gobbledygook means is that schools became publicly pressured to "get kids to pass" their standardized tests, which is the marker by which districts were judged to be able to receive the much-needed money to educate the students who needed the most help. Schools were publicly rated Exemplary down to Unacceptable (in our state—other states may have had other ratings names), and schools that did not meet the expectation were met with the tsk-tsk of being a "bad school." Banners were given out (naturally) to the "best" schools. The trickledown was (and is) huge: home prices surged or dropped in response to

> **Like most ideas in education, the intention was good: educate all kids with the best teachers so all kids have a better shot at life when they got out of school. Like many other well-intentioned moves in education, this one also had a downside.**

local school academic ratings, schools were sought after or run from, and the insatiable focus on standardized testing went through the roof. Districts sought to align their curriculum and graduation requirements so that more and more students could pass more and more tests, while at the same time, the entire focus and responsibility of educating students increasingly went to the school and its employees, cutting the parents and even the student out of the process (as crazy as that sounds) by ignoring the fact that students must be interested in the education they are being given and parents must help and actively be involved in the educational process at home. Just this brief description should give you tired-head. I must point out that you should know that this system does not represent everything that is going on in schools every day despite the restrictive and prescriptive boxes placed around educators as a result of this process. There is still much happening every day in schools that is positive, inspiring, and productive.

As all of this racing around for high ratings was going on, state educational leaders continued to adjust the state graduation plan, or classes required for students to graduate, in order to meet the requirements of

NCLB and to improve education as a whole. The tweaking of graduation requirements is also a result of philosophical pendulum shifts about "what is important in education" and "what kids need" and the educational evolution over the last thirty years has been a shift toward academic (as illustrated above) and away from vocational, at least in our state. The years of woodshop and auto mechanics disappeared for many schools into old black and white yearbooks (annuals in those days), and therein lies the rub: those classes were the "hook" for many students who, for reasons that were their own, had no plans for college but had many plans for successful vocational trades as a career. NCLB led many states to focus everything on academics and "meeting the standards," which led to a lot more testing and to a reduction or cutting of some of the very classes that students loved about school. Essentially, students felt (and still feel) over-tested and, as a result, some became disinterested in school.

In our state, students must pass five state tests in high school to be able to graduate, and state testing begins in 3rd grade. As a high school counselor, I have worked with more than one student who has NEVER passed a single state test from 3rd grade on. I don't have to spell out for you how discouraging that is for students, particularly by the time they reach high school. Many of these kids will go on as adults and work in a trade earning a solid living (because they are interested in the trade, not because they had to "settle for" working in a trade), and their education while they are in school should be more well-rounded and less driven by state academic tests. I will point out that our state currently offers many career and technology programs, and some school districts do this better than others; our current state graduation plan also requires an elective focus that can include these classes. In its simplest form, however, when we talk about kids being apathetic toward school, we have to look at the big picture—the evolution of education, and not just label the kid as "apathetic." But I digress.

Meanwhile, back in the 1990s, at the opposite end of the spectrum we also entered a time in which high-achieving students increasingly felt pressured both internally and externally to succeed academically, to be the best, to earn the highest grades and class rank for college admissions. Naturally, it followed that stress and a certain level of anxiety came with the territory. While kids feel the pressure to be the best, their parents react by doing what parents do—they help their kids. The tendency for some parents in this evolution, however, was to pressure the teacher for better grades, and that tendency has become increasingly aggressive over the years to what seems now to be a breaking point in education. A cartoon that gets passed around social media illustrates this change. In the first cartoon box, the yesteryear parents of a student with poor grades are yelling at the student about the grades; in the second cartoon box, the parents of today's student with poor grades are yelling at the teacher about the grades. Any current or recent educator can tell you this cartoon is painfully true and not an exaggeration. Some current teachers do not want or are afraid to talk to parents because of the aggression with which parents sometimes speak to teachers in defending their kids. Parents—we all know it comes from love, but this is not helping your child. Parents and teachers must maintain open lines of communication and support for each other.

Some modern parenting styles have been called on the carpet because of the negative impact of those parenting styles on kids, and those parenting styles have been given less-than-flattering names, such as "helicopter parent." Bayless (N.D.) traced the term "helicopter parent" back to a 1969 book *Parents & Teenagers* in which teens said their parents would hover over them like a helicopter. Similar terms include "lawnmower parenting," "cosseting parent," or "bulldoze parenting," and the term "helicopter parenting" became a dictionary entry in 2011 (para. 1). Bayless quotes Carolyn Daitch, Ph.D., director of the Center for the Treatment of Anxiety Disorders near Detroit and author of *Anxiety Disorders: The Go-To Guide*, who says helicopter parenting refers to "a style of parents who are over focused on their children. They typically take too much responsibility for their children's experiences and, specifically, their successes or failures" (para. 2). Bayless also quotes Ann Dunnewold, Ph. D., a licensed psychologist and author of *Even June Cleaver Would Forget the Juice Box*, who calls it "overparenting. It means being involved in a child's life in a way that is overcontrolling, overprotecting, and overperfecting, in a way that is in excess of responsible parenting" (para. 2).

Bayless identifies triggers that lead parents to go down the path of helicopter parenting:

Fear of dire consequences, such as the child not making a team.

Feelings of anxiety and worry.

Overcompensation for something that happened in the parents' own lives.

Peer pressure from other parents and the guilt from perceived "bad parenting" that goes with it (para. 4).

Perry, Dollar, Calkins, Keane, and Shanahan (2018) studied helicopter (and similar) parenting styles in 307 families of 422 children over a span of 8 years beginning when the children were toddlers and found that an over-controlling parenting style can lead to a child's inability to manage his own emotions and behavior as the child moves into adolescence (p. 1542). Bayless points out that although the term "helicopter parenting" is most often applied to parents of high school or college-aged students who do tasks for their child, such as arranging a class schedule or contacting a professor about poor grades, helicopter parenting can apply at any age (para. 3). Dunnewold says when their child is a toddler, the parent may constantly shadow their child and direct their behavior, while in elementary school, a parent might ensure a child has a certain teacher or coach, select the child's friends and activities, or provide disproportionate assistance for homework and school projects (para 3.)

As I have pointed out before, many parenting styles come from a place of love, and it is natural for a generation of parents to understandably want "better" for their kids than what they had growing up. Parents who adopt a helicopter parent style undoubtedly love their kids and may even feel that their parenting style is evidence that they love their kids more than other parents who adopt a different parenting style, but like other well-intentioned plans or ideas, there can be a downside. Bayless points out that there are negative consequences to these styles of parenting for the child:

*Decreased confidence and self-esteem.

*Undeveloped coping skills.

*Increased anxiety.

*Sense of entitlement.

*Undeveloped life skills (doing laundry, etc.) (para. 5).

A very telling blog post on the popular *Grown and Flown* website addressed this parenting style:

I'm concentrating on something, but out of the corner of my eye I see the elevator doors slide open. It's a teenage girl and a middle-aged woman, presumably her mother. The parent walks into my office, with the girl trailing sheepishly behind. The mother says, "My daughter will be starting here in the fall. We want to change one of her elective classes." I try to make eye contact and address the girl as I politely give them directions to the Office of Student Services down the hall, but it's the mother who apologizes for interrupting me. They leave my office, Mom leading the way with the class schedule in her hand (para. 3).

As a high school counselor, we are faced each year throughout the year with scenarios like this one that cover a variety of topics, not just class schedules. One might think that the example above was written by a high school counselor, but this post was written by a college professor. I include this example to drive home a point that I make to my students and their parents every opportunity I get: when kids leave high school and go on to their next stop, whether it is college/work/etc., they will take with them every habit they have been honing their entire lives. There is no magic that happens between May/June when they graduate high school and August/

September when they are dropped off at their dorm on a college campus. This is true for academic habits, obviously, but for life habits and soft skills as well. When parents habitually do too much for their kids K-12, the end result usually does not benefit the kid in that the kids have to learn these skills at some point, and parents can't (and shouldn't) plan to go with them doing for them for life.

So if doing too much for kids doesn't work, what is a loving parent to do? What can parents do to build resilience, self-efficacy, and grit, and promote a growth mindset in terms of allowing their kids to experience imperfection and failure so they learn to not fall apart the first time they experience it after they have left home? First, it should be noted that simply allowing your kids to "do life" in all its messy glory helps build resilience and their own personal, inner strength. In its simplest form, it is the "over doing" and "overthinking" that drives parents to try to be one step ahead of their kids so that "everything goes exactly to plan." Using this parenting method, no one gets hurt, but that's the problem. Life is messy, and painful, and stinky. Let it be, and let your kids experience it. You will not (and should not be) always there to save the day as your kids grow up and move on from their childhood home and life. We as humans learn through our experiences, and if all we are allowed to experience is (seemingly) painless perfection where everything always works out, it is no wonder kids are in shock when their first real pain occurs, whether it is from trying out and not being selected for a team or group, or from the stabbing pain caused by the first person to break their heart, or any other painful life experience that makes life just that—life (which might even be being unfriended/ unfollowed on social media).

It should be noted that your child will eventually run into failure at some point, on some level, and it is what your child has been taught/believes to be true about how to react to failure that will kick in, whether you are with him/her or not. For some kids who have been protected by their parents from every known difficulty, it is the fall of freshman year in college that kids will run into trouble—whether it is a poor grade that cannot be fixed or reversed, a professor your child "can't stand" or "can't understand," a class that cannot be passed, a rejection by a friend or love interest, homesickness, loneliness, or a bad impulsive decision with irreversible consequences. It really can be life or death with kids and impulsive decisions. We must teach kids how to weather failure and adversity, that these are normal parts of life, and that they will get through it.

Allowing your child to experience life, however, does not mean stepping back fully and allowing a free fall to happen to your child; it still means being a strong, guiding parent who sets limits for your kids. It is being mindful of the little things, or little ways we handle things, that over time break down any resilience a student may naturally have. In meeting with parents of high school students, I have found

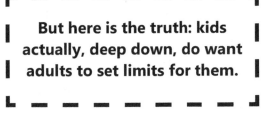

But here is the truth: kids actually, deep down, do want adults to set limits for them.

that some parents are not sure of how much to pull back in high school. Some do not pull back enough, and others hand over the reigns to their kids. One thing about kids that I know to be true is this: kids say they do not want limits, or rules, or adults telling them what to do. They will shout it at you at home from the top of the stairs, and sullenly give teachers the death stare when it is doled out at school (or they may just tell you in their inappropriate-for school-or-anytime language).

It is a developmentally natural part of growing up for kids to push back against and pull away from adults, especially parents and educators. **But here is the truth: kids actually, deep down, do want adults to set limits for them.** It is the kids whose parents have fully checked out and provide no limits whatsoever (some might call them the "cool" parents) who can feel the worst deep down because even though on the surface level they love the freedom (and perceived respect they get from other kids for having the "cool" parents), they know in their gut that having limits is actually a good thing, and they will respond to limits that are set for them. As we say in education—no matter low or high you set the bar for kids, they will reach it, and it is true for parents setting limits for their kids. Communication with kids is key in setting limits, so decide what your limits are as an adult, but talk through them with your kids, and you are likely to get more buy-in than by using sheer force. Remember, talking about limits (or other expectations) with your kids doesn't mean you are changing your mind; it's just a discussion.

One very common opportunity to help your student build resilience concerns what you do and how you react when your child fails a test or earns a "poor" grade. Just a reminder—"poor" is in the eye of the beholder; for one child poor is a 98; for others, poor is a 52. If your child gets a poor grade on or fails a test, first tap the brakes on your own emotions—about your child, about the grade, about the teacher whether you like him/her or not, about what grade you think your child's friends made—just some of the examples of hot-button reactors that may typically set people off emotionally. In this moment, work to recognize your own reactionary emotions or actions and avoid immediately acting (reacting) on/to those feelings.

Instead, if your child fails a test or gets a poor grade, talk with your child about what he or she feels went wrong (even if it seems overly obvious to you—remember, their brains are not fully developed yet). Through calm conversation with your child, talk about the steps that your child took that led up to earning the failing or low grade, then help your child formulate a plan for "doing better" the next time (self-responsibility). It is worth noting that perfectionism is a huge stressor for kids in the academic world (more on that in another chapter), so a helpful hint would be to encourage your child to set increments of improvement rather than shooting for a 100 on the test or future grade. For example, a plan might include setting aside reasonable amounts of time to study or do school work leading up to the next test or assignment deadline and then helping your child stick to the routine. As this series of acts becomes more routine over time, most kids will see a huge improvement in grades and confidence in themselves on how to earn them.

Some of the most damaging things a parent can do in terms of building resilience in their kids occur during stressful situations like finding out about their child's failed or low grades. Warning, what I am about to talk about may offend or even anger some readers, but you should know that *that is not my goal.* PLEASE KEEP READING. As I have mentioned—all of this book may not apply to all people, but the goal is for all of us to have a hand in changing our current anger-driven society for the better, and I am trying to speak as openly and honestly as I can. In life, honesty is sometimes welcomed but at other times may seem too harsh. My goal is not to "call anyone out" or judge people from a "high and mighty" standpoint. Rather, I want all of us to be able to work together to create genuine change, and the only way to create change is to discuss, head-on and openly and honestly, the issues that we are facing in today's world.

A typical scenario that plays out goes something like this: The parent learns of the failed test or low grade, usually at home in the evening (or possibly during the day via a text from the child or by viewing the grade online in an electronic grading portal or something similar available to parents), then lets his/her own emotions take over. The parent becomes angry at the child and may or may not show it to the child. The parent gets the child's story about what happened, which is likely to be pro-child when told by the child because sometimes kids, when faced with an angry parent, will give those facts and leave out others. (No, I am not saying your child always lies to you and the teacher is always right. What I am saying is that people naturally protect themselves when someone is angry at them and questioning them, especially if it is their parent, and they will protect themselves by making themselves look innocent of any wrongdoing and leave out other parts of the story. This scenario has happened to me personally more than once during my almost three decades in education.)

The parent then becomes judge and jury, and what happens next is key.

Rather than focusing the angry energy in a positive, future-thinking, child-centered self-improving way (which can help build the child's resilience), the parent, in an effort to "fix" the grade or help their child, may fire off an emotional (possibly aggressive) email to the teacher making an assortment of demands that may include pressure on the teacher to allow a re-do, defending the student's actions, insulting or blaming the teacher, threatening to go meet with the principal, or better yet, copying the principal on the email or going to visit the principal before ever speaking to the teacher. **When we are emotional, we sometimes do and say things we regret.** You get the picture. (See the chapters about communication and having control over how we react to something when it happens to us.)

Once angry words are delivered, they cannot be unsent or unsaid, and this is true in any emotional situation or relationship, not just parent/educator relationships (obviously). The teacher is likely to react with wearied frustration and his or her own level of anger because if one parent is willing to send an email like this, chances are other parents are equally willing to send their own. It is no wonder teachers—young new teachers or seasoned veteran

> **Once angry words are delivered, they cannot be unsent or unsaid, and this is true in any emotional situation or relationship, not just parent/educator relationships (obviously).**

teachers—can be reluctant to talk to parents. When angry/aggressive emails are sent (or equally bad, the aggressive yelling-at-the-teacher phone call or voicemail), it just does not make for a good working relationship or open communication. The importance of relationships and communication will come up again and again throughout this book.

I want to point out that I am not saying parents are not allowed to be angry or to express frustration with teachers (or anyone else for that matter). What I am saying is that we are all human, and when any of us (educator or not) are approached in an angry, aggressive way, any communication that occurs after that moment can (and in many cases will) be affected by that anger. What I am proposing, instead, is that we become aware of our own emotions when communicating with others, whether it is our child's teacher, our co-worker, the person behind the counter or answering the call at any business, or anyone else we interact with so that we can all truly "hear" each other and find more productive ways of resolving conflicts as they occur. Just as our culture of communication and behavior has reached a point in which angry aggression has become more common, we can and should work to reverse that trend in our society.

I also want to point out that just as "everything" in this book does not apply to "all" kids, *all* parents do not send angry/aggressive emails (or leave angry/aggressive voicemails) solely blaming the teacher and/or the school. Many times parents are upset, frustrated, or even angry, but their frustrations are aimed at the problem and their child's role in the problem, and they genuinely want help in getting their kids "back on track" or with resolving the issue in general. But I cannot say that these angry/aggressive scenarios are "exceptions" or are "few and far between." They occur too frequently to describe them that way. The examples I give in this book are those that we as educators have experienced, and because those cases can be so aggressive (compared to average conversations), they are seared in the minds of educators, and I am certain anyone who works with people has examples from their own line of work. My point is that our world in general has become more angry and more aggressive, and schools are not immune to that trend. We cannot dismiss angry/aggressive behaviors and actions between parents and educators as separate from and unrelated to those same behaviors and coping habits that shock and appall all of us when they happen in the "real world." Schools are our, and our teens', real world, and we must start there when working to reverse the trend of violence, outrage and aggression in the world. As adults we must start with ourselves.

We discussed communication skills in another chapter, but as an aside here I want to point out a general rule of thumb that I believe can go a long way toward improving communcation and, as a result, building strong relationships between not only parents and educators but also between humans in general. If you find yourself writing an email that takes more than a few sentences, stop. Gather your thoughts, and call that person. It is true that it is hard for teachers to talk on the phone because they are in class, but it still needs to happen. I can tell you from my own personal experiences that a phone call—a personal, human-to-human conversation—is much more powerful and effective than a multi-paragraph email (whether heated and emotional or run-of-the-mill mundane). Just because electronic forms of communication exist, it doesn't mean those are the always the best forms of communication. A good conversation has the power to heal wounds, build relationships, clear assumptions, clarify miscommunications (including perceived tone), and resolve anger. I can't stress this enough.

So back to honesty. I read a shared Facebook post recently in which a weary teacher (not someone I know; rather, a passed-on post) commented about grades and parents' views of what constitutes a "good" teacher and thus learning environment for kids versus reality. This writer made the point that parents equate a student's good grades with proof of effective learning and a good teacher. The writer went on to point out that in many situations, the best teachers and best learning environments are actually the ones in which your child does not make the best grades because of the very situation described above.

It goes like this: In a worst case scenario, low grades can equal angry/aggressive parents. Angry/aggressive parents can equal emails and phone calls demanding the teacher do again what he/she already did—teach and provide everything needed to be successful on the test or work. Student made choices (did not have a good plan for success) and failed the test or achieved a "bad" grade. For a teacher in this situation to avoid the parent emails or phone calls, it is much easier on the teacher to just let everyone get good grades. Problem solved. Everyone wins; no one gets hurt; no one complains. The parent fully believes it was a great school year because the child earned (received?) all As, but is everything the way it seems? A good education is truly in the eye of the beholder. Buyer beware.

I agree fully with the Facebook writer—some of the best classrooms and thus teachers are those in which the tests are hard; the reading challenging; the class discussion equally challenging and genuine. In other words, those in which the grades are truly earned and indicative of learning, not ones in which the teacher feels pressured or goaded into awarding sameness to everyone to avoid confrontation with parents and an educational system that is weary of complaints and the associated outrage, anger and aggression.

Professional ex-English teacher hint here: If you have ever read your own child's work for any given class, and you recognize the lack of quality in the work, but your child received an A on the work, you must acknowledge the difference between your child getting a good grade versus your child being truly educated. If your child writes poorly on one assignment, you cannot tell yourself things like "he was rushed" or "this is a one-time thing—she is an excellent student who always makes As" etc. Kids graduate from schools every year with poor skills but passing grades. These skills do not magically improve when kids leave high school. Parents must be willing to see what is happening with their own kids, hold their kids accountable for the quality of their kids' work, and look beyond the grade on the report card. Is this scenario true of every kid and every teacher every time? No. Does it happen? Absolutely. In its simplest form, it is about people avoiding conflict. Teachers avoiding conflict with parents and students. Parents avoiding conflict with their kids. All sleep well at night because of avoiding

> **If you have ever read your own child's work for any given class, and you recognize the lack of quality in the work, but your child received an A on the work, you must acknowledge the difference between your child getting a good grade versus your child being truly educated.**

the conflict, but is there real learning going on in the process? If it sounds too good to be true, it probably is.

So what are parents to do? Below are some pointers when navigating the stressors and anger that accompany your child's less-than-stellar school performance:

When you find out about the grade and feel yourself becoming angry, temporarily remove yourself from the situation. Go into another room, count to 10, breathe deeply, and remind yourself that your child is making decisions like, well, a child. This process will all get easier the more you (and your child) practice it. Once the conversation isn't driven by anger, it will be a much more productive conversation and situation.

Ask your child questions that get him/her to walk through the decisions and choices he/she made that led up to the earning of the poor grade. Note: Do not list them off for your child, which can create defensiveness in the child. It must be in the form of a conversation so your child takes ownership of his/her own decisions and behaviors. Maybe he/she procrastinated or skimmed through the study guide, or maybe he/she didn't do the required reading. Maybe he/she doesn't regularly participate in class for a variety of reasons from the age-old problem of friends in the classroom to the modern problem of being on his/her cell phone instead of listening. It happens in schools across the country every day.

On a side note—many students do not have effective study skills, and with the age of smart phones/internet/at-your-fingertip on-demand information, they also do not see the logic in learning how to appropriately study (more on electronics later). Many students believe scanning over something for a few minutes equates "studying for a test" and are surprised when they fail. A quick internet search will reveal a variety of study skill lists and techniques that you can help teach at home. Yes—you teach at home. Depending on your age, you may or may not be old enough to remember or notice that in previous decades, there was a crisp line drawn between education and home that has been blurred into today's expectations that

EVERYTHING be taught at school with little or nothing taught at home, and I can tell you it is not working very well. There is a saying that it takes a village…Education takes all of us—professional educators and parents/guardians at home.

I should add, too, that good, old-fashioned study skills are still effective but for many students, have fallen by the wayside. Study techniques such as using notecards to write out words (etc.) on the front and definitions (etc.) on the back so that students can quiz themselves or each other are still effective. Kids who have been raised in the electronic age still need to be taught these skills in that they often believe that skimming over an electronic page on a computer (or their phone) is an effective way to study, yet their grades and actual knowledge reflect poor study skills. In its simplest form, skimming does not equal memorizing, and lots of students use skimming to "study" for a test or quiz. Sometimes information simply needs to be memorized. The simple act of writing the words and definitions out is itself an effective learning tool that many students do not experience because they receive class notes, etc., via electronic means such as an electronic "blackboard" system in which notes, homework, etc. are posted for the student to download. The lack of writing itself is just one missing link in modern students' study skills.

Help your child set up a routine for studying/doing school work at home that includes a specific place to work. For some families, the kitchen table does the trick; for other families, the child's room works for this. Have a frank discussion with your child about what works best for your family and your child, then set it up and stick to it. Every day as needed.

Have your child develop and follow a routine at school in which your child talks to his/her teachers and attends tutoring as needed. When many students reach high school age, they believe going to tutoring only needs to happen when they have a failing average, but the opposite is true. Students should attend tutoring when they sense they do not fully understand the class work before the grade ever becomes failing so that the student can ask questions and interact with the teacher. Not only does tutoring help students to improve in the class, but the act of going to tutoring and talking to a teacher builds so many other qualities and skills in the student—practicing communication skills; learning to advocate for him/herself without the parent intervening; figuring out what the student actually needs help with or is not understanding; following a positive academic routine; and more. These skills will benefit your child throughout high school and beyond—college, the workplace, real life problem-solving, etc.

Create a family system of reward that motivates the child to meet set goals. Very often parents focus on taking away what their child wants to encourage the child to do what the parent wants the child to do (and what the child should do). Removing what the child wants is a very common disciplinary system. A suggestion is to flip that mindset into setting up a system in which your child works to earn the things he/she wants. Have a discussion with your child about what motivates the child the most. (Be sure to take into account and apply the discussion we had in an earlier chapter about motivation in general.) You probably already have a good idea of what motivates your child, but the discussion with your child makes your child a part of the plan rather than the victim of a plan you created and forced on the child—perception is reality. Create a family system that incorporates earning that valued thing—whether it is driving privileges, TV or screen time (again, more on electronics in another chapter), participating in activities, which very often cost money (competitive sports, dance lessons, etc.), or a material item such as a new pair of tennis shoes, etc. Write the plan down in the form of a contract that kids and parents both sign, then follow.

For high school kids, earning the use of their phone is an excellent motivator as most kids want their phone more than they want food or, for some, driving privileges. Taking the phone away as punishment is a far more difficult routine to enforce and maintain, and the onus is on the parent to enforce it. By setting up phone usage as a reward for meeting earned goals each week, the onus is on the child to meet the set and agreed-upon expectations—it is a win-win situation. As your child follows the plan you both came up with, a reward system can be in place in which, in exchange for earning a certain grade (remember, discussion is key here as well—it is not always about the number), your child earns something—what he/she earns depends on your system. It could be points toward something, a certain number of minutes of something, getting to watch a show or movie. Be creative!

> **For high school kids, earning the use of their phone is an excellent motivator as most kids want their phone more than they want food or, for some, driving privileges.**

On a side note—many times in my career, parents have talked to me about how they have punished their child for his/her poor grades by not allowing their child to participate in a school group he/she is a part of, whether that is the football team, the marching band, or any other organized activity the student is involved in. I have always discouraged parents from going this route because for many kids, that group is a main reason their child enjoys school and looks forward to coming to school. Because of state rules such as "No Pass No Play," the adult leaders of those groups are another set of eyes on your child's grades and progress and will step in to support your child if he/she is going off-track with his/her grades or behavior in class. To cut your child from these groups as a punishment for "bad" grades is very often the best way to disengage your child from school in that the group could be the very thing that motivates the child to "do better" that a parent is looking for.

No swooping in. If your child earns a failing grade (by his/her own choices and decisions), focus on the child's ownership of the grade and next steps. The grade did not *happen to* your child—the child earned the grade he/she received. Help your child to reframe his/her worldview about how grades (and any other outcomes) work in life. Refrain from blaming others for the grade and reset using the tips above for helping your child get a better grade next time. If your child forgets his homework at home, do not take it to him. Do not email the teacher asking for extended time. Over time, your child will learn from the frustrated feeling of forgetting something at home how to be a responsible kid and a future responsible adult, especially when it is paired with not meeting a goal the child was working toward. Will your child be upset the first time you refuse to save him/her? Absolutely. But it will get better. If you save him or her every time something is forgotten, resilience and grit can never be honed.

Along these same lines, it also goes without saying—do not do the work for your child. Ever. No matter how much you feel it makes your life easier. This feeling of relief for parents is only temporary as it glosses over the immediate and does not address the real issue, which will happen again. If a parent "fixes" it this time, the child learns very quickly and expects that the parent will fix it every time. It doesn't take long following this routine for a child to lose motivation to get anything done on his/her own by a deadline because the child knows the parent will "handle it," and the parent is the one left working all hours of the night while the child is doing... whatever he/she is doing. This applies to filling out college applications and any assortment of high school paperwork. For example, when it comes to high school class scheduling, of course you need to discuss your child's plans and choices with your child, but your child should fill out his/her own scheduling paperwork. The same is true for college recommendation or transcript requests. Parents—do not complete your child's college applications for him/her. It is your child's education, and/he she must take ownership of it. Other than official school enrollment forms, all high school paperwork should be completed by the child/student with the parent involved as needed. Remember—kids do not magically grow up and learn to do these things when you drop them off at their dorm the fall after graduating high school or when they start their first job. Every habit (good, bad, or never learned) will go with them. Teach your child, and let your child.

You may be thinking at this point in the reading that your role as a parent is to be hands-off, but that is not the case, either. You are still the parent, responsible for raising your child in the style that you feel is the best fit for your family and for your child. It is more difficult and scarier for some parents, however, to allow their child to do and be for him/herself, at least in the beginning if this is not how you have been parenting. Some parents may perceive that it is easier to do it for their child (whatever "it" is—filling out the form, doing the work *just this one time*, etc.) rather than taking the harder, messier, and more time-consuming route of letting your child do "it" and learn from his/her own experiences (AKA the "hard" way) if he/she doesn't ace "it" the first time.

Parents, you are still the parent. Monitor what is happening at school, and if there is a situation that you know requires you to talk to the teacher, counselor, or principal, please do it. This book is not about backing off from the educational system or from parenting your child as you see fit. This book is about allowing your child to experience life's challenges with your guidance so that your child can build his/her own resilience when you use a potentially different approach to helping your child deal with the educational system and the stressors and challenges in his/her life. As parents, talk through the issue with your child and keep an open mind when you reach out to the school so that your conversation with the school can be productive.

Just as teaching is hard, parenting is hard. For many of the years I taught, I had a poster in my classroom with the message that doing what is right is not always popular (and thus easy). This poster applies to all of us—educators, parents, and kids. The key to being part of genuine, effective, positive, real change in our world lies in and begins with all of us. We must start with ourselves—parents and educators—and we must work together to make real change happen.

Chapter 9

Bullying

Chapter 9

Bullying

Most parents want nothing more than to shield their kids from hurt and pain. I have seen parents in my own circle of friends post on social media that seeing their kids in pain and not being able to do anything about it is one of the hardest parts of being a parent. If a parent suspects or finds out their child is being bullied, the parent will most often (and understandably) respond with anger and protectiveness. In previous generations, the parent might redirect their anger into working with their child to help empower the child to be strong and stand up to the bully. For some that meant fighting fire with fire, for others it meant working with their child to help them be a stronger person and not let the bully get to them as much. Coping mechanisms such as ignoring the bully were typical go-to's in previous generations. Or, the parent might have reached out to the parent of the bully directly to have a conversation about what is going on in their children's relationship with each other. While these tactics are probably still used by some parents today, in the past it was a different, simpler time, and the school was largely not part of the process unless an altercation took place at school.

Before we dive into the definition of bullying, let me say that regardless of whether a student's behavior is or is not bullying, educators want to help your child. If your child is experiencing or is the recipient of negative behavior from another person, we want to know about it, and we want to help. We do not want to debate whether it is or is not bullying. It is important to recognize, however, that with anything at school, an allegation of bullying is one that school administrators must look into, and that is where the definition of bullying truly comes into play. I cannot emphasize enough that parents and students

> Before we dive into the definition of bullying, let me say that regardless of whether a student's behavior is or is not bullying, educators want to help your child.

should reach out to educators (teachers, counselors, administrators, etc.) if another person's behavior is making them uncomfortable so that we can help your child and help address the situation, no matter what "category" of behavior that other behavior falls into.

In today's world, the term "bullying" and its definition have broadened vastly for kids and parents compared to previous generations, and the onus has been put on the school to "fix" the issue of bullying. This is true of many areas of life that were once considered strictly issues that would be handled at home—very similar to the grades discussion from a previous chapter. Because kids' and parents' perception of the term bullying has become so broad and all-inclusive, school districts have had to develop a technical working definition so that all stakeholders—parents, kids, teachers, administrators, etc.—understand each other and are on the proverbial "same page." It is important to note from the beginning of this chapter that "bullying" can encompass a wide, all-inclusive set of behaviors that differs from person to person and varies depending on whether that person is a parent, educator, etc. There is a perceived public definition of bullying, and there is a more technical definition of bullying. In an effort to clarify the definition of and to dispel any myths about bullying, all will be discussed in this chapter. Before we begin the discussion of bullying, however, I again want to make something clear on behalf of all educators: we want to help your child. We do not want to get bogged down in the definition of bullying when it comes to helping your child deal with someone else's behavior, so if you feel someone is hurting your child, please contact the school. Immediately.

Many consider hateful, aggressive behavior to be bullying, and this is true for many teens. Unfortunately, this behavior is not limited to schools. Just turn to social media for five minutes, pick any news story or article that might warrant differing opinions, and read the comments. Virtually any story will be filled with hateful, personal, low-blow, presumptive, and just plain mean comments personally aimed at other people leaving comments. And these comments are written by adults meant for other adults the writer has never even met. We will dedicate another chapter to social media and electronics specifically, but it is clear that the internet and social media embolden people to do and say things online that they might NEVER do in person. When applied to the teen world, social media becomes a hunting ground for the haters and the hated. We discussed the reality of controlling other people's behavior in a previous chapter, yet when it comes to cyberbullying, today's schools and educators are expected to control and punish the actions of kids that occur off school grounds in the middle of the night in a teen's room at home.

> **One assumption by many today is that all suicides and school shootings are caused by or linked to bullying, whether directly or indirectly.**

Bullying is a hot-button topic in that it has been an assumed go-to link to suicides and school shootings as well as fights in schools. One assumption by many today is that all suicides and school shootings are caused by or linked to bullying, whether directly or indirectly. This is not to say that there is never a causal relationship between bullying and suicide or school shootings, but like most things in life, it is often more complicated than that. It is understandable that when a child's suicide or a school shooting occur, people want answers. We all want to be able to understand why something happened so that someone can be held accountable and we can work together to keep it from happening again. It is human nature. Sometimes bullying is part of the situation; other times, it is not. Regardless of one's perceptions of bullying and fault, it is easy to see that bullying is a high-stakes topic for schools, students, and parents.

> **We all want to be able to understand why something happened so that someone can be held accountable and we can work together to keep it from happening again. It is human nature.**

Like the rest of this book, I am going to write as honestly as possible in hopes of initiating change. As an educator, I absolutely do not condone bullying or mean behavior any more than any student or parent who has dealt with it. In terms of discussing bullying, however, it must be clarified that all mean behavior is not bullying, and everyone accused of bullying is not a bully. Sometimes people are mean, and since the dawn of time, there are people who have been mean. People are mean to their spouses. People are mean to wait staff at restaurants. People are mean to educators and police officers and nurses. People are mean to animals. People are mean to each other on highways and in parking lots and at little league games. Were (or are) these people bullies? Possibly but not necessarily. Do we need to work to help those people? Absolutely. Will we ever be able to completely eradicate meanness in humanity? Probably not. And therein lies the rub with the perceived (common worldview) definition of bullying.

Many people equate the term bullying with mean behavior, but bullying is often more than just mean behavior. *Stopbullying.gov* (N.D.) defines bullying as "unwanted, aggressive behavior among school aged children that involves a real or perceived power imbalance. The behavior is repeated, or has the potential to be repeated, over time (What is Bullying, para. 1). According to *stopbullying.gov*, **in order to be considered bullying, the behavior must be aggressive and include:**

An Imbalance of Power: Kids who bully use their power—such as physical strength, access to embarrassing information, or popularity—to control or harm others. Power imbalances can change over time and in different situations, even if they involve the same people.

Repetition: Bullying behaviors happen more than once or have the potential to happen more than once. Bullying includes actions such as making threats, spreading rumors, attacking someone physically or verbally, and excluding someone from a group on purpose (para. 1).

Bullying can also take different shapes. *Stopbullying.gov*: identifies three types of bullying:

Verbal bullying is saying or writing mean things. Verbal bullying includes teasing, name-calling, inappropriate sexual comments, taunting, and threatening to cause harm. **Social bullying**, sometimes referred to as relational bullying, involves hurting someone's reputation or relationships and includes leaving someone out on purpose, telling other children not to be friends with someone, spreading rumors about someone, and embarrassing someone in public. **Physical bullying** involves hurting a person's body or possessions and includes hitting/kicking/pinching, spitting, tripping/pushing, taking or breaking someone's things, and making mean or rude hand gestures (Types of Bullying, para. 1-3).

Stopbullying.gov addresses cyberbullying separately from bullying:

Cyberbullying is bullying that takes place over digital devices like cell phones, computers, and tablets. Cyberbullying can occur through SMS, Text, and apps, or online in social media, forums, or gaming where people can view, participate in, or share content. Cyberbullying includes sending, posting, or sharing negative, harmful, false, or mean content about someone else. It can include sharing personal or private information about someone else causing embarrassment or humiliation. Some cyberbullying crosses the line into unlawful or criminal behavior (What is Cyberbullying, para. 1).

According to *stopbullying.gov*, bullying can occur during or after school hours, and most reported bullying happens in the school building. Cyberbullying, however, can occur many places, including social sedia, such as Facebook, Instagram, Snapchat, and Twitter; SMS (Short Message Service) also known as text message sent through devices; Instant Message (via devices, email provider services, apps, and social media messaging features), and Email (para. 2).

According to *stopbullying.gov*, there are special concerns when it comes to cyberbullying in that online information, regardless of forum, can be shared and viewed by many people, which creates a public record of a person.

> *The content an individual shares online – both their personal content as well as any negative, mean, or hurtful content – creates a... permanent public record of their views, activities, and behavior. This public record can be thought of as an online reputation, which may be accessible to schools, employers, colleges, clubs, and others who may be researching an individual now or in the future. Cyberbullying can harm the online reputations of everyone involved – not just the person being bullied, but those doing the bullying or participating in it (para. 3).*
>
> *...Cyberbullying can be **persistent** (online availability 24 hours a day, so difficult to get away from); **permanent** (most information communicated electronically is permanent and public; and **hard to notice** (may not be easily observed by others such as parents or teachers) (para. 4).*

According to *stopbullying.gov*, "although all states have laws requiring schools to respond to bullying, many states do not include cyberbullying under these laws or specify the role schools should play in responding to bullying that takes place outside of school. Schools may take action either as required by law, or with local or school policies that allow them to discipline or take other action" (para. 5).

As a frame of reference, *stopbullying.gov* cites recent national bullying statistics. For youth bullying, the 2015 School Crime Supplement (National Center for Education Statistics and Bureau of Justice Statistics) indicates that, nationwide, about 21% of students ages 12-18 experienced bullying (Frequency of Bullying, para. 1). The 2017 Youth Risk Behavior Surveillance System (Centers for Disease Control and Prevention) indicates that, nationwide, 19% of students in grades 9–12 report being bullied on school property in the 12 months preceding the survey (para. 2). For cyberbulling, the 2017 Youth Risk Behavior Surveillance System (Centers for Disease Control and Prevention) indicates that an estimated 14.9% of high school students were electronically bullied in the 12 months prior to the survey (Frequency of Cyberbullying, para. 2).

Parents, it is important to realize that all mean behavior does not necessarily fit the category of "bullying," but if your child is experiencing any the above, whether it ends up meeting the "definition" of bullying or not, please do not hesitate to reach out to your child's school counselor or administrator for help. Again, educators want to help your child, regardless of the technical definition or category of the behavior your or your child is reporting about someone else. Although exact rules and procedures may vary state-to-state, generally when an accusation of bullying has been made at a school, school administrators are required to investigate to determine if the actions of the students meet the definition of bullying based on the district's definitions and guidelines similar to the guidelines listed above.

Using a high school example, when bullying is reported to someone at school, whether it is a teacher, counselor, or administrator, the administrator will conduct an investigation in which he/she will talk to your child, to the accused bully, and to other witnesses to determine what has happened and when. Typically and understandably, when a parent and student come forward and accuse another student of bullying, the parent and student already fully believe the other person is a bully and want the school to "prosecute" the other student to the full extent of the (school) law (worldview; perception is reality). In its simplest form, meanness has occurred, that meanness is unacceptable, and someone needs to be punished. Very often, however, the definition of bullying is not met; very often it is found that the aggressive behavior has come from both sides/both kids, neither of whom has an imbalance of power over the other. Very often, too, the behavior is not repetitive.

Rather, in its simplest form, two kids disagreed over something, argued about it, possibly got into an altercation at school about it, and, as a result, got into disciplinary trouble. Because there was arguing and disagreement between the two kids and mean words were said, the assumption is made (by the parents and students) that one or both children were bullied (by each other). After the investigation is completed by the administrator and the accused is not found to have committed "bullying" in the eyes of the district based on parameters like those listed above, and particularly when the students will both still have to serve his or her disciplinary punishment (suspension, etc.), parents (and students) may become angry because their worldview tells them that mean behavior is bullying, and schools must do something about it. When schools do not find that bullying has occurred (and do not reverse the disciplinary consequences of the students involved), the assumption by some parents and students is that the school and the educators who work there do not care (about their kids or about what happened) or that they condone bullying. The working relationship between the parent and school is damaged in the process.

Reminder: People (adults and kids) have a level of self-responsibility for their actions and make choices every day. The better-informed that kids and parents are when it comes to the dynamics of getting along with both kids and adults at school, the better off everyone is in the process, and, as a result, fewer hurt and angry feelings occur (as well as potential disciplinary consequences).

It is very important for students and parents to report incidents of aggressive behavior to the school so that the school can investigate. There are times when aggressive behavior is occurring at school that goes unreported until something blows up (and kids get into trouble at school), and at that time, the student and parent "tells all" and gets angry at the school for "doing nothing about it" because "this has been going on since 7th grade!" (even though the student is now in high school, and nothing has been reported at that school). The school cannot help with something they know nothing about. They can only step in when a behavior is reported or observed by someone at school. There are many reasons students and parents do not want to report, but it is critical that they report in that, maybe most importantly, even if the school's bullying investigation does not reveal a specific instance to be bullying, it documents that the behavior took place so that if it happens again, evidence mounts and shows a pattern of behavior (repetition) that may eventually be found to be bullying. Or, the investigation itself might be enough to stop the behavior altogether so everyone can live in peace. As part of the investigation, school counselors or interventionists very often are able to step in and work with the students and, if the students on both sides of the disagreement agree to take part, can use conflict resolution techniques such as peer mediation or other strategies to help students resolve their conflict with each other in a peaceful way for all parties.

There are many good resources and strategies for parents to help their children if they suspect their child is being bullied or is a bully, and your school counselors, interventionists, and administrators can help you with those resources. Remember—one of the hardest parts of parenting is being totally honest about what your own children are doing and saying, especially during the teen years when teen personalities are naturally becoming more independent. Parents of teens will identify with the eye rolls, heavy sighs, slammed doors, and other teen behaviors that accompany the developmental human need to pull away from parents and become independent people. It is up to parents to decide how they will navigate this emotional time, and educators are here to help you!! But parents must be vigilant and honest with their own kids' behaviors and step up if they see their child as the recipient of bullying behavior or as the bully him/herself. The key is to be in tune with your child and to foster open communication with your child.

> ...parents must be vigilant and honest with their own kids' behaviors and step up if they see their child as the recipient of bullying behavior or as the bully him/herself.

We will discuss social media and electronics more in-depth in another chapter, but parents must be in tune with what their kids are doing online. As I mentioned in the chapter about grades, the best, seemingly most well-behaved kids will not always tell their parents everything, and parents sometimes choose to look the other way because it is easier or because they do not like confrontation themselves. Parenting is hard, and parenting in the age of the internet and social media is the most difficult of all. Parents must be vigilant in knowing what their kids are doing in the virtual world just as they would in the physical world because, again, people are emboldened and far more brave online, and this includes kids.

According to *stopbullying.gov*, there are are many warning signs that may indicate that someone is affected by bullying—either being bullied or bullying others. Recognizing the warning signs is an important first step in taking action against bullying. Not all children who are bullied or are bullying others ask for help. It is important to talk with children who show signs of being bullied or bullying others. These warning signs can also point to other issues or problems, such as depression or substance abuse. Talking to the child can help identify the root of the problem (Warning Signs for Bullying, para. 1-2). *Stopbullying.gov* recommends that parents look for changes in the child. However, parents should be aware that not all children who are bullied exhibit warning signs (para. 3).

Some signs that may point to a bullying problem are:

*Unexplainable injuries

*Lost or destroyed clothing, books, electronics, or jewelry

*Frequent headaches or stomach aches, feeling sick or faking illness

*Changes in eating habits, like suddenly skipping meals or binge eating. Kids may come home from school hungry because they did not eat lunch.

*Difficulty sleeping or frequent nightmares

*Declining grades, loss of interest in schoolwork, or not wanting to go to school

*Sudden loss of friends or avoidance of social situations

*Feelings of helplessness or decreased self esteem

*Self-destructive behaviors such as running away from home, harming themselves, or talking about suicide (para. 4).

Stopbullying.gov recommends that if you know someone in serious distress or danger, don't ignore the problem. Get help right away (para. 5). While it is obviously very important for parents to keep a watchful on their kids in looking for signs that they are being bullied, it is also critical that parents are equally concerned about noticing whether their child is a bully him/herself.

Kids may be bullying others if they:

*Get into physical or verbal fights

*Have friends who bully others

*Are increasingly aggressive

*Get sent to the principal's office or to detention frequently

*Have unexplained extra money or new belongings

*Blame others for their problems

*Don't accept responsibility for their actions

*Are competitive and worry about their reputation or popularity (Signs a Child is Bullying Others, para. 1).

With so many resources available, and the discussion of bullying being on the forefront of both educators' and parents' minds, one might wonder why more kids who are being bullied don't reach out for help. Stopbullying.

gov provides insight and data on that point as well. The 2012 Indicators of School Crime and Safety show that an adult was notified in less than half (40%) of bullying incidents (Why don't kids ask for help, para. 1).

Kids don't tell adults for many reasons:

Bullying can make a child feel helpless. Kids may want to handle it on their own to feel in control again. They may fear being seen as weak or a tattletale.
Kids may fear backlash from the kid who bullied them.
Bullying can be a humiliating experience. Kids may not want adults to know what is being said about them, whether true or false. They may also fear that adults will judge them or punish them for being weak.
Kids who are bullied may already feel socially isolated. They may feel like no one cares or could understand.
Kids may fear being rejected by their peers. Friends can help protect kids from bullying, and kids can fear losing this support (para. 2).

While all "bad" behavior is not bullying according to the formal definition of bullying, kids still need guidance at school and at home about appropriate and inappropriate behavior. Parents are encouraged to reach out to their school counselors or administrators for help, and there are many resources available to help. Good communication is key both at home and at school with school personnel. Holding kids accountable for their behavior both at school and at home is necessary in helping kids learn what is appropriate, positive behavior, even if it is hard to do. Being an educator is hard, and being a parent is harder, but they are both such important jobs that educators and parents must team up to work together and support each other.

> **Holding kids accountable for their behavior both at school and at home is necessary in helping kids learn what is appropriate, positive behavior, even if it is hard to do.**

Working with your child's school is the best place to start because you and your child's educators best know your child (and observe his/her behavior first-hand), but it is important for all parties to be honest in the discussion of your child's behavior so that all parties are not dancing around the real issues in order to keep the conversation from blowing up or falling apart due to heightened emotions. Like the communication skills we discussed in a previous chapter, good communication skills in which parents and educators are able to openly give and receive information are going to be the most productive when dealing with a topic as sensitive and high-stakes as bullying and mean behavior. When parents come to a school and say their child is being bullied, educators know the parents' (and the child's) emotions are already on high-alert, and they are ready to help and support you and your child and get the situation resolved. Lean on them, and don't push them away with anger if the school investigation does not turn out as you had hoped. It does not mean the school does not care.

Some parents may be wondering at this point if they are alone in feeling that not only is their child a bully, but that the parent himself/herself is the victim. I can tell you from my own school counseling experiences, you are not alone. Many times over the years parents have come to my office at the end of their proverbial rope with dealing with their child. Sometimes parents have shared that they are afraid of their child and that their child has physically abused them or other family members. Unfortunately in these cases, the police or protective services have had to or should have become involved.

According to a *Psychology Today* blog post, Grover (2016) says there are **three types of kids who bully their parents.** The **defiant bully** is the child who is aggressive, confrontational, and oppositional; the child who will openly in-your-face reject a parent's attempt at controlling the child's behavior (para. 2). The **anxious bully** is the child who oscillates between clinging to their parents and pushing them away…they cling to the parent for comfort and, once received, reject and push away their parents again (para. 12). The **manipulative bully** is the child who finds the parent's own insecurities, guilts, and fears about your parenting and takes advantage of them using a variety of tools to get what he wants by preying on the parent's own insecurities (para. 24).

So what can a parent do if he/she is being bullied by his/her own child? According to Grover:

…*The bullying styles discussed here offer a lens through which to view your own child's behavior. With a clearer understanding of his or her bullying style, you will gain a deeper understanding of the child's inner life and be better prepared to steer your relationship in a new direction. Keep in mind that beneath the tough exterior of every bully is a scared child, constantly wrestling with insecurities and worries. Bullying is an expression of this internal unrest. By understanding what makes your bully tick, you will gain insight into the nature of her fears, better understand the forces that fuel her bullying, and become poised to take action to restore balance (para. 26).*

Parenting a child-bully comes back in many ways to working on good communication skills on the part of the parent but also on the part of the child as well as parenting skills, and practicing these skills from when the child is very young helps. There are many free resources available online, and just as with any kid-to-kid bullying situation, reach out to your child's counselor or administrator. Many schools have resources they can offer for counseling and other professional intervention to help support parents, including parenting classes, which are often free. Again, if your child is violent towards you or other family members, calling the police is sometimes necessary and will sometimes be enough to turn the situation around (along with some family counseling and other professional interventions). Just know that you do not have to live in fear of your child, and as with any parenting situation, it is not always easy to "fix" the situation, but you still must try for your sake and for your family's sake. Just as with any other difficult situation, doing nothing and taking the path of least resistance will not fix the situation.

When it comes to tolerating abusive, aggressive behavior, the path of least resistance can encourage that behavior to continue.

I should add at this point a reminder about the importance of follow-through. Many times parents come to school to get help from counselors and are referred for counseling and other resources, and too often, parents do not follow through with the resources. Family and individual counseling is one example of an intervention that can help not only with child-bullies but with all types of family issues (divorce, death in the family, substance abuse, blended families, etc.). When parents come to me asking for help and clearly needing outside help, I go through the process with the family on what resources our district offers and how to take advantage of those resources. In the moment, the parent is very relieved and glad to have some type of option to help. But the next steps are crucial—did the parent schedule an intake for counseling? Did the parent follow through to get the counseling? Too often the parent does not follow through with getting the help.

Following through is the most critical step in parenting and in getting help. Whether it is with consistent discipline at home (no means no) or with homework routines or with going to the counseling appointments—follow-through is key. Parents cannot be frustrated and surprised that there is no change when they themselves do not commit to the change. In defense of parents, sometimes the follow-through for counseling and other services is difficult due to personal circumstances, but even in those difficult situations, finding a way to follow through and get the help is better than the alternative of getting no help. We will discuss this more in another chapter.

Chapter 10

Combating Meanness & Bullying:
Empathy, Apathy & Being a Friend

So now that we understand what bullying is and isn't, the fact remains that whether the behavior meets the "definition" of bullying, the behavior is still mean, and parents must step up and step in. So what can parents do? As with everything else in this book, the key is to do something. Even though your kids and their behaviors may make you scratch your heads some days, they are still like sponges in that every day they soak up the world around them, and you are a key part of that world.

Oxford Dictionaries defines **empathy** as "the ability to understand and share the feelings of another." Empathy is not to be confused with sympathy. When one feels empathy, he is able to understand what the other person is going through. In modern slang, we feel empathy when we have "been there and done that" and (in a lighter, less serious form of emotion) respond to our friends by saying (or commenting online)—"I feel ya!" We might feel empathy when our friend is upset that her favorite pants no longer fit because she ate too much over the holidays. Or we might feel empathy for someone when their dog dies because we remember the distinctive pain that occurs when your own beloved pet passes away. We have been there.

It hurts, and you hurt with them. Sympathy, on the other hand, is a feeling we get when we feel something for someone else, such as feeling sorry for someone when their boyfriend breaks up with them or their purse gets stolen. Admittedly, empathy and sympathy are similar depending on what our life's experiences have been, and it is easy to see how they are confused and interchanged.

Oxford Dictionaries defines **apathy** as "lack of interest, enthusiasm, or concern." I have had many (in the hundreds if not thousands) of conversations with parents and students about the student's apathy towards all things school—grades, homework, tests, attendance—you name it. Based on my personal experiences in schools, apathy is alive and well, and it has progressively worsened during my three decades in education.

Because bullying involves a person being "mean" to another person, one might assume that kids who bully lack empathy. Experts are not consistent in terms of the connection between empathy and bullying. According to a *Psychology Today* blog post, Lamia (2010) says empathy can be used to help or hurt others. Rather than bullies lacking empathy, Lamia says:

Bullies are notorious for their ability to recognize weaknesses or shame in others. They do have a capacity to empathize. However, they destructively use their empathy to manipulate, control, exploit, or to cause pain. And they are able to withhold their compassion for the distress they cause others to feel (para. 7).

Van Noorden, Cillessen, Haselager, Lansu, and Bukowski (2017) studied how empathy is related to bullies and their target peers in 264 7-12 year-olds and found that it varies depending on characteristics of the bully as well as the target (p. 260). Van Noorden et al. pointed out that we often think that varied levels of empathy are due to individual differences (meaning the bully lacks empathy more than the victim or witnesses, which in turn allows him/her to bully without caring about the other person), but in the study they found that the bullies, victims, and bully/victims showed less empathy for each other than for noninvolved peers (p. 260).

In other words, rather than lacking empathy altogether, all of the kids in the study (bullies and bully victims) had a level of empathy but applied it differently towards those they were bullying/being bullied by compared to their uninvolved peers.

So if bullies have the capacity to care, why do they behave the way they do? And can we step in and make a change? Yes, we can all step in and make a change by doing what we have always done at home and at school—by teaching and guiding our kids. Much of the research about bullying is aimed at just that—teaching and modeling appropriate behavior because, in its simplest form, kids (and adults) don't know what they don't know. Left unchecked, the worst behavior humans exhibit will continue. Why should it stop if there are no consequences? To understand more about why kids behave the way they do (bullying and otherwise), it is important to understand the basics of what they are experiencing emotionally as they grow up. Based on my experiences working with kids and their parents, there are kids who could use some work on their skills at becoming more empathetic and sympathetic and becoming less apathetic. Part of this behavior is simply "being a teen," but that's where adults need to step up and step in.

According to the Centers for Disease Control and Prevention, young teens between the ages of 12 and 14 experience (among others) the following emotional/social changes as well as with thinking and learning:

*show concern about body image, looks and clothes

*focus on themselves

*experience moodiness

*show interest in and influence by peer group

*seem rude or short-tempered toward their parents

*feel stress from more challenging school work

*have more ability for complex thought

*are better able to express feelings through talking

*develop a stronger sense of right and wrong (para. 2-3).

"*Wait,*" you may be thinking. "*Earlier you said they didn't know what they were doing until age 25!*" Not exactly. Brains are not fully mature until the age of 25, but as kids are growing up, they are maturing. It's not like they don't know anything and are off the hook for all of their behaviors!

When teens reach the ages of 15-17, parents can start to see a noticeable change in most kids. According to the CDC, young teens at this age experience (among others) the following emotional/social changes as well as with thinking and learning:

have more interest in romantic relationships and sexuality

go through less conflict with and more independence from parents

have a deeper capacity for caring and sharing and for developing more intimate relationships

spend less time with parents and more time with friends

learn more defined work habits

show more concern about future school and work plans

might be better able to give reasons for their own choices, including about what is right or wrong (para. 2-3).

Many studies exist regarding what makes a bully and how to "bully-proof" your child. I encourage you to read for yourself what is out there. Experts differ on whether empathy and other personal characteristics have a direct connection to whether someone is a bully or not. Some experts say that bullies still possess the ability to be empathetic towards others but choose not to be; others say that bullies need to work on their empathy skills. I would say this is true for many kids, not just those who seem to be bullies (and adults as well—again, check the comments section on social media and tell me if you see empathy when the discussion is controversial).

Some basic recommendations for helping bully-proof your child (or just basically teach him/her how to be a good human being and role model for others...) include:

Teach problem-solving skills by helping your child walk through and navigate a problem rather than fixing the problem for them. I talked about this extensively in another chapter using the example of helping your child come up with a plan and then executing the plan for improving his/her grades and relationship with his/her teacher at school. This is just one example.

Build relationship skills by modeling appropriate behavior at home in relationships and working on those relationships if needed (getting family counseling, etc.). As parents, do you fight with your spouse? Do you have your own relationship patterns to work on, including how you interact with your children? Chances are, if you are human, the answer is yes. Being self-aware of your own behaviors and reactions to others and working to improve them will go very far with how your child learns to navigate his/her own relationships with you and with his/her friends.

Work with your child to empower them to handle difficult people. A difficult person in high school is likely not the last difficult person your child will encounter; just ask any adult who has a job or goes out in public or gets on social media.

Find ways to instill resilience into your child. Remember, saving and protecting are two different things, but don't pull away altogether in an effort to teach your child to go it alone. Kids need guidance *and* resiliency.

Work with your child on building his/her self-efficacy (or belief in him/herself). This goes hand-in-hand with building resiliency and building a growth-mindset in your child. Remember, swooping in and saving your child can reinforce your child's belief that he/she cannot be successful without you stepping in. If this is the go-to coping mechanism that you reinforce in your child, you cannot complain when he/she has those same qualities at 22 or even 32. Slight exaggeration? Possibly, but I think it is more accurate than not. A very common discussion I have with students and parents in high school about their student's study habits is that there will be no magic when the student graduates from high school and the parent drops the student off at his/her dorm a few months later. ALL of the student's habits will go with him/her to that college campus and college classroom. Very often students struggle extensively the first semester or year of college, and many do not make it beyond that first year because they simply do not have the skills (soft skills such as time management, leadership, and communication skills, not to be confused with a lack of academic ability) or belief in themselves to make it on their own if they are so accustomed to their parents saving and fixing everything for them leading up to that point in life. It can be very difficult and painful for parents to let their children live imperfect lives and "learn the hard way" when they are younger, but these difficult life experiences are the very way kids can learn to be strong on their own.

Reinforce appropriate behavior at home from a very early age. If you see your children bullying or being mean to each other, step up and step in to model better, more appropriate behavior so that later, when your child is part of a peer group at school, the more appropriate behavior comes naturally to them.

Teach your child how to treat others with kindness and respect, including how to behave when they disagree with someone. Model appropriate behavior at home. Again, kids do not know what they do not know. If they witness hateful, aggressive behavior at home, whether it is toward each other or toward others (television shows, newscasts, social media, adult friends, politics, etc.), they are likely to imitate that behavior themselves when they get into similar situations with their peers. Teach your child that it is wrong to judge and criticize others based on looks, beliefs, money, etc.—all the different things people are judged by every day. (Just because it happens doesn't make it right, and we have to start somewhere!)

Talk to and meet your child's friends and families. Get to know them and be involved. Build relationships with all involved.

Get mental health and counseling services when they are needed. Reach out to the schools for help with this. Remember that your conversations with school personnel are confidential.

Read to and with your child. Wait, what? Yes. Reading to and with your child can help your child in more ways than just his/her reading skills. Reading to and with your child gives you automatic examples to use as conversation-starters to show your child how people deal with problems (good and bad). On a side note, many kids today do not consider themselves to be "readers," and following that line of thinking, I will mention that I hear parents very often telling their kids or telling an educator in front of their kids things like "you know you are not very good at math," or "he's never been a reader," etc. I'm not condoning telling your child he is the best at everything (I think we covered that in a previous chapter...), but avoid constantly reinforcing his/her belief that he isn't something or can't do something. Maybe he had a bad experience with an elementary grade math teacher. That doesn't mean parents should repeat for the rest of eternity how bad their son is at math, or that he just doesn't like math teachers, or whatever the case may be. Perception is reality, and very often your kids are going to believe exactly what you tell them, even if they actually do have the potential to do more or be more, and even if a specific situation may have occurred earlier in his/her life that suggested otherwise (such as being "bad at math" etc.). This goes along with building resilience and self-efficacy in your child—it's all connected!

So back to reading—there are so many books out there that can teach valuable life lessons when your child lives vicariously through the character.

We will discuss electronics in another chapter, but I think we can all agree that today's kids have so many options other than reading to keep them busy. Never mind the fact that reading is a skill that all kids need to be successful in school (and not just in their language arts or high school English class). It is up to parents to reinforce a love of reading at home from as young of an age as possible. It's never too late to start! "Not a reader" yourself? What a great way to connect with your child. Help your child find a book your he/she might enjoy (do not pick for him/her) and get a copy for yourself. Read the book at the same time as your child and have discussions with your child about the characters and events of the book. You will be amazed at how you can connect with your child through these conversations. You can use these conversations to reinforce "good" behaviors and teach about avoiding "bad" behaviors, you can discuss the difficult situations the book's characters found themselves in and how the characters handled those situations, plus you are building your child's academic and conversational skills at the same time. This is a total win-win that video games in isolation cannot provide—but more on that later.

(Again) reach out to your child's school counselor for help as needed. Your child's counselor has resources that can help you help your child. This is true from the earliest years in school all the way up through graduation.

Be proactive. The bottom line/main point/main idea is that, as we discussed about school shootings and focusing on the "wrong" things, with bullying and mean behavior, we cannot just wait for someone else to come along (in most cases, the school) and fix the issue by punishing the bully. Parents have so much power in their own hands to instill skills in their children at home that can then be reinforced at school. Waiting for the school to do everything will likely be a long, arduous wait. Again, not because the school doesn't care, but rather because of simple math. You, as a parent, are responsible for a limited number of children. Schools are responsible for hundreds of children, with a main focus being academics. You ultimately hold all of the power over the things that your child really wants and is motivated by, and that power can be used in many ways to raise strong, well-adjusted children.

Teach your child how to be a friend to others and actively work on and practice those skills with your child.

We might assume that kids naturally learn to be a friend to others and instinctively become that person, and to some extent that is true. Sometimes, however, kids genuinely struggle to make friends and do not know how to be a friend to other kids. But as with all skills in life, adults can step in and help build, reinforce, and model those skills at home and in school. Another poster I had on my wall for many years as a teacher was a Garfield poster that said "I don't raise 'em; I just teach 'em." What was seemingly innocuous and cute at that time has gained meaning the longer I have been an educator, and I call upon parents to step up and step in when it comes to helping your child learn to be a friend to others. There is no one perfect way to do this, but it starts with thinking about what you as an adult might want in a friend—someone who:

*is a good listener

*is there for you in good times and bad

*asks you questions (rather than making all the conversations one-sided about him/herself)

*is reliable and follows through

*is loyal and says what he/she means (is not a backstabber or one who talks about you behind your back)

*has similar interests, yet also might be distinctly different and stretches you as a person to grow

*might be on your athletic team, or in your class at school, or lives in your neighborhood

And just as a reminder, it is far easier for your child to be a good listener, make friends and be a friend when the earbuds are out of his/her ears. I had a conversation with a parent who was concerned about her child making friends (at the high school level), and she added that rather than reaching out to other kids and making himself available to talk to others, he kept his headphones on at all times, which effectively shuts everyone else out. When talking to your kids about their struggles in making friends, please talk to them about the absolute basics of communication, which include listening and simply making oneself available to being a friend. When kids walk around with earbuds in/earphones on at all times, there are many missed opportunities not only for being a friend and making friends but also for simply experiencing life and the growth, maturity, and empathy for others that comes along with going through those human experiences with others.

We will discuss more on earbuds and electronics in a later chapter, but something that may seem so insignificant can actually have a significant impact on your child's life, and it shouldn't be ignored. If you have a hard time getting your child to take the earbuds out when he/she is with you, then it seems evident that your child is comfortable with that behavior and will likely choose that same behavior everywhere else. If you have trouble communicating with your child when he/she is your captive audience, then so will everyone else out in the hustle and bustle of life, including a busy high school setting. Kids learn more than academics through their school experience. Kids learn to communicate with and interact with other people (kids and adults), and that growth doesn't happen when the child isn't having those experiences because he/she has shut out the world via earbuds or headphones.

The list of ways to be a friend goes on and can include any variety of qualities. The key is teaching your child to value those qualities in others but also to model those qualities him/herself. One of my favorite sayings is to lead by example, and being a friend as well as a leader in a social group begins with just that. Will it always be easy? Probably not. But most things in life that are worth something are not easy, which is again why parents should abstain from doing everything for their kids and instead support and teach their kids as they live their lives. Any parent who has ever had a child be disappointed by another child (not invited to a party by the child; the child didn't come to your child's party; two friends become mad at a third friend; etc.) knows how hard it is to stand by and not swoop in and make it right. It is even harder, but more valuable sometimes, to help your child learn from the experience and go on to pay it forward through kindness and inclusiveness to another child when the opportunity arises, and there are opportunities for kindness EVERYWHERE in our world today.

Which leads us back to **apathy**, or the perceived lack of caring. In a *Psychology Today* blog post, Pickhardt (2012) breaks down different types of apathy in kids, including **boredom, defiance, defense, indifference, cynicism, substance abuse, and depression, and points out that apathy can mask a variety of problems** (para. 6-22). Apathy can affect many aspects of your child's life, including motivation (for grades, for friendships, for school attendance, etc.) and should be taken seriously by parents. Everyone has bad days, but if parents see an ongoing pattern of apathy in their child, and moreso if parents see that the pattern is affecting parts of your child's life about which he/she cared in the past (such as quitting a sport or other school activity, or a serious drop in grades), it is important to reach out for professional help. Again, your child's counselor or administrator is a great place to start. The key is to not ignore it or dismiss it as a phase and hope it gets better on its own.

loser i hate u X*@#! leave me alone i hate school ur ugly go away
whatever nobody likes u i'm stupid u just don't get it i don't have any
friends i don't care ur a freak everybody else gets to BFF i'm bored it's
not fair it's all your fault i don't know help me i'm so sad loser i hate u
X*@#! leave me alone i hate school ur ugly go away whatever nobody
likes u i'm stupid u just don't get it i don't have any friends i don't care ur
a freak everybody else gets to BFF i'm bored it's not fair it's all your fault
i don't know help me i'm so sad loser i hate u X*@#! leave me alone i
hate school ur ugly go away whatever nobody likes u i'm stupid u just
don't get it i don't have any friends i don't care ur a freak everybody else
gets to BFF i'm bored it's not fair it's all your fault i don't know help me
i'm so sad loser i hate u X*@#! leave me alone i hate school ur ugly
go away whatever nobody likes u i'm stupid u just don't get it i don't
have any friends i don't care ur a freak everybody else gets to BFF i'm
bored it's not fair it's all your fault i don't know help me i'm so sad loser
i hate u X*@#! leave me alone i hate school ur ugly go away whatever
nobody likes u i'm stupid u just don't get it i don't have any friends i don't
care ur a freak everybody else gets to BFF i'm bored it's not fair it's all
your fault i don't know help me i'm so sad loser i hate u X*@#! leave
me alone i hate school ur ugly go away whatever nobody likes u i'm
stupid u just don't get it i don't have any friends i don't care ur a freak

Chapter 11
The Internet, Social Media,
Television & Electronics

everybody else gets to BFF i'm bored it's not fair it's all your fault i don't
know help me i'm so sad loser i hate u X*@#! leave me alone i hate
school ur ugly go away whatever nobody likes u i'm stupid u just don't
get it i don't have any friends i don't care ur a freak everybody else gets to
BFF i'm bored it's not fair it's all your fault i don't know help me i'm so
sad loser i hate u X*@#! leave me alone i hate school ur ugly go away
whatever nobody likes u i'm stupid u just don't get it i don't have any
friends i don't care ur a freak everybody else gets to BFF i'm bored it's
not fair it's all your fault i don't know help me i'm so sad loser i hate u
X*@#! leave me alone i hate school ur ugly go away whatever nobody
likes u i'm stupid u just don't get it i don't have any friends i don't care ur
a freak everybody else gets to BFF i'm bored it's not fair it's all your fault
i don't know help me i'm so sad loser i hate u X*@#! leave me alone i
hate school ur ugly go away whatever nobody likes u i'm stupid u just
don't get it i don't have any friends i don't care ur a freak everybody else
gets to BFF i'm bored it's not fair it's all your fault i don't know help me
i'm so sad loser i hate u X*@#! leave me alone i hate school ur ugly
go away whatever nobody likes u i'm stupid u just don't get it i don't
have any friends i don't care ur a freak everybody else gets to BFF i'm
bored it's not fair it's all your fault i don't know help me i'm so sad loser
i hate u X*@#! leave me alone i hate school ur ugly go away whatever
nobody likes u i'm stupid u just don't get it i don't have any friends i don't
care ur a freak everybody else gets to BFF i'm bored it's not fair it's all
your fault i don't know help me i'm so sad loser i hate u X*@#! leave
me alone i hate school ur ugly go away whatever nobody likes u i'm
stupid u just don't get it i don't have any friends i don't care ur a freak
everybody else gets to BFF i'm bored it's not fair it's all your fault i don't

Chapter 11

The Internet, Social Media, Television & Electronics

A ny person who grew up without the internet and social media can see the difference in kids today who have grown up with the internet and social media. You do not have to be a parent of teens or an educator to notice it. The most obvious changes are evident and easily observable in public places worldwide, and, to be fair, the changes are evident with adults as well as kids. Most adults grew up with a television, but today's television choices hardly compare to the simplistic viewing options of yesteryear. And what adult hasn't joked about their childhood telephones being in a main room of the house tethered to the wall? It was really difficult in those days to "pull a fast one" on your parents using the family phone.

Before we dive into this chapter, I will readily admit that I, like most everyone else, am a consumer of the internet, social media, television, and some electronics. I admit I have shared article after article about the detrimental effects of electronics and social media *on social media*, and I admit I feel a certain level of hypocrisy every time I do. As I have said in other parts of this book, however, too much of a good thing can be very bad, and the overuse of just about anything can be very harmful for the user.

Chapter 11

The research articles (that we pass along on social media) tell us every day: Too much sugar/red meat/carbs/alcohol (you name it, you can probably find an article on it): bad. Too much awake time: bad. Too much sleep: bad. Too much sitting: bad. Too much running: bad. Too much medicine: bad. Too much worrying: bad. Too much sun: bad. Too much time indoors: bad. Reckless overuse of just about anything can lead to terrible or at least negative consequences, and this also applies to our use of electronics and the 24-hour electronic world. The best-made bulb in the world burns out at some point.

This chapter and this book are not about bashing the electronic world we live in. We live in a world of modern inventions and innovations that have literally changed how we all live, and these inventions have in many ways greatly improved our world. Want to talk to someone you went to college with 30 years ago? Get on social media and send him/her a note. Want to show your high school friend who now lives on the other side of the world pictures of your baby? Email or get on social media. Want to find out an obscure fact or tidbit about just about anything that comes up in conversation? Look it up on the internet. Want to read a magazine while waiting at the DMV? Look it up. Tired of the same old thing and want a new recipe? A new set of curtains? A new anything? Voila! The internet has it all. The downside is that the internet has it all. *All. The. Time.* And it's not just the internet. Want to see what your pets are doing at home while you are away? There's an app for that. Want to know how many calories you burned walking from your car into the grocery store? Check your app. Want to know how many calories that donut you just ate set you back? Look it up. Looking. Checking. Reacting. Responding. Over and over and over. All day. Every day. We live in a 24-hour, always-on world.

We know that too much of a good thing can be a very bad thing. So, this book is not about getting rid of these wonderful, modern inventions that have in many ways changed our lives for the better. It is about recognizing the "bad," having an action plan for educating our kids, and addressing "it" before "it" becomes too much for our kids to handle.

This chapter is data- and research-driven more than opinion-driven. I think it has to be due to the complexity of the issue. Without looking at any data at all, I think we can all agree that while virtually everyone (kids and adults) takes part in using social media/using the internet/using a smart phone/watching television shows/etc., comparatively speaking, a small percentage of people become violent criminals. Research does show definite connections, however, between teens' behavior and development and the electronic/online media they are exposed to.

Current data helps put the conversation about social media and electronics into perspective. The Pew Research Center is a self-described nonpartisan fact tank that informs the public about the issues, attitudes and trends shaping America and the world via public opinion polling, demographic research, content analysis and other data-driven social science research. Anderson and Jiang (2018) found in a Pew Research Center May 2018 survey of 1,058 parents who have a teen ages 13 to 17, as well as interviews with 743 teens that:

YouTube, Instagram, and Snapchat are the most popular online platforms among teens. 95% of teens have access to a smartphone; 45% say they are online 'almost constantly'. 51% say they use Facebook, notably lower than the shares who use YouTube, Instagram or Snapchat (p. 1-2).

Anderson and Jiang found no clear consensus among teens about these platforms' ultimate impact on people their age. 45% believe social media has a neither positive nor negative effect on people their age; 31% say social media has had a mostly positive impact; 24% describe its effect as mostly negative (p. 2). Teens who say social media has had a mostly positive effect tended to stress issues related to connectivity and connection with others. 40% say that social media has had a positive impact because it helps them keep in touch and interact with others (p. 5). There is slightly less consensus among teens who say social media has had a mostly negative effect on people their age. 27% say social media leads to more bullying and the overall spread of rumors (p. 6). 17% feel these platforms harm relationships and result in less meaningful human interactions; 15% think social media distorts reality and gives teens an unrealistic view of other people's lives; 14% think that teens spend too much time on social media (pp. 6-7).

Twenge, Martin, and Spitzberg (2018) examined the media use of more than one million teens in the United States between 1976 and 2016 and found:

> *Digital media use has increased considerably, with the average 12th grader in 2016 spending more than twice as much time online as in 2006, and with time online, texting, and on social media totaling to about 6 hr a day by 2016. Whereas only half of 12th graders visited social media sites almost every day in 2008, 82% did by 2016. At the same time, iGen adolescents in the 2010s spent significantly less time on print media, TV, or movies compared with adolescents in previous decades. The percentage of 12th graders who read a book or a magazine every day declined from 60% in the late 1970s to 16% by 2016, and 8th graders spent almost an hour less time watching TV in 2016 compared with the early 1990s. Trends were fairly uniform across gender, race/ethnicity, and socioeconomic status. The rapid adoption of digital media since the 2000s has displaced the consumption of legacy media (p. 1).*

Put more simply:

> *Compared with previous generations of teens, iGen teens in the 2010s spend more time online and less time with older media such as books, magazines, and TV. Time on digital media appears to have displaced time once spent reading and watching TV (p. 1).*

So, we get it. Teens are on some form of electronic media more than they read books or other tangible materials, and just about all teens have access to some form of electronic media. And parents and teachers alike can tell you that the small percentage of kids who may not have personal access to it (i.e. their own phone), still have access to it through their friends' phones or their computers.

A wealth of research about the connections between electronics and teens exists. A sampling of this includes:

*A possible predisposition between internet addiction and psychological disorders such as ADHD and depression exists (*The Brown University Child and Adolescent Behavior Letter,* 2009).

*Students who have a high level of internet addiction are more likely to be low in self-control and self-management, which makes sense in that they are not able to self-limit their own time on the internet (Akin, S. Arslan, N. Arslan, Uysal, & Sahranc, 2015).

*In terms of Facebook usage specifically, Facebook users who are able to resist an impulse or temptation, are more self-disciplined, and do not focus on negative emotions are less likely to develop Facebook addiction (Blachino & Przepiorka, 2016).

*When teens use communication technology usage such as text messaging, e-mail, instant messaging, and social networking sites, it may not interfere with their identity development process itself, but it may negatively impact those who struggle in real life, face to face, social interactions and may affect their abilities to form positive relationships in person (Cyr, Berman, & Smith, 2015).

*The more that teens reported being addicted to the internet or their smartphones, the higher they scored on nine subscales of psychopathology and problematic behavior. This study found that greater smartphone addiction correlated with an increased likelihood of somatic symptoms, withdrawal, depression or anxiety, thought problems, delinquency, attention problems, aggression, and internalizing and externalizing problems (Boschert, 2013).

*A wealth of research exists about cyberbullying, which, by definition, occurs using social media and/or the internet. We discussed cyberbullying extensively in a previous chapter.

145

Ehmke (N.D.) cites a Royal Society for Public Health (United Kingdom) study of 14-24 year olds that found that Snapchat, Facebook, Twitter and Instagram all led to increased feelings of depression, anxiety, poor body image and loneliness (para. 2). Ehmke explains the downside of screen time on teens developmentally:

> Teens are masters at keeping themselves occupied in the hours after school until way past bedtime. When they're not doing their homework (and when they are) they're online and on their phones, texting, sharing, trolling, scrolling, you name it. Of course before everyone had an Instagram account teens kept themselves busy, too, but they were more likely to do their chatting on the phone, or in person when hanging out at the mall. It may have looked like a lot of aimless hanging around, but what they were doing was experimenting, trying out skills, and succeeding and failing in tons of tiny real-time interactions that kids today are missing out on. For one thing, modern teens are learning to do most of their communication while looking at a screen, not another person (Indirect communication section).

Ehmke addresses a wide range of ways teens can be negatively impacted by social media/electronic use:

*By communicating via text and other electronic means, kids are not able to learn to read other people's nonverbal cues such as body language, facial expression, and even changes in other people's voices (citing Dr. Catherine Steiner-Adair, Indirect communication section).

*Communicating electronically allows kids to avoid the risks it takes to make and keep a friend in person, especially when teens disagree on topics of discussion. By communicating electronically, teens do not have to witness the impact that their words have on other people. Kids are not getting the practice to relate to real people in person, and this lack of practice continues as the stakes become higher as the teen ages and enters relationships and jobs (Lowering the risks section).

***Communicating electronically makes it easier for teens to be cruel to each other.** Teens (and adults) say things in an electronic format that they would never be brave enough to say to someone's face (Cyberbullying and the imposter syndrom section).

***Girls are more socialized to compare themselves to other people (other girls in particular) in forming their identities, and a downside of electronic formats is that it makes comparing easy to do.** As girls feel insecure and bad about themselves, they often react by tearing other girls down so they feel better themselves (citing Steiner-Adair, Cyberbullying and the imposter syndrome section).

***Because peer acceptance is very important to teens developmentally, teens judge themselves and their worthiness to other teens by the number of "likes" they get, and they spend an enormous amount of time trying to project the most perfect image of themselves.** Teens agonize over which picture to post to project their best self to others and wait for the confirmation of others through their reactions after the post (Cyberbullying and the imposter syndrom section).

***Kids, in comparing themselves to each other, believe everyone else's life must be perfect because of the perfection the other kids are projecting, which in turn makes kids (and adults) feel worse about their own lives** (Cyberbullying and the imposter syndrome section). (Note: Adults do this, too.)

***Because of the constant "on" of technology and social media, kids are never alone, and the activity never stops.** Kids do not give themselves a break or a chance to relax and let it go (Stalking (and being ignored) section).

***Although kids are never alone and are always on, they simultaneously experience loneliness in the midst of all the activity because it is very obvious when they are being ignored, and the wait-time for an electronic response or "like" can be excruciating for teens.** When friendships or romantic relationships suddenly end when the friend or romantic partner ceases electronic communication (with no explanation), kids are left assuming the worst about themselves because they have not had live communication with the other person about what happened (Stalking (and being ignored) section).

Social media and internet use are only part of teens' electronics use. Video gaming is another area that researchers have studied and that has garnered attention in connection with school shootings. Anderson and Jiang (2018) found in the Pew Research Center Survey:

A majority of both boys and girls play video games, but gaming is nearly universal for boys. 84% of teens say they have or have access to a game console at home; 90% say they play video games of any kind (whether on a computer, game console or cellphone). 75% of girls report having access to a game console at home; 83% of girls report playing video games in general; 92% of boys have or have access to a game console at home, and 97% say they play video games in some form or fashion (p. 9).

Violent video games and media have been linked to aggression and an inability to positively navigate anger and frustration. According to Anderson (2010):

Repeated consumption of media violence over time increases aggression across a range to situations and across time...First, it creates more positive attitudes, beliefs, and expectations regarding aggressive solutions to interpersonal problems. In other words, youth come to believe that aggression is normal, appropriate, and likely to succeed.

It also leads to the development of aggressive scripts, which are basically ways of thinking about how the social world works. Heavy media violence consumers tend to view the world in a more hostile fashion. Additionally, it decreases the cognitive accessibility of nonviolent ways to handle conflict. That is, it becomes harder to even think about nonviolent solutions.

Media violence also produces an emotional desensitization to aggression and violence. Normally, people have a pretty negative emotional reaction to conflict, aggression, and violence, and this can be seen in their physiological reactions to observation of violence (real or fictional, as in entertainment media). For example, viewing physical violence normally leads to increases in heart rate and blood pressure, as well as to certain brain wave patterns. Such normal negative emotional reactions tend to inhibit aggressive behavior and can inspire helping behavior. Repeated consumption of media violence reduces these normal negative emotional reactions.

Finally, repetition increases learning of any type of skill or way of thinking, to the point where that skill or way of thinking becomes fairly automatic. Repetition effects include learning how to aggress (pp. 28-29).

Very often when there is a school shooting, the topic of violent video games and kids' desensitization to the value of human life comes up. Anderson addresses the connection between violent video games and school shootings:

Mainstream media violence researchers do not believe that an otherwise normal, well-adjusted child who plays violent video games is going to become a school shooter. The best way to think about this issue is the risk factor approach. There are three important points to keep in mind.

First, there are many causal risk factors involved in the development of a person who frequently behaves in an aggressive or violent manner. There are biological factors, family factors, neighborhood factors, and so on. Media violence is only one of the top dozen or so risk factors.

Second, extreme aggression, such as aggravated assault and homicide, typically occurs only when there are a number of risk factors present. In other words, none of the causal risk factors are "necessary and sufficient" causes of extreme aggression. Of course, cigarette smoking is not a necessary and sufficient cause of lung cancer, even though it is a major cause of it. People with only one risk factor seldom (I'm tempted to say "never") commit murder.

Third, consumption of media violence is the most common of all of the major risk factors for aggression in most modern societies. It also is the least expensive and easiest risk factor for parents to change. Playing a lot of violent games is unlikely to turn a normal youth with zero, one or even two other risk factors into a killer. But regardless of how many other risk factors are present in a youth's life, playing a lot of violent games is likely to increase the frequency and the seriousness of his or her physical aggression, both in the short term and over time as the youth grows up (p. 29).

So, according to research, not all teens who play violent video games are destined to become a school shooter, but playing violent video games is a risk factor in and precursor of teens' aggressive behavior and one of the risk factors in people who become school shooters. McLean and Griffiths (2013) found that exposure to violent video games is associated with less concern being reported for victims of crime. Young people who play more violent video games reported less concern for general victims and for culpable victims, and these effects could not be explained by gender or age differences (p. 1). In other words, young people who play violent video games showed that they cared less about victims, regardless of gender or age of the player.

It is not the use of the internet/online media alone that can be a detriment to youth. A personal observation I have made as an educator involves students' use of their phones to listen to music (etc.) via earbuds. The use of earbuds to listen to music (etc.) in itself seems innocuous, however, there are two huge negative impacts of this habit. First, per my own personal observations over the years as an educator, many students have earbuds in all the time (and almost all have their phone with them at all times). In its simplest form, students cannot learn when they have earbuds in (because they are not participating in the class lesson/discussion/ etc. when they cannot hear it). For the same reason, students cannot form meaningful relationships with others around them when they have earbuds in. Students isolate themselves from the world when they have earbuds in. Students will not magically learn to interact with others when they leave high school and enter the "real world." School and the process of growing up, which obviously includes students' time outside of school, is their real world.

To give an example, I once walked into a classroom to retrieve a student, and a quick glance across the room looking for my student revealed that the entire class had earbuds in. The teacher was in the middle of teaching the lesson. Yes, I agree that this is as much a poor classroom management/ low expectations issue on the part of the teacher. But it also speaks to the academic motivation of all the students in that room who chose to tune out their education and tune in to their music, and clearly no one wanted to fight them over it even though it was the right thing to do. I will readily go to bat for teachers and educators. Teaching and working in education is hard. Every day. Parenting is hard. Every day. But this is a perfect example that doing what is easy is not necessarily doing what is right. If we all give up and let kids carve the least resistant path they want just because they "really don't want to do it," (whatever "it" is—homework, chores, class participation, cleaning up after themselves, etc.), then we have all lost our way. We as adults are all responsible for molding our kids' futures, and it is just not helpful when we allow them to sit passively and tune the rest of the world (never mind academics) out.

The same can be said for general phone/electronic usage and human interaction, and parents, teens, and educators are equally guilty on this one. The use (overuse?) of phones/electronics is pervasive in society just about world-wide. To drive home a point about internet/electronics usage and our world, as I am sitting working on this book, I am doing (you guessed it) online research. I am using online articles found on the world wide web (like I said, you can find anything you want to find out there), and I am using research databases, which are also online. As I was researching information on parenting and phones, on the very page with the article I was reading online (about the dangers/downsides of too much media use), a pop-up ad for a parenting app appeared (which obviously requires the use of electronic media). Another electronic rabbit hole that pulls us further into the online electronic world. But I digress.

Kids are not the only ones whose lives have changed with the proliferation of the cell phone. Adults have not been immune to the downsides of electronics and social media, and their kids have noticed it. Niz (N.D.) says kids feel unimportant to cell-phone addicted parents. Niz cites a June 2015 study by AVG Technologies that surveyed more than 6,000 children, ages 8 to 13, from Brazil, Australia, Canada, France, The United Kingdom, Germany, The Czech Republic and the United States. The survey discovered that 32 percent of children felt unimportant when their moms and dads were distracted by their phones. The kids said they had to compete with technology for their parents' attention, and 28 percent of mothers and fathers agreed (The Lowdown section).

"I do feel like the balance between the degree to which I use my mobile device to stay connected to work and my ability to be more present, available to my family, is quite out of balance," one of the parents in the study said.

In addition, 54 percent of the kids think their parents spend too much time on their phones. Fifty-two percent of moms and dads agreed with their children and worried that they were setting a bad example for their kids.

"With our kids picking up mobile devices at an increasingly younger age, it is really important that we set good habits within the home, early on," said Tony Anscombe, senior security evangelist at AVG Technologies. "Children take their cues from us for everything

else, so it is only natural that they should do the same with device use. It can be hard to step away from your device at home, but with a quarter of parents telling us that they wished their child used their device less (25 percent), they need to lead by example and consider how their behavior might be making their child feel" (The Lowdown section).

To again point out the irony that we are all faced with when navigating our modern electronic world, at the bottom of the online article above in which parents are being admonished to be more present with their kids and to put down their phones/electronic devices, a link asking the reader to "like us on Facebook and Twitter" glows like a beacon saying "Come on in. The water is warm." I admit it. It's a problem, and it's a hard one to solve, but in its simplest form, it comes down to self-control and personal choices. We must continue to teach this to our kids both at home and at school, and we all have to be mindful of our own habits and choices.

While this book is mainly focused on teens, the impact of phones and electronic media usage by parents can obviously affect kids well before their teen years. Research exists showing negative consequences of parents using cell phones too much when parenting infants/small children (distracted parenting). Research also exists showing negative consequences of parents using cellphones to distract their infants/small children (parenting via distracting children using cellphones/electronics).

According to a *Psychology Today* blog post, Matthews (2017) says parents need to turn off their phones and cited a compilation of research supporting this:

Young children are closely attuned to their parents' attention. They depend on that attention for their survival, of course, but also for their social and emotional development. Several recent research studies show the damage parents can do when they're physically present, but distracted and less responsive because they're attending to their smartphones (para. 1).

153

Matthews says parents on devices distress children and reduce their resilience and cites a 2016 study in which Myruski, Gulyayeva, Birk, Perez-Edgar, Buss, and Dennis-Tiwary found that moms on cellphones have children who are more negative and less resilient. The researchers reported that children expressed more distress, and were less likely to explore their environment, when their mothers were using their cell phones. The young children whose mothers reported greater habitual use of mobile devices outside the lab showed more negativity, and less emotional recovery, when their mothers did turn off their phones (Study #1 section).

Matthews cited the 2015 AVG study that found that children and parents have an opinion about the parents' cell phone usage:

54 percent of the children questioned...felt that their parents checked their devices too often; 36 percent chose, as their biggest grievance (when given a list of possible, bad device habits)...that their parents allowed themselves to be distracted by their device during conversations – something that made 32 percent of the complainants feel unimportant.

When asked about their device use, 52 percent of all parents agreed that it was too frequent, and many also worried about how this looked to the younger generation. 28 percent felt that they didn't set a good example for their children with their device use (AVG para. 2-3).

Anyone who has been to a public place and observed the behaviors of people around them in recent years can identify with the observations documented in another study Matthews cites that was highlighted in an NPR article (Neighmond, 2014). In this study, Dr. Jenny Radesky, a pediatrician specializing in child development, along with two other researchers spent one summer observing 55 different groups of parents and young children eating at fast food restaurants. While Radesky characterizes this more as anthropological observations rather than a formal study, she has concerns over the use of cell phones while parenting. Radesky noticed that when the families sat down to eat, many of the caregivers pulled out a mobile device right away and began looking, scrolling and typing, only putting it down intermittently (Neighmond, para 3.). Radesky pointed out that face-to-face interactions are the primary way children learn, and expressed her concerns about what kids are missing when their parents are on their phones instead of interacting with their children:

> They learn language, they learn about their own emotions, they learn how to regulate them. They learn by watching us how to have a conversation, how to read other people's facial expressions. And if that's not happening, children are missing out on important development milestones (para. 3-5).

Finally, Matthews cited the work of clinical psychologist Dr. Catherine Steiner-Adair, which revealed kids' reported feelings when parents use cellphones:

> (Dr. Steiner-Adair) interviewed a thousand children between the ages of four and eighteen, asking them about their parents' use of mobile devices. She reported that many of the children described themselves as "sad, mad, angry, and lonely" when their parents were on their devices. Several young children reported damaging or hiding their parents' cellphones. (Dr. Steiner-Adair) concluded that parents should think twice before picking up a mobile device when they're with their kids. She said, "We are behaving in ways that certainly tell children they don't matter, they're not interesting to us, they're not as compelling as anybody, anything, any ping that may interrupt our time with them" (Study #5 section).

Neighmond (2014) also referenced the work of Steiner-Adair, who reported stories from her interviews like the following:

> One 4-year-old called his dad's smartphone a "stupid phone." Others recalled joyfully throwing their parent's phone into the toilet, putting it in the oven or hiding it. There was one girl who said, "I feel like I'm just boring. I'm boring my dad because he will take any text, any

call, anytime — even on the ski lift!" (para. 9).

Matthews concluded her research compilation by pointing out that kids thrive when they receive consistent, dependable, focused, loving attention. Matthews says:

> *We're not talking about staying off your phone 100% of the time, more like 90%. It's okay to answer an urgent text or make a quick call, especially if it includes your child. But, really! As much as possible, when you're with your child, be with them. Put away that phone and other electronic devices. Enjoy the brief moment you have to help your child grow into the delightful adult you hope they will become (para. 11).*

So, parents, are you feeling guilty yet? Believe it or not, bringing out all of our guilty feelings is not the purpose of this book. Bringing real attention to real issues and encouraging parents to do something about it is the purpose of the book, so it is important that we are all open and honest about our own behaviors. The overuse of technology in any given family may not be limited to the kids in the family. When parents come in to talk to me about needing counseling help for their student (for other types of issues/concerns), I have the conversation with them about getting/how to get counseling for their child, but I remind them that very often, the issues being experienced by the student are actually issues being experienced by the family. Getting counseling is not taking the child to get him/her "fixed" by the counseling so the family can live happily ever after with the "pesky problem" gone. Family counseling is very often a more appropriate path for a family to take (depending on the issue, obviously). It is important for parents to see the difference between viewing the "problem" as your child's problem, one in which you as the parent have no involvement and are independent of, and recognizing that most often, the "problem" is relational and affects more family members than the child, making family counseling (in addition to individual counseling) a more appropriate path to take. This mindset is the same with technology. It cuts both ways. Problems with overuse of technology affect all of us to varying degrees. What is important is for parents to take note if there is a problem with tech overuse in the family and find balance in the use of technology by *all* members of the family, including the parents themselves.

Overuse and distraction are not the only issues with phone and electronics. Not surprisingly, there are more issues with technology that warrant discussion in this chapter. As I mentioned in the beginning of this chapter, in yesteryear, it was very difficult to put yourself in danger or act inappropriately using the family phone because you were usually on the phone in front of your entire family tethered to the wall. If you were lucky, your parents bought a long phone cord so you could drag the phone into a nearby closet, or if you were even more lucky, you had a phone in your own room. Regardless of where the phone was in those days, for most kids, because using the phone required talking out loud, any trouble you were trying to create using the phone was easily detected by your parents. Not so today. Through their cell phones, kids today have access to anything and everything all the time; kids more often use their phones silently because they prefer electronic interaction rather than actually talking on the phone; and kids who want to use their phones furtively have every opportunity to do so. Phones in yesteryear could also be used for negative, harmful reasons, but even prank-calling other kids required you to talk.

In its simplest form, teens can, if they choose, use their phones to access anything they want, and we already know teens do not always use the best judgment in their decision-making. As I tell parents and kids all the time in my work as a school counselor, people are going to find what they are looking for, whether it is the boy or girl their parents don't want them to date, the drugs their parents don't want them to take, the inappropriate media content their parents don't want them to watch, the party their parents don't want them to attend, etc. The list of "what's out there for teens to find" is infinite. Again, I am a daily consumer of the cell phone and the internet, and I am not bashing either technology, but the cell phone and internet are the host for kids to find exactly what they are looking for, even if they don't know it until they find it or someone sends it to them unsolicited. While I know most recognize this to be true, to drive home the point, it's similar to how many of us found out about *very important topics* in our youth in yesteryear. First, we heard it from our friends, who heard it from their friends or older siblings or whomever. Then, we looked for the Judy Blume book in the library to read about it for ourselves. It just took a lot more effort and time to get to that point in yesteryear. In today's world, kids get their information in seconds in mere clicks, and they can get a lot more than Judy Blume.

Patchin (2017) cited data compiled from more than 5500 middle and high school students from across the United States published on the Cyberbulling Research Center website that revealed 12% of students had sent an explicit image of themselves to another person at some point in their lifetime; 4% said they had done it within the last month; 19% said they had received a sexually explicit image from someone else at some point in their lifetime; 6% within the last month (para. 2). Patchin's research revealed that older students were more likely to report that they had participated in sexting. Specifically, almost one out of every five seventeen-year-olds had sent an explicit image of themselves to someone else at some point in their lifetime, compared to less than 6% of twelve year-olds. Boys were significantly more likely to send and receive sexts (para. 3-4).

Patchin clarified the definition of sexting used in this research and noted it varies widely by how teens and how researchers define it:

When we inquire about sexting, we tell students that sexting is when "someone takes a naked or semi-naked (explicit) picture or video of themselves, usually using their phone, and sends it to someone else." We then ask to whom they sent these images and from whom they received them. The numbers above include only those images sent or received between romantic partners or interests (para. 6).

Hinduja and Patchin (2018) published a Teen Sexting guide for parents and educators available on the Cyberbulling Research Center website. In this guide, they highlighted high-profile stories such as one in which a female student's ex-boyfriend circulated nude pictures of her to their high school peers which resulted in the female student's suicide, and a similar story of a middle school student who sent a male student topless photos of herself which were also shared with their peers and which also resulted in the suicide of the female student (p. 2). These are tragic stories that are most parents' worst nightmares, and it should be noted that sexting situations may occur far more frequently than any adults are fully aware in that students may not report these situations to adults out of embarrassment or the desire to keep it secret or hidden from adults. It is important to note that sexting can carry serious legal consequences for students involved. While the law varies in each state, Hinduja and Patchin say twenty-five states have enacted legislation to address sexting as of July 2018, with penalties ranging from educational programming for first-time offenders, to fines, felony charges, or short-term incarceration (p. 5).

Yet another slippery slope of the online world for teens involves their social media presence and their future. Bhardwaj (2017) says students' online presence is fair game for college admissions offices, and they do look. The same is true when applying for jobs (para. 4-7). Bhardwaj reports the rise of social media coaches to help with this, but in its simplest form, adults—parents and educators—need to continually remind students that they live in a world in which they will someday likely be judged by something they have posted online, and because of this, they must think it through before they post. Therein lies the obvious challenge based on everything we have discussed about the way teen and adolescent brains work—remember, impulsivity is key. Despite those developmental truths, we as adults must still continue to deliver the message that students are responsible for content they post. One real lesson for this might be to show teens any of the examples of students who boasted online about blowing up/shooting up/otherwise doing something to a school and who were, as a result, arrested for making terroristic threats or something similar.

It is natural for teens developmentally to pull away from their parents and become more independent from their parents, yet as we have discussed, teens do not think through their decisions. Think of the teen years as the last years that humans truly live in the moment. When we become adults, we tend to evaluate decisions before we make them (more often than not). For example, as adults we might be invited to a social event with our co-workers on a Thursday after work. As adults, before we even consider going with our co-workers we might run through a host of thoughts—

Ugh, I have a meeting in the morning. Do I really want to be tired for it?

Ugh, I cooked last night, and there are leftovers in the refrigerator that will go bad if no one eats them tonight, and tomorrow I have to go to (insert your child's name here) (insert your child's event here). Do I really want to go to happy hour?

Ugh, I love my co-workers, but I had recorded (insert favorite show here) and really just wanted to have dinner at home then settle down to watch it on my comfy couch.

Remember, everyone, we are adults, and we are tired. Teens—not so much. A teen's decision-making strategy is likely to be much more in-the-moment and friend-driven, which is what we miss when we are adults saddled with adulting, but it is also what makes teen life so fraught with the dangers of poor decision-making. I made poor decisions when I was a teen, and I daresay every adult who reads this book has, too, whether they will admit to it or not.

So, in order to live in the moment and to exhibit their independence from their parents (even if they are not aware that is why they are doing it), modern teens will use their online world to explore and push the limits, which gets them into eyebrow-raising situations that adults may or may not ever know about. The online world evolves continuously, but way back in 2012 (the Dark Ages in terms of how fast technology seems to evolve!), McAfee, the online security software company, conducted an online survey of 2,017 people, which Sutter (2012) profiled in a CNN article. Sutter points out that admittedly, the reason for the survey was a product they were pushing that helped parents monitor their kids online, but the information they found is still informative and alarming, especially for parents who believe their child is only using the online world for innocent, socially healthy and developmentally appropriate reasons (para. 2).

The McAfee study surveyed 1,013 parents and 1,004 teens between the ages of 13 and 17 via online interviews (para. 14) that revealed:

Seventy percent of teens "hide their online behavior" from parents... That's up from 45% in 2010... These hidden behaviors include some things you might expect — such as accessing violent (43%) or pornographic (32%) content online — but also a few surprises. Fifteen percent of teens have hacked into social networks; 9% have hacked into e-mail accounts; 12% have met face to face with a person he or she met on the Internet; and 16% of teens surveyed said they had used their phones to cheat on tests at school. McAfee said parents are often unaware of these behaviors (para. 3-5).

Sutter includes McAfee's list of the "top 10 ways teens are fooling their parents":

1. Clear browser history (53%)

2. Close/minimize browser when parent walked in (46%)

3. Hide or delete IMs or videos (34%)

4. Lie or omit details about online activities (23%)

5. Use a computer your parents don't check (23%)

6. Use an Internet-enabled mobile device (21%)

7. Use privacy settings to make certain content viewable only by friends (20%)

8. Use private browsing modes (20%)

9. Create private e-mail address unknown to parents (15%)

10. Create duplicate/fake social network profiles (9%) (para. 16).

Remember, this list is circa 2012, so the list today would likely contain other methods specific to particular apps, etc. To that end, the list of "what to look for" continues to evolve, so parents must use (wait for it) the very same internet to do their own research to stay on top of "what the kids are doing now." Below is a list of ten apps beings used by teens that parents need to know about compiled by the Bay City (Texas) police department in April 2018 published by a Houston, Texas, news station. Teens who read the list below may laugh at the ignorance of the adults trying to "figure them out," but it is a place to start:

Calculator—*This app looks like a calculator but functions like a secret photo vault.*

Omegle—*A free online chat website that promotes chatting anonymously to strangers.*

Yellow—*This app is designed to allow teens to flirt with each other in a Tinder-like atmosphere.*

Whisper—*An anonymous app where the creators promote sharing secrets and meeting new people.*

Ask.fm—*Ask an anonymous question and get an answer. This app has been linked to the most severe forms of cyberbullying.*

Hot or Not—*Strangers rate your profile. The goal is to lead to a hookup.*

Burn Book—*People post anonymous rumors about others through audio messages, texts, and photos.*

Wishbone—*An app that allows users to compare kids against each other and rate them on a scale.*

Kik—*A messaging app. Kik has built apps and web content that can be filtered on your home computer.*

Instagram—*Many kids are now creating fake accounts to hide content from their parents. Kids also like to text using Instagram because messages are deleted once the user leaves the conversation (para. 4-13).*

Admittedly (again, at the risk of sounding old), I will say that many of the above apps sound more like trendy new restaurants or fodder for *Saturday Night Live* comedy sketches. Because I, like you, am an adult, I have not used any of these apps, and I have heard of only the more mainstream ones on the list (and remember, this list is likely ancient in terms of keeping up with the latest apps, but you get the picture). One of the best strategies I can recommend to parents to keep up with this part of technology is to enlist your own older children or the older children of your friends or co-workers who are young enough to know, but old enough to know better, and as a result are willing to share the information with you. Obviously, fostering and maintaining an open, honest, communicative relationship with your kids can also go a long way toward keeping you in-the-know about what your kids are doing online.

What it boils down to is this. Teen insecurity has been around as long as teens have been around. Teens feel insecure about themselves, about what others think about them, about their bodies, their relationships, what someone said to them in second period…A lot of things make teens feel insecure and anxious. Like most everything else we have discussed in this book, being a teen is hard. Social media ratchets up this insecurity for many teens because it adds the ability for teens to constantly compare themselves to others with real-time pictures; to constantly see what others are doing (even if all teens are presenting their "best selves" on social media and avoiding presenting anything imperfect); to constantly feel left out of both formal and informal events as otherwise innocuous as a group of people running into each other at any random place, snapping a pic and posting it. The left-out teen may immediately feel a twinge of "why wasn't I invited?" or "why wasn't I there?" The opportunities for teens (and adults) to feel a twinge of self-doubt with every endless scroll, like, or lack of a like is exactly that—endless.

Shafer (2017) posted an article on the Harvard University Graduate School of Education website that provides parents with information to help parents navigate the digital world with their teens. As I have mentioned throughout this book, Shafer confirms that it is complicated:

…many of the pressures teenagers feel from social media are actually

consistent with developmentally normal concerns around social standing and self-expression. Social media can certainly exacerbate these anxieties, but for parents to truly help their children cope, they should avoid making a blanket condemnation. Instead, parents should tailor their approach to the individual, learning where a particular child's stressors lie and how that child can best gain control of this alluring, powerful way to connect with peers (para. 3-4).

Shafer cites a 2017 study in which Twenge, Joiner, Rogers, and Martin found that 48 percent of teens who spend five hours per day on an electronic device have at least one suicide risk factor, compared to 33 percent of teens who spend two hours a day on an electronic device. And Shafer points out that "we've all heard anecdotes, too, of teens being reduced to tears from the constant communication and comparisons that social media invites" (A Link Between Social Media and Mental Health Concerns section).

Shafer makes an excellent point, too, about the connection between social media and teen depression and anxiety:

But the connection between anxiety and social media might not be simple, or purely negative. Correlation does not equal causation; it may be that depression and anxiety lead to more social media use, for example, rather than the other way around. There could also be an unknown third variable — for instance, academic pressures or economic concerns — connecting them, or teens could simply be more likely to admit to mental health concerns now than they were in previous generations (Teenage Challenges and Stressors, Exacerbated section).

Shafer cites Lenhart's 2015 Pew Research Center study that revealed a range of teen social media stressors, including:

*Seeing people posting about events to which you haven't been invited.
*Feeling pressure to post positive and attractive content about yourself.
*Feeling pressure to get comments and likes on your posts.

Having someone post things about you that you cannot change or control (What's Triggering About Social Media? section).

Shafer also cites the work of Harvard researcher Dr. Emily Weinstein, who along with her colleagues analyzed thousands of adolescents' reactions to digital stressors and found other teen challenges:

Feeling replaceable: If you don't respond to a best friend's picture quickly or effusively enough, will she find a better friend?

Too much communication: A boyfriend or girlfriend wants you to be texting far more often than you're comfortable with.

Digital "FOMO": If you're not up-to-date on the latest social media posts, will it prevent you from feeling like you can participate in real-life conversations at school the next day?

Attachment to actual devices: If your phone is out of reach, will your privacy be invaded? Will you miss a message from a friend when he needs you? (What's Triggering About Social Media? section).

So what can parents do? Shafer suggests individualizing your approach. One size does not fit all in the case of social media anxiety. Shafer suggests not making the blanket decision to take the phone away but instead helping your teen understand where the anxiety in insecurity are coming from—getting to the heart of the matter. Shafer also suggests setting screen-free times, monitoring your own screen time in order to model positive behavior and make time for real-life activities. Most importantly, Shafer says, parents should work with their teen to come up with social media expectations in order to achieve your teen's buy-in to the plan (For Parents, Strategies on Mitigating Anxiety—Without Overreacting section).

Research continues to confirm and point out the negative effects of social media. A 2017 UK study from the Royal Society for Public Health and the Young Health Movement lists the negative effects of social media they found in their study:

Anxiety and depression

Poor sleep, which affects mental health

*Negative body image

*Cyberbullying

*Fear of missing out (p. 8-12).

While we know there are many negative effects of social media, the UK study lists the positive effects of social media they found in their study:

*Access to other people's health experiences and expert health information

*Emotional support and community building

*Self-expression and self-identity

*Making, maintaining, and building upon relationships (p. 13-16).

This 2017 UK-wide survey of 1,479 14-24 year olds asked them about five of the most popular social media platforms: Facebook, Instagram, Snapchat, Twitter and YouTube. Participants were asked to use 14 health and wellbeing-related questions about topics such as depression, loneliness, body image, community-building and bullying to rank each platform. YouTube was ranked most positive, Twitter ranked second, Facebook ranked third, Snapchat fourth, and Instagram fifth, or most negative (p. 17-23).

According to a blog post by Giesler (N.D.), a registered nurse, on the Children's Hospital of Los Angeles website:

Researchers at Case Western University found that high school students who spend too much time texting or on social network sites are at higher risk for other issues including smoking, risky sex, depression, eating disorders, drug and alcohol abuse and absenteeism. This is a problem because some 75 percent of 12 -to 17-year-olds now own cell phones (up from 45 percent in 2004). Some 88 percent of adolescent cell phone users are text messagers. The study identified 'hyper-texters' as teens that have sent over 120 text messages each day. Among adolescent texters, one in three teens sends more than 100 text messages a day, or 3,000 texts a month (Lenhart, Ling, Campbell, & Purcell, 2010) (Hyper-Texters section).

Giesler referenced a 2007 survey of teens ranging in age from 13-

18 conducted by Teenage Research Unlimited (TRU) for Fifth & Pacific Companies, Inc. (formerly Liz Claiborne Inc.). Because this survey is from 2007, we can imagine that the cyber world has become even more sophisticated since then, but the information is compelling:

> *...an alarming number of teens in dating relationships are being controlled, threatened and humiliated through cell phones and the Internet with unimaginable frequency. The research also reveals disturbing data that a significant majority of parents are completely unaware of this type of dating abuse and the dangers facing their teens (Break the Cycle para. 1).*

Other key findings include:

> *Teens report dating abuse via technology is a serious problem.*

> *Cell phone calls and texting at unimaginable frequency mean constant control day and night.*

> *Parents do not know about dating teens' constant contact.*

> *Cell phones and Internet have become weapons of teen dating abuse.*

> *Parents do not know about this abuse.*

> *Parents believe technology makes dating abuse more prevalent and more hidden — yet few are doing anything about it.*

> *Parents also do not know that their teens are victims of physical and sexual abuse (Break the Cycle para. 2).*

Giesler confirms something that is very evident to those of us in education—cell phones are associated with cheating. Giesler cites a study that found that up to 39% of parents of boys are concerned about cheating on tests by text messaging or cell phone compared with 31% of girls (Cell Phones and Cheating section). Paul (2018) cites studies that show that cell phones are shortening the attention spans of teens (para. 6).

We discussed in a previous chapter the need for parents to ensure their kids are actually learning and getting an education, which is not always evident from the grades the student earns. A grade of 100 does not necessarily mean the student actually has acquired the skills necessary for the next level of education, and the issue of students (of all ages) using technology to cheat is a huge part of this problem. The educational system makes great efforts to block students from cheating, but with the online era comes online learning, both in the classroom and at home, where no teacher is present to cast a watchful eye on the student as he/she works. In its simplest form, there is just no way to eliminate all electronic cheating (never mind old-school paper and pen cheating that has been around as long as school has been around).

Quality of sleep is another major area in teens' lives affected by teen cell phone usage. Twenge (2017) found that the number of U.S. teens who reported sleeping fewer than seven hours a night jumped 22% between 2012 and 2015, and by 2015, 43% of teens reported sleeping less than seven hours a night on most nights (sleep experts agree that teens need at least nine hours of sleep a night). Twenge attributes this change to more teens owning smartphones (para. 2-3). Twenge found that teens who spent more time online and on social media were more likely to sleep less, and teens who spent more time with their friends in person or on sports or exercise actually slept more (para. 6). Twenge points out a psychological contributing factor: the blue light emitted by smartphones and tablets stimulates daylight, inhibiting the brain's production of melatonin, the hormone that helps us fall asleep and stay asleep (para. 13). Twenge cites a 2014 study that found 80% of teens admitted to using their phones when they were supposed to be sleeping—a practice some call "vamping" (para. 15).

> **As an educator, I would add that many teens lack sleep not only due to cell phone usage but also due to a lack of overall balance in their lives, or because they are overscheduled.**

As an educator, I would add that many teens lack sleep not only due to cell phone usage but also due to a lack of overall balance in their lives, or because they are overscheduled. We discuss the pressures of students' academics in another chapter, but I can add here that when students select many or all high-rigor classes for their school academic schedule and pursue a variety of activities outside of school, whether that is school extracurriculars and/or non-school activities such as club sports or competitive anything (dance, cheer, music, etc., which are all demanding in their own right), students naturally run into a situation in which they must stay up late just to manage their responsibilities. It is the modern-day equivalent of burning the candle at both ends. Again, I am not criticizing students' class selections or outside-of-school pursuits, but I do encourage students to maintain balance, even if that means taking fewer high-rigor courses or being more selective about activities (which is very different from quitting all activities and taking no rigorous courses or from quitting all activities and overloading the course schedule).

I can say with absolute certainty that no educators are surprised by any of these findings, especially those with a little experience under their belts. Ironically (or maybe not), despite all of the downsides to teens' use of electronics, educators are increasingly pressured to keep kids engaged (remember—shortened attention spans) by utilizing the latest in technology, which often includes apps students can access on their cell phones. It is a vicious cycle.

Based on my own experiences, I can say that the problem is not just the cell phone. Many schools require their students to use a laptop in class, and many districts provide those laptops to their students so that all may have access to the same electronics. Like every well-intentioned deed in education, this one has a downside that I have personally experienced. As school counselors, we go into classes from time to time to present to students about a variety of topics. I was recently in a classroom walking a class through (fittingly) an online program our district provides for our students. The program itself is a very good one that gives students access to academic and career planning. I was behind the students presenting and walking around the room so that I could see the students' screens and ensure that they were able to keep up with the log-in process, etc. Just moments into the process, one student collapsed the page we were working on and pulled up an interactive video game that involved chasing others and shooting them and had the face of another person (player) at the bottom corner of the screen (similar to Facetime or Skype). Plenty of other students were visibly off-task—one was instant messaging another, others were trying to check their phones (even though they had been asked to put them away), and yet others hadn't brought their laptops at all and were sitting with their heads down, which is another downside of the use of electronics in the classroom. This is one brief snapshot of a classroom that can be multiplied again and again and again on any given day across our nation, and it doesn't take an educational expert to see that electronics in general are negatively affecting the level of education a student is getting. When you as a parent envision a day in the life of high school today, you must not envision your own high school experience because very likely your vision is way off. I am not taking a hard stance against all electronics, but I am acknowledging that there is a definite problem that needs to be addressed.

The effects of the cell phone on basic classroom management have been profound, but that is another book. I would ask parents, however, to picture the typical high school classroom before attempting to place blame solely on the teacher for just about anything. Just picture how difficult it probably is to get your own child to put down his/her phone and help with household chores or do his/her homework. Then multiply that task by 35 kids in each class, then multiply that by 6, 7, or 8 classes—remember, just like it's not 1995 at home, it's not 1995 in the classroom anymore, either. Then add to it, for each kid in each class, the caveat that some students believe they really do not have to listen to you because, well, their parents will call you or come see you and tell you to back off (or worse). Be sure to picture your most aggressive friend or acquaintance who is a parent of a teen yelling at you about this, and you can easily see that parents must be part of the solution instead of going to war with the teacher and school district over their efforts to discipline their child. In terms of putting down the cell phone, schools need parents' help, and parents need the school's help, so the sooner we band together to help each other, the better for our kids.

So, social media is the obvious biggy, but what about television? Since so much of teens' time is spent online, what are teens' viewing habits? You can probably guess there is a study on those habits, too. McAlone (2017) cited a 2017 survey of 1500 U.S. teens commission by Awesomeness TV, which produces video for 31 different platforms. Among their findings: On average, teens spent 34% of their video time watching YouTube, compared to 27% watching Netflix, and 14% watching live TV. This puts YouTube and Netflix way ahead of their streaming competitors: Hulu and Amazon came in at 4% and 3% respectively (para. 1). As to what devices teens are using, topping the list was a smartphone (34%), followed by computer (26%), and TV set (24%) (para. 4).

As an adult, reading this chapter up to this point about the ins and outs of social media and electronics might be overwhelming, and frankly, the data and research that exists is exactly that. A vast sea of information on the topic exists. I have included a broad overview of research that is out there, and I encourage parents to do your own research. It's all out there on the internet—articles, studies, blogs—and much of it is free. Plus, the electronic world and the research that accompanies it is constantly changing, so parents must stay vigilant and current to remain informed. What parents should not do is ignore the issues with electronics because the issues are "silent" or "invisible" in that kids are quiet (for the most part) when they are engrossed in something online and virtual. Out of sight/out of mind will not work here.

Ultimately, we end where we began, with the confirmation that it is complicated. And like everything else kids and parents have been faced with throughout history, it can't be about adults hiding all the "bad stuff" from kids and hoping kids don't find it. It also can't be that parents are frustrated with their teen's behaviors with their electronics at home (i.e.

never putting them down even when you ask/tell again and again) yet assume that when the teen goes to school, this habit magically disappears and the child transforms into the perfect student, leaving the teacher as the "bad guy" who asked the child to put the phone away and it turned into "a disciplinary thing" when the child refused/argued/etc. The big picture is about educating ourselves and our kids about navigating the world of electronics responsibly. It is the same as when a teen gets a driver's license—with that license comes the responsibility of operating a vehicle and being cognizant of the human lives that can be affected by each decision the driver makes. Teens must approach the electronic world with the same seriousness, and they must be educated about the dangers and responsibilities that accompany the use of electronics and the electronic world.

> **The big picture is about educating ourselves and our kids about navigating the world of electronics responsibly.**

Ultimately, parents need to know what their kids are doing, but as has been the case with teens since the dawn of time, parents are unlikely to know everything their teens are doing. So the next best strategy is good old-fashioned strong parenting, building strong relationships, and fostering an open line of communication with their kids. Like in *Romeo and Juliet*, the minute a parent bans a kid from doing something, "it" becomes the number one thing on the teen's list to do, so it can't be about a ban, plus most bans are just not realistic to enforce. So instead of banning the use of social media and phone/electronics use, parents can work with their teen to first educate them on the dangers of usage, and then work with them to set reasonable limits for usage.

As one example, teens might be required to leave their phones in their parents' room to charge overnight, eliminating the temptation to use them all night long. The same would go for laptops, etc. As we discussed in a previous chapter about using things the teen likes as a reward to be earned, the cell phone can be one of those things teens can earn after achieving X, Y, or Z. Having a discussion about the importance of human interaction and family time is also an appropriate and important step for parents to take with their kids.

Remember, people don't know what they don't know. Today's kids have known technology since Day 1, and it's our job as adults to educate them about it so they realize there is a downside. Picture what you would do if instead of holding a phone, your child was holding a cigarette, a bottle of liquor, a dangerous drug, a weapon, pornography, etc. Most parents would be highly unlikely to ignore those scenarios. Each scenario would likely warrant a serious conversation about the dangers of each as well as the rules of your household in relation to each scenario. At first glance, a phone seems much more innocuous than the scenarios above, but research confirms it can be equally detrimental. Your teen's phone usage should not be ignored and warrants the same type of serious conversation with your child.

I would also point out that we are in a unique moment in time in that electronics/cell phones/social media/etc. are all new enough to our existence that many (most?) current parents of teens and many current teachers grew up without these devices interfering with kids' development and educations and teachers' classrooms. Because of this reality of time and age, at the current time, the interference by and negative effect of these devices on kids is noticed the most by (ahem) "older," more experienced people who have been around the block without the devices and can personally compare things now to how things "used to be." As time marches on, those more experienced educators will retire, leaving the next (ahem) "younger" generation of teachers in schools, and the next generation of parents of teens will be ushered in, all of whom will have come of age only knowing life with the devices.

The concept of sounding like the stereotypical older person of the 1950s lamenting about "kids today" and "all their rock and roll" is not lost on me (shaking my head; lol), but I am genuinely concerned that the time is now to recognize the potential damaging effects modern electronics and their extensive reach can have on the development of kids before those of us who know differently are no longer in a position to notice. One simple way I see it is this—the Walkman (a precursor of current electronics and earbuds) came out in 1979, just before I entered junior high school. No one was allowed to walk up and down the halls of a school, never mind sit through class, with a Van Halen tape blasting in his/her ears. EVERYONE would have noticed and pointed out the obvious—"You can't hear with that thing on! Take it off!" Armed with that simple knowledge, schools did not allow them at school. Just because modern technology is sleeker and less noticable than a 1980s Walkman, it doesn't mean the effect is any different, yet virtually all kids have access to this modern technology all day and all night.

And yes, when we dicuss electronics, earbuds are only one of the issues. Social media or texting (even texts and phone calls from parents) is the modern-day equivalent of students from all over the school walking into the classroom (or across the room), interrupting the teacher's lesson and the student's learning to pass neatly folded notes to each other all period long, all day long, (and all night long!), every day. It also means that any teen drama (friends or family) that in yesteryear that would have needed to wait until lunch or after school can continue to interrupt the teen's learning and emotional state 24-7, which can (and does) spill over into fights and other disciplinary or emotional issues for the student at school. Virtual note-passing is seemingly impossible to stop, yet taking the path of least resistance with it doesn't seem to be an effective answer to addressing the problem, thus this chapter and the concerns outlined in this chapter. As time marches on, the younger generation who have grown up with electronic devices, social media, and apps galore, will need to take the driver's seat in guiding the next generation through the use of technology while ensuring that our young humans become educated and socially adjusted in the process.

I think we can all agree that electronics are not going away; the internet is not going away; social media is not going away; and kids' temptation and curiosity of pursuing "bad things" is not going away. And I am not arguing for a ban against a use of all electronics all the time. Part of being a teen developmentally means pushing their limits and being social. Teens will continue to pursue their social existence via electronic means, but parents and schools must continue to educate teens about the rabbit holes of too much media use and the same basic "dangers in society" that existed before electronics became a mainstream part of life. There is a funny meme being passed around social media that basically compares our standards in the past (don't talk to strangers, don't talk to strangers on the internet, don't get into cars with strangers) with our modern standards (use the internet to summon strangers and get into their cars—referencing transportation services like Uber/Lyft/etc.) that accurately and humorously illustrates how times have changed. Just as our yesteryear parents shook their heads when we climbed on the roof of our friend's house, doused ourselves in baby oil, and lay there for hours tanning (i.e. burning/aging/prematurely destroying) our skin, we continued to do so until someone's parent came out and demanded that we "come down off that roof this instant!" Yesterday's suntanning roof is today's electronic world, and it is up to adults everywhere, as with everything else that comes with the responsibilities of adulting, to stand up and step up.

I see the current evolution of electronics and smart phones as similar to society's delayed reaction to the dangers of cigarette smoking, as an example. An undated CNN report outlines the history of tobacco, highlights of which include:

Tobacco was introduced in Europe in the 1500s. The first successful commercial crop was cultivated in Virginia in 1612 and within seven years was the colony's largest export.

Cigarettes became widely popular after the Civil War.

The negative health effects of tobacco were not initially known, and most early European physicians agreed with the Native American belief that tobacco can be an effective medicine.

*By the early 20th century, articles addressing the health effects of smoking began to appear in scientific and medical journals, and in the 1930s, German researchers made a correlation between cancer and smoking. As research grew, the general public still knew little of the newly-discovered statistics.

*A 1952 Reader's Digest article detailed the dangers of smoking, and similar reports became more mainstream. Sales dropped for the first time. By 1954, U.S. tobacco companies mass-marketed "healthier" cigarettes that were low-tar and filtered. Sales boomed again.

*In the early 1960s, the Surgeon General's Advisory Committee on Smoking and Health concluded that scientific evidence showed a causal relationship between smoking and cancer.

*Bans on smoking began. 1965—Surgeon General's warnings on all cigarette packages; 1971—all broadcast advertising banned; 1990—smoking banned on all interstate buses and all domestic airline flights lasting six hours or (fewer); 1995—President Clinton announced FDA plans to regulate tobacco, especially sales and advertising aimed at minors (para. 2-11).

Despite this decades-long clear chain of events and warnings, according to the Centers for Disease Control and Prevention Fast Facts, today smoking is the leading cause of preventable death. Worldwide, tobacco causes nearly 6 million deaths per year, and current trends show that tobacco will cause more than 8 million deaths annually by 2030 (Smoking is the leading case of preventable death section).

As an aside—in other smoking/other negative habit news, parents, do some research on teens and JUULing/smoking e-cigarettes, and you will see the history above playing out again right before our eyes. An October 2018 CDC report showed:

Sales of JUUL, an e-cigarette shaped like a USB flash drive, grew more than seven-fold from 2016 to 2017, and held the greatest share of the U.S. e-cigarette market by December 2017...Use of JUUL by youth in schools, including in classrooms and bathrooms, has been widely reported. Most e-cigarettes contain nicotine, and JUUL contains among the highest nicotine content of any e-cigarette on the U.S. market. Nicotine is highly addictive and can harm a child's brain development, which continues into the mid-20s.

"The popularity of JUUL among kids threatens our progress in reducing youth e-cigarette use," said Robert Redfield, M.D., director of CDC. "We are alarmed that these new high nicotine content e-cigarettes, marketed and sold in kid-friendly flavors, are so appealing to our nation's young people" (para. 1-3).

In September 2018, FDA announced the issuance of more than 1,300 warning letters and civil money penalty complaints to retailers who illegally sold JUUL and other e-cigarette products to minors. The FDA has also requested information from JUUL, and several other manufacturers, related to marketing, youth appeal and product design, including details on the companies' plans to address the problem of youth use of their products (The use of e-cigarettes is unsafe for children, teens, and young adults section).

The irony should not be overlooked that a JUUL/e-cigarette is both a smoking device and an electronic device, but I digress. The point is that we are still essentially at the beginning of the time period in which cell phones/electronics and all that that entails are a mainstream part of life. Just as we did with cigarette smoking, we are becoming more educated about the potential damaging effects and impacts of electronics on kids (and adults, for that matter), but we will continue to see the effects real-time and will hopefully react accordingly, as we have with cigarette smoking (despite the very high current stats about the negative impact of smoking).

The bottom line is this—kids will find what they want to find, whether it is an app, an internet site, a YouTube channel, a JUUL/e-cigarette or whatever else they are looking for. Am I saying that cell phones (and other electronics) will kill 6 million people a year fifty years from now? No, but we do not know the full, long-term impact electronics/cell phones/social media/etc. will have on human learning/human development/human ability to cope with difficulty/etc. (But smoking e-cigarettes...that remains to be seen. I recently walked a teen smoker of e-cigarettes through the brief history of how cigarettes went from being considered cool and mainstream to being proven as deadly over several decades. I explained to her how no one knew how deadly cigarettes were until decades into the use of them. We are in the very early stages of finding out what effects smoking e-cigarettes will eventually have on its users. As I explained to my student, she and her peers will not find out how they are being affected for many years to come. At this time I have no additional report on whether my very informative speech had any impact on her and her e-cigarette habits or beliefs.)

What I am illustrating with the history of tobacco example is that people want what they want, even when evidence suggests there is inherent harm in whatever the behavior is. Just because electronics can be silent and seemingly invisible, parents cannot be complacent about their kids' use of them (all age kids—not just teens). It would be highly irresponsible to do so, and endless research exists backing it up. In closing, as a side note, parents should know that JUULing/smoking e-cigarettes is equally invisible and very difficult to eradicate in and out of schools. Parents should also not assume it is a "certain (stereotypical) type" of kid partaking in e-cigarettes. Trust me on this one. History, experience, and time have shown us the dangers of tobacco use and smoking and lying in the sun too long. Only the passing of time will show us the "big picture" culminating effects of electronics/smart phones/social media/etc. on our young people (not just teens). We should not passively wait to find out those results. Parents, consider yourself informed.

Teen Mental Health, the Perfect Student & the Decidedly Imperfect Student

Teen Mental Health, the Perfect Student & the Decidedly Imperfect Student

S o parents, here we are. You've hung in there and gotten to this chapter because you care about your kids and may also see the need for a change moving forward. In the beginning of this book, I asked for your open-mindedness and warned that a goal of this book was to rip the bandages off touchy subjects and begin a dialogue of real talk between parents and educators. The evidence presented in this book alone, which is a tip of the proverbial iceberg, shows an alarming need for this conversation to not only begin, but to evolve quickly into a full-on, deep, open, honest conversation between parents, educators, and the kids we all care about.

One simple way I can illustrate the need for a real conversation is to discuss the reality school counselors and educators are facing in today's educational landscape when it comes to teens' mental health. A conversation I find myself as a high school counselor having with parents with increasing regularity concerns counseling at school. Parents come to meet with me because of serious mental health concerns they have about their child, and some believe that we have the capabilities at school to provide the appropriate level of ongoing mental health treatment to help their child, the same as they would receive from a dedicated mental health professional. To help dispel the myth of what the role of a school counselor is compared to a professional mental health provider, we need to look at the official roles of school counselors according to the national professional leadership we are provided as well as the scope of the education we received when we became school counselors.

School counselors are employed by the school to help students in a variety of ways. The American School Counselor Association (ASCA) is a national professional guiding organization that focuses on providing professional development, enhancing school counseling programs and researching effective school counseling practices. ASCA defines a school counselor as:

> ...certified/licensed educators with a minimum of a master's degree in school counseling, making them uniquely qualified to address all students' academic, career and social/emotional development needs by designing, implementing, evaluating and enhancing a comprehensive school counseling program that promotes and enhances student success (The Role of the School Counselor, para. 1).

The role and duties of a school counselor are both broad and specific simultaneously. For example, according to ASCA, examples of activities school counselors should be involved in include:

*providing individual student academic program planning

*providing counseling to students who are tardy or absent

*providing counseling to students who have disciplinary problems

*collaborating with teachers to present school counseling core curriculum lessons

*analyzing grade-point averages in relationship to achievement

*interpreting student records

*helping the school principal identify and resolve student issues, needs and problems

*providing individual and small-group counseling services to students

advocating for students at individual education plan meetings, student study teams and school attendance review boards (Appropriate Activities for School Counselors list).

Just as there are activities at school expected of a school counselor, examples of activities that are not appropriate for school counselors according to ASCA include:

coordinating paperwork and data entry of all new students

signing excuses for students who are tardy or absent

performing disciplinary actions or assigning discipline consequences

teaching classes when teachers are absent

computing grade-point averages

supervising classrooms or common areas

assisting with duties in the principal's office

providing therapy or long-term counseling in schools to address psychological disorders (Inappropriate Activities for School Counselors list).

I share this information to illustrate the role of a counselor when it comes to providing counseling for students' serious mental health needs. School counselors are tasked with the responsibility to provide responsive services—activities and interventions designed to meet students' immediate needs and concerns. **Responsive services** may include counseling in individual or small-group settings or crisis response (The Role of the School Counselor, Delivery section). Examples of this include small group topics such as grief, anger, or study skills. **Crisis response** counseling occurs when something has happened that impacts students at the school, such as a student suicide or a bus accident. The purpose for both of these areas of school counseling is to help the student get to a place mentally where they can successfully function in the classroom. Both group and crisis counseling in schools are intended to be short term.

According to ASCA, school counselors provide counseling sessions in individual or small-group settings that:

help student overcome issues impeding achievement or success help students identify problems, causes, alternatives and possible consequences so they can make decisions and take appropriate action

are planned and goal-focused and are short-termed in nature

According to ASCA, school counselors do not provide therapy or long-term counseling in schools to address psychological disorders. However, school counselors are prepared to recognize and respond to student mental health crises and needs. School counselors address those barriers to student success by offering education, prevention and crisis and short-term intervention to include group counseling until the student is connected with available community resources. When students require long-term counseling or therapy, school counselors make referrals to appropriate community resources (The School Counselor and Group Counseling, The School Counselor's Role section).

So, as a school counselor works with a student, it may become evident to the school counselor that the student may need further professional intervention. I say "may need" because ultimately it is up to the professional mental health care provider to determine the next steps for a student. When a student needs ongoing, professional mental health services, that is where a school counselor's role stops, and a professional mental health provider's role begins. I will note, however, that when students are receiving professional mental health services outside of school, school counselors and interventionists want to know about it so we can continue to provide mental health support for that student at school. School counselors are not able to provide therapy or long-term counseling. When a student's needs reach this point at school, a school counselor will help the parent and student by providing a referral for additional professional assistance, and many school districts have referral resources to

> **When a student needs ongoing, professional mental health services, that is where a school counselor's role stops, and a professional mental health provider's role begins.**

help kids and their families get the appropriate help they need. It is critical for the parent/guardian of the student to follow through at this point to seek professional mental health care for the student as recommended by a mental health professional.

It is necessary for me to bring this up to illustrate first, where the school's boundaries end when it comes to ongoing mental health care, and second, that the overall expectations sometimes put on schools by society have become unmanageable. In its simplest form, schools do not have the manpower or expertise to provide students with both an education and with full-service mental health treatment. As students' mental health needs have risen, however, school counseling offices (along with school intervention specialists' offices) have become a daily revolving door of crisis intervention and referrals for professional mental health services—i.e. the services of a mental health provider (psychologist/psychiatrist) or facility (in-patient/out-patient/etc.).

An increasing number of students are exhibiting signs of mental health distress and are in need of help that is beyond the scope of a school or school counselor or interventionist, requiring referrals for ongoing professional mental health care. A similar example would be when a student goes to the school nurse because he fell in a physical education class. If the nurse is able to treat his injury at school, such as having the student ice his knee and go back to class, the nurse may provide that treatment and contact the parent. But if it becomes evident that the student needs further medical treatment, the parent is contacted and a referral is made for further medical treatment by a professional medical provider (i.e.—take him to the doctor or hospital). To put it simply, the nurse would not attempt to operate on the knee at school.

Current statistics on teen mental health help put things into perspective in terms of numbers of kids served by mental health providers. According to the National Alliance on Mental Illness (NAMI), one in five children age 13-18 have or will have a serious mental illness:

*20% live with a mental health condition.

*11% have a mood disorder.

*10% have a behavior or conduct disorder.

*8% have an anxiety disorder (Fact section).

*50% of all cases of lifetime mental illness begin by age 14.

*The average delay between onset of symptoms and intervention is 8-10 years.

*70% of youth in the juvenile justice system have a mental illness (Impact section).

*Suicide is the third leading cause of death in youth ages 10-24.

*90% of those who died by suicide had an underlying mental illness (Suicide section).

NAMI lists the following warning signs for parents to look for in their teens:

*Feeling very sad or withdrawn for more than 2 weeks (e.g., crying regularly, feeling fatigued, feeling unmotivated).

*Trying to harm or kill oneself or making plans to do so.

*Out-of-control, risk-taking behaviors that can cause harm to self or others.

*Sudden overwhelming fear for no reason, sometimes with a racing heart, physical discomfort or fast breathing.

*Not eating, throwing up or using laxatives to lose weight; significant weight loss or gain.

*Severe mood swings that cause problems in relationships.

*Repeated use of drugs or alcohol.

*Drastic changes in behavior, personality or sleeping habits (e.g., waking up early and acting agitated).

*Extreme difficulty in concentrating or staying still that can lead to failure in school.

*Intense worries or fears that get in the way of daily activities like hanging out with friends or going to classes (Warning Signs section).

NAMI makes the following recommendations for parents when they have a concern about their child's mental health:

  Talk with your pediatrician.
  Get a referral to a mental health specialist.
  Work with the school.
  Connect with other families (4 Things Parents Can Do section).

Parents, I must point out that:

It is critical to add that *when your teen talks about killing himself/herself* **(**"I just don't want to be here anymore" or "Everyone would be better off without me here" etc.**)**

and says he/she has a plan ("I would take pills," or "I would shoot myself," etc.)

you need to seek professional help immediately.

Even if your teen follows up with "I'm just kidding" or something similar, **it is important to take all statements teens make about killing themselves seriously.**

Many times, the teen will not say it to parents directly, just as they don't say a lot of other things to you directly. A very typical scenario involves a teen posting something online or saying something in passing to a friend (often via text), and the friend tells someone, and eventually someone tells the teen's parent. If this type of exchange is reported to someone at a school, the school professional will communicate with the parent as part of working with the student, but this type of information is not always reported to someone at school, and these scenarios do not always play out during school hours or school months. So, parents, however the information gets to you, it is important to act quickly. If this happens at home over the weekend, for example, do not wait until Monday morning to go to the school.

A direct resource for help is to call the National Suicide Prevention Lifeline (or other similar resource): 1-800-273-8255. Help is available at this number 24 hours a day every day. Healthychildren.org provides an inclusive list of recommendations for parents for suicide prevention, including not letting your teen's depression or anxiety snowball, listening (even if your teen is not talking), and never shrugging off threats of suicide as typical teenage melodrama (sections 1-3). There are many resources available, and parents are urged to use them when needed.

> **A direct resource for help is to call the National Suicide Prevention Lifeline (or other similar resource): 1-800-273-8255. Help is available at this number 24 hours a day every day.**

In its simplest form, to contrast this to a typical scenario of delayed action in seeking medical help: there are times we as humans feel like we are getting sick with a cold, for example, and we make the decision to "wait and see" how we feel, to "watch it" for a few days, thinking maybe we will start feeling better on our own without any medical intervention, and sometimes we do feel better on our own. When your child has made statements to you or to someone who has reported the information to you (such as the school counselor) about thinking about hurting or killing himself (herself), it is not a time to "wait and see." It is time to take action and get help.

Very often when parents suspect their children need mental health care, they do reach out to the school, and I urge parents to continue to do so. For many families in today's world, the school is the first stop for help on many fronts, and schools are there to provide that help or to connect the family with the resources for help. The level of mental health intervention that a student needs may be beyond the scope of what a school can provide, however, and it is important for parents to take the mental health referral the school provides and follow through with getting your child the treatment he/she needs. It is also important to follow up with your child's school after your child has had professional mental health treatment. If your child threatens suicide or is hospitalized for suicidal thoughts or intervention outside of school (especially if the school was not involved in the referral for that help and doesn't know anything about it) please follow up with your child's school by letting the counselor or interventionist know so that the school can provide mental health support for the student when the student is back at school.

A wide range of mental health help and services are potentially available in a community or area, but the process of getting mental health services for their kids can feel overwhelming for parents. A series of real and/or perceived roadblocks can keep a child from receiving appropriate mental health services. Some interventions may be free, but others can be expensive. All interventions require time and a commitment to treatment. Just as medical treatment for broken bones or high blood pressure requires continued doctor's visits and "following doctor's orders," so too does getting help for mental health.

The personal worldview of the parents as well as the mental health needs of parents themselves can have an impact on whether the child receives mental health services after the school makes the referral. Studies have shown that mental health beliefs vary culturally as well as generationally, and it makes sense that the household view and beliefs that the parent grew up with him/herself would have an impact on whether a family proceeds with getting mental health treatment for their child. Sometimes, parents do follow up and get their child professional help, and the child or parent has a bad experience or does not connect with the specific provider (therapist, hospital, etc.) and stops seeking treatment because they do not like or connect with the provider. Like finding any other type of doctor or medical practitioner, we like some better than others, and this will be true in seeking mental health help as well. So, as with everything else in this book, it's real life, and it's complicated, but this is yet another time that taking the path of least resistance and doing nothing is not only inappropriate but also potentially dangerous.

In discussing teens and mental health, we cannot discuss mental health without discussing the concept of perfection and its relationship to teen mental health. While teens' mental health needs have risen, so, too has teens' pursuit of perfection. The pursuit of perfection (or the image of perfection) is evident and prevalent in teens' and young adults' worlds. We discussed it at length in the chapter on social media, and we see it daily in our roles as educators. Curran and Hill (2017) broadly defined **perfectionism** as a combination of excessively high personal standards and overly critical self-evaluations. This study of 41,641 American, Canadian, and British college students found that recent generations of college students are demanding higher expectations of themselves and attaching more importance to perfection than previous generations. According to Curran and Hill:

> As to why self-oriented perfectionism is rising, we speculated earlier on several cultural shifts that include competitiveness, individualism, meritocracy, and anxious and controlling parental practices that may be promoting perfectionism generally (p. 10).

Curran and Hill looked at different types of perfectionism:

Self-oriented perfectionism is defined as when individuals attach irrational importance to being perfect, hold unrealistic expectations of themselves, and are punitive in their self-evaluations.

Socially prescribed perfectionism is defined as when perceived to come from others, individuals believe their social context is excessively demanding, that others judge them harshly, and that they must display perfection to secure approval.

Other-oriented perfectionism is defined as when perfectionistic expectations are directed toward others, individuals impose unrealistic standards on those around them and evaluate others critically (p. 1).

Curran and Hill found that American students reported a higher "self-oriented perfectionism" than Canadian or British students. The researchers speculated that this is due in part to cultural shifts that have evolved in the U.S. since the 1980s in which individualism and the pursuit of individualized liberty and self-gain have become increasingly valued and emphasized. They also referenced American beliefs and values regarding the American dream, in which college is seen as a means of individuals rising up the social and economic ladder (p. 10).

Curran and Hill found that U.S. students report having much higher academic expectations of themselves, and the demands of education itself are also higher compared to previous generations:

> As young people's expectations have increased, so have the educational demands placed on them. Intense competition for elite college admission has meant that, relative to previous generations, current high school students in the United States, Canada, and the United Kingdom are subjected to more numerous and stringent standardized tests (p. 4).

As a long-time educator in our state, I can verify that our students feel the pressures of being over-tested to the point that some students apathetically tune out of education altogether, particularly those who struggle year after year to achieve (note to the state: more testing does not necessarily mean students have better reading, writing or math skills). Other students, particularly those accustomed to "getting everything right" with relative ease, react to the barrage of testing at the opposite end of the spectrum by trying in vain to achieve perfect results (or at least among the best as compared to their peers). It is when these students meet a test they cannot easily master (classroom or standardized) that the gloom and spending doom of "I am a complete and total failure" mentality sets in.

Academics are (clearly) not the only source of teen perfectionism and stress. As we discussed earlier in the chapter on teen development and social behavior as well as teens' use of social media, Curran and Hill found a connection between college students and social perfectionism:

> Perhaps the most important finding from this research is that more recent generations of college students are reporting higher levels of socially prescribed perfectionism than previous generations. This finding suggests that young people are perceiving that their social context is increasingly demanding, that others judge them more harshly, and that they are increasingly inclined to display perfection as a means of securing approval (p. 11).

In line with our discussion in previous chapters about teens and mental health, Curran and Hill also found a seeming relationship between increased levels of perfectionism and psychological difficulties. Specifically, Curran and Hill pointed out that perfectionism is related to a variety of disorders, symptoms, and syndromes:

> ...socially prescribed perfectionism was revealed to be positively related to a range of psychological disorders and symptoms of disorders (e.g., social phobia, body dissatisfaction, bulimia nervosa, and suicide ideation) and had the largest relationship of other dimensions of perfectionism with depression and anxiety (p. 12).

Curran and Hill suggest that since the 1980s:

> As American, Canadian, and British cultures have become more individualistic, materialistic, and socially antagonistic over the period, with young people now facing more competitive environments, more unrealistic expectations, and more anxious and controlling parents than generations before (p. 12).

In referencing Curran and Hill's research, Simmons (2018) said:

> Perfectionism is caused by a variety of factors, not only Parents. Young adults have described pressure to appear flawless in every domain, often effortlessly so — in schoolwork, athletics, activities,

and looks —since the early 2000s. Social media has raised the bar in the pursuit of teen perfection, introducing a place where the drive to project success, as much as a wish to connect, draws youth like moths to the digital flame. As kids hungrily seek the "likes" of their peers, it is not uncommon for many to delete posts that don't receive enough "likes." (The one-like-per-minute ratio is most desirable, according to the many teens I speak with).

But the parental push to raise an uber-successful child has never been more keenly felt, so much so that researchers have a name for it: "child-contingent self-esteem," or the tendency for a parent to base their own self-worth on the success of their child. Parents now spend more time than ever on school work with their children, while time spent simply hanging out has declined. Meanwhile, between 1986 and 2006, the number of kids who said their parents surveilled their every move doubled.

In other words, teens are not the only ones guilty of "putting too much pressure" on themselves — the push to fulfill others' expectations has never been higher, for parents, too (para. 4-6).

So parents, it truly is time to stop, drop what you are doing, and roll up your sleeves when it comes to helping your child. One key area a parent can help is in the academic arena. A very typical area that both perfectionism and mental health issues arise during high school is the arena of academics:

high school class selections

college admissions

grades, GPA, class rank, and the resulting academic competition internally within the student but also externally against all the other students in the class, very many of whom are experiencing the same inner turmoil over all things academic.

Add to that the demands of just being a teenager and learning how to grow up, plus any additional family stressors such as divorce, money problems, drug problems, housing problems, deaths in the family, etc. It's easy to see what a melting pot of STRESS and the resulting anxiety students can be faced with every day.

To add to this already potentially Code Red scenario, while kids of today can be stressed to the max, so too are the educators. In defense of educators everywhere—educators are faced with their own increased demands and high-stress working conditions, not to mention that they are also humans with their own life stressors and mental health needs. Due to proverbial ongoing "cuts in funding," class sizes in general are larger than I have ever seen in my three decades of experience, and teachers are overwhelmed (as are many school counselors) with their class loads/caseloads alone. Not only are the class sizes and caseloads larger, but more students have more needs both emotionally and academically, which increases the stress load for students and educators. So, to summarize:

*class sizes are up;

*student anxiety levels and needs for mental health intervention are up;

*many students with anxiety become even more anxious in large classes;

*large classes can be boisterous, chaotic places just based on the larger size alone;

*large classes have more individual student behaviors in each classroom that both the teacher and students must deal with;

*some (many) students (anxious or not) need a quiet, calm place in order to learn.

To put it simply, stress levels are up in education for everyone.

The load of daily mandates put upon teachers is heavier than ever as well. In its simplest form—the more students struggle academically as evidenced by state tests (at least in our state), the more demands the state (and federal government as well) put on educators to "fix" it. Many of these additional mandates are tied to testing, and almost all of them require additional paperwork and meetings and jumping through hoops that (you guessed it) take educators' physical time and mental energy away from their primary purpose of helping the classes of humans sitting before them each day. So it is a vicious cycle—kids are stressed academically and emotionally; educators are stressed, stretched thin, and overwhelmed with mandates; educators need kids to perform academically; and classrooms and schools everywhere are bursting at the seams. You do not have to be an academic expert to see this is a recipe for a high-stress situation, and it is playing out in schools across our country every day.

I should note again my personal bias in discussing school issues. I am speaking based on my own personal experiences in education as well as the other documented evidence I have provided throughout this book. To give context to my personal educational experiences, which have all been in Texas public schools, according to U.S. News & World Report's ranking of education by state, Texas ranks 37th of 50 overall, 34th in higher education, and 33rd in PreK-12 (website list). I must add, too, that not ALL students are overwhelmingly stressed, and many students are very successful academically. As I say to students when I talk to them about academics, an education is not something that adults must force on you— an education is yours to get. It won't happen by accident. All individuals must take ownership of their education, regardless of what the individual student's situation is. I can give you examples of students who came from backgrounds that were not for the faint of heart, and they persevered and succeeded academically, so it does happen. But the fact remains that based on statistics, teen anxiety and stress are up, and many parents are at their wits' end about what they can do to help their kids.

So what can a parent do to help alleviate stress when it comes to your child's academic and possibly perfectionistic life? To reference our chapter about control—we can only control ourselves and our own choices. As a parent, one of your roles is to guide your kids' academic choices without selecting for him/her or unwittingly pressuring him/her. Remember, parental opinions carry a lot of power; proceed with caution. Most teens in today's academic climate already feel the pressure without any parental input, but kids still need guidance about class choices.

College admissions, GPA (grade point average), and class rank are terms parents of high school students will become very familiar with. Students strive for a high GPA and class rank for a variety of reasons. Bragging rights alone is a leading reason, but it is deeper than that for most teens. Some colleges are very rigorous and selective with their admissions, meaning without a certain class rank or GPA, admission most likely will not happen. Other colleges provide automatic admission that is tied to class rank/GPA, and many scholarships are tied to class rank/GPA, so good grades (especially relative to a student's classmates) can open academic and financial doors for students.

High schools/school districts vary greatly in how they compute GPA and whether they rank or do not rank their students, and there are pros and cons to the various methods schools choose for their procedure. There really is no one right way to do it. It should be noted that student mental health is part of the conversation when districts consider whether to rank/not rank/set up GPAs a certain way.

Some high schools choose to rank or not rank its students, others choose to include all classes in the GPA and class rank, while others choose to include only certain classes in a student's GPA (ex. "core" classes such as English or Algebra vs. "elective" courses such as a computer science, fine arts, or business course). Regardless of what method individual high schools choose to follow when it comes to calculating GPA and thus class rank, most colleges look at the actual classes (and the rigor level of those classes) that are listed on the student's transcript, or academic record of all classes attempted and grades earned in those classes. And regardless of the GPA and class rank calculated by any individual school district, many colleges have their own ratings system to rank a student based on what classes a student took, what "level" that class was, and the grade earned in the class.

Typical levels of classes might include "on level" (or in old school terminology "regular"), "honors," "AP/Pre-AP or Advanced Placement/Pre-

Advanced Placement," "IB or International Baccalaureate," or some form of "dual credit" college class that counts as both a high school and college credit. School districts determine what type of GPA points are awarded to these classes, but typically the highest level classes (AP, for example), are awarded the most GPA points. Ultimately, though, because colleges look at the actual transcript (and not just at the apples and oranges of school district -to-school district variations of GPA calculation), the answer does not lie solely in which method of GPA calculation your local high school uses or whether they rank or do not rank. The answer lies in your own child and the decisions you and your child make when it comes to high school load, class selection, and maintaining balance in your child's life.

When a teen sits down to select his/her classes for high school each year, everything we have discussed in this book so far goes into the decisions and class choices the student makes, either actively and overtly or subconsciously. So, students who are "pushing themselves academically" tend to select not only the highest rigor of classes in order to make themselves competitive against their peers for all the reasons outlined in this book, but some also choose the highest number of those rigorous classes on their schedules. For example, if a student has an 8-period day, some (many) students will select the highest level of class for all 8 periods despite discussions about balance. So let's discuss a few things here.

First of all, while there are many students who struggle in the world today, there are those who, as far as any of us know, are able to handle a rigorous class schedule without obvious mental anxiety and struggle. So, a major disclaimer needs to be made that "hard classes" do not automatically cause students to develop mental health problems. But as I discuss with students and parents all the time, once students get to high school, it is about more than just being smart. Many, many students are smart and highly capable of success in rigorous classes. What it comes down to for many students is the concept of "balance," or, as I say to kids and parents so often—how late can you stay up at night to get your work done, stay on top of things, and achieve the grade in the class that you hope to achieve and will be happy with? (Not to mention balance in life in general.)

To add to the mix, many colleges want to see a well-rounded student who has done more than just academics in his/her high school career. Out of the pressure to succeed, or seeing it as a "guarantee" of a higher GPA/class rank, and thus a better chance at a competitive college, some students will leave/quit their other activities such as sports or fine arts, or will forego trying classes with a lower GPA level that they are interested in because of the "hit" those classes will make on their GPA and will instead load up on the most rigorous classes in an effort to "ensure" the mathematical possibility of a high GPA.

As you can probably predict, not all students ace every one of their most rigorous classes. Some students will struggle because they do not have enough time in the day to achieve everything they want to achieve. Others struggle because they are taking the class based on the GPA value, not because the student is genuinely interested in the class. Others struggle because the student lacks skills in certain areas (math skills needed for a high level science class, for example) to truly ace the class. For other students, because school has been "easy" in earlier years (meaning the student has been able to achieve a high grade with minimal work or studying outside the classroom), as they reach the most rigorous classes of high school (and take several simultaneously), they lack the study skills and routine to achieve maximum success in a class.

It should be noted that study skills are simply habits that can be worked on and improved. A simple internet search will reveal endless lists of study skills and methods that parents can help their kids hone at home (and also use at school). As I tell my students all the time—you will be amazed at how less stressed you are before a test when you know that you are adequately prepared for that test.

With all of this in mind, it is important for parents to help guide their kids' decisions when it comes to picking their high school cla ss sch while at the same time remembering that it is your child's education and not yours. When it comes to participating in high school activities or electives, parents have a lot of influence in what their kids value and will try. When a student is meeting with me as their counselor making class selections, I educate them on everything I have mentioned above. There have been times when a student has shown interest in selecting a class that the parent did not want their student to take, which becomes evident when the parent says something along the lines of "You're not doing that," or "You know you're not good at that," or "No, we tried that with your sister and you saw how that turned out," etc. There are times that the words from the parent are along the lines of "No, that will kill your GPA. Do you have an AP class he (she) can take?" In defense of parents, many times, it is the kid saying he/she must take a certain AP or other rigorous class, and it becomes evident it is because his/her friends are taking that class, and the kid doesn't want to miss out. Somehow we have lost our way when our kids' educational careers are determined this way.

Parents best know their kids, and kids best know themselves. We as counselors talk to kids and parents all day long about balance, but parents have the most influence on their child's class choices. If parents see their child struggling academically due to the student's class load, it is important for the parents and child to discuss it together, with the child's teachers, and with the child's counselor to find a path that works, regardless of the GPA impact. It is also important to remember that every student in a high school class can go on to attend college and earn a college degree. Many colleges have much less selective (or restrictive) admissions and provide an excellent (and often less expensive) education, so it is important for parents and kids to recognize the self-imposed stresses they place on themselves during the high school class selection and college choice selection process.

While it seems obvious to most educators and non-educators that so-called "high flyer" students who choose all high-rigor classes every year may run into potential stress and anxiety at some point, academic stress can be found in all levels of students, especially those who struggle academically. When students go through high school (and the earlier years) not applying themselves academically (not participating in class, studying, reading, completing work on time, or choosing to listen to music instead of the lesson, etc.), far more than their GPA and class rank are hurt. The cumulative lack of education a child has simply from not applying himself/ herself through the K-12 educational years has a clear impact on what choices a child has for himself/herself after high school.

This cumulative lack of education can translate to a very difficult high school career, which can be a serious source of stress for students, especially as they reach the age of 18, the typical age of high school graduates. Very often this academic stress and struggle play out as discipline problems in the high school classroom, which comes across to the naked eye the student choosing to act out for no apparent reason ("bad parenting" is a typical assumption made by the general public), when what is actually playing out is the student's frustration and anger that is the culmination of years of struggling to learn and "do school." Despite the obvious difficulty a struggling student might have getting there, many students (struggling or not) do make it to high school graduation and do go on to college, whether it is a four-year college or a two-year college, but as we discussed in a previous chapter, graduating from high school is not a guarantee of possessing the skills to be successful in college.

A startling 2016 statistic from the Center for American Progress drives home this point:

The national rates of remediation are a significant problem. According to college enrollment statistics, many students are underprepared for college-level work. In the United States, research shows that anywhere from 40 percent to 60 percent of first-year college students require remediation in English, math, or both. Remedial classes increase students' time to degree attainment and decrease their likelihood of completion. While rates vary depending on the source, on-time completion rates of students who take remedial classes are consistently less than 10 percent (p. 1).

In the defense of students everywhere, these numbers only tell part of the story. While students' academic expectations of themselves is definitely part of the problem, another part is the responsibility of schools across the United States and their academic expectations of students, as is evidenced by a Baltimore educator's comments in a PBS article (Butrymowicz, 2017):

Sonja Brookins Santelises, chief executive officer of Baltimore City Public Schools, is well aware of the gap between the knowledge needed to earn a diploma in the district and what college professors expect students to be able to do on day one. She served as chief academic officer for the district before going to the D.C.-based think tank Education Trust in 2013, where she studied this issue nationally. She returned to the Baltimore school district in the summer of 2016.

It's "more like a chasm," she said. "We've had too low a standard for too long." The district is working to increase dual-enrollment opportunities, through which high school students can enroll in college courses, as well as increase general exposure to higher education, Santelises said. It's also trying to equip schools with the tools to deal with trauma in students' lives and to better support teachers in raising standards to challenge students more in high school.

"If we've been giving kids worksheets with simplistic answers for years and then get upset when they can't write a five-paragraph essay or recognize subject-verb agreement, that's not the kids," she said. "That's us" (para. 22-25).

As I said in the beginning, this book is meant to begin an open, honest conversation between parents and educators so that we can work together for positive change on a variety of issues. It is not meant to be a critical analysis of issues plaguing the American educational system. To help parents of struggling students, however, we must acknowledge the reality that many students are facing when it comes to "getting a good education." We know that in addition to students struggling due to a lack of motivation through the years, students may have a learning disability or difficulty that is or is not diagnosed that adds to the struggle, and certainly mental health issues can have an impact on a student's education.

Ultimately, parents, know your kids, and help educators know your kids. If you suspect your child is struggling academically for any reason (well before high school but certainly throughout high school), communicate with the school. It may not be an easy fix, and it will definitely be a team effort, but educators want to work with you. All cannot be "fixed" by schools alone; schools must have the help of parents. But just as I tell my students who might be struggling in a particular area—please do not wait for the teacher who has just met your child to figure it out on his/her own because by that time, your child may already have at least one failing 6-weeks average as the evidence and documentation of a struggle, which can potentially be repeated year after year after year.

Because so many students get by with turning in late work and redoing tests (this includes "high flyer" students), it is sometimes very difficult for teachers to get a good read on a student's abilities and struggles. A struggling student (in today's educational landscape) is highly likely to be inconsistent with turning in work, etc. When a struggling student is habitually not turning in work, the teacher has no real way (other than standardized test data, etc., which can also be suspect if the struggling student did not put in genuine effort when he/she took the test) to know the exact struggles a student is having, so it is a vicious cycle that can repeat itself for years. Parents, talk to your student's teachers and counselors before you see the same issues pop up with your student each year, and continue to have high expectations of your student throughout high school. Sometimes parents of struggling high school kids give up on some level when their kids reach high school and hope that the school will take care of it without them, but I can tell you we need your help, parents, so please hang in there. As a team, we can make so much more progress than schools can trying to do it alone.

> Whether your child is the consummate perfectionist who takes every challenging class available or the one who lost every high school credit in 9th grade, your child is just that—a child who is learning to become an adult.

Whether your child is the consummate perfectionist who takes every challenging class available or the one who lost every high school credit in 9th grade, your child is just that—a child who is learning to become an adult. The teen years are just hard for a lot of kids (and for a lot of parents). As "they" say—the struggle is real. But you do not have to struggle alone. You may also feel that you are the only one whose child has ever (fill in the blank here—there are many potential choices—skipped school, had drug problems, failed all his/her classes, etc.), but based on my experiences alone as an educator, I can tell you—you are definitely not alone. So please, reach out to your school for help, and follow through with the help that is given. It may not be easy, but it will be worth the struggle.

Chapter 13

School Shooters: What the Research Shows

Chapter 13

School Shooters:
What the Research Shows

Most adults who grew up and attended high school in the 1980s or before continue to be baffled by the very idea of kids bringing guns to school and purposefully killing other people. For those of us who grew up and attended high school in the 1980s, one of our main goals when we were teens was to have as much fun as possible, in and out of school. Just the idea of bringing a gun to school would have been far-fetched for most, and the idea of using a gun or any type of weapon against our peers was unfathomable. And now, our generation represents the adult leaders of schools across America—we are now the superintendents, principals, teachers, school nurses, counselors, librarians, secretaries, and custodians of today's schools, and we want change. Depending on one's own upbringing and life experiences, some believe school shootings are a relatively new occurrence (new since the 1980s), while others wonder if the explanation is that we notice them more because of the increase in 24-hour media coverage that we all live with in modern society. Whatever one's belief about school shootings, most believe they must stop. We just cannot allow this to be our new normal.

Many articles have been written on the topic of school shootings, but I wanted to look first at the facts in an effort to make sense out of the senseless, or at least confirm patterns and trends. Paradice (2017) compiled an analysis of school shooting data spanning 1840-2015 that sheds light on what we know about school shootings through that time. It is important to acknowledge that Paradice's research covers shootings through 2015, and shootings have occurred or been thwarted since that time. Paradice outlines his work:

> This paper describes the construction and descriptive analysis of a data set of United States school shooting events. Three hundred forty-three shooting events are included, spanning 175 years of United States educational history. All levels of US educational institution are included. Events are included when a firearm is discharged, regardless of whether an injury occurs. The analysis defines a mass shooting as an event in which four or more persons, excluding the shooter, are injured or killed. It defines a mass murder as an event in which four or more persons, excluding the shooter, are killed. The data reveals that US high schools are where most shooting events occur. Relatively speaking, there have been few mass murder events in US campuses, but they have occurred with much greater frequency in the last 50 years. In most cases, shootings are premeditated. No prescription related to firearms at educational institutions is made (p. 135).

It is worth nothing that in response to his research Paradice is not proposing any specific steps (or politics) to resolve gun violence in schools, but rather is simply compiling and reporting the factual evidence:

> This study describes shooting events at educational institutions in an objective manner. The data was compiled from news accounts of the events, along with the use of court documents and other primary source materials when found. The study does not seek to advocate

for or against a specific policy related to the possession of firearms at educational institutions. Instead, the author is hopeful that the study will inform decision makers and policy makers in a way that resources can be allocated wisely (p. 144).

Many believe if we are able identify a "profile" of a school shooter, we might be better able to predict (and prevent) a shooting from occurring. Paradice's analysis of the data revealed background on the shooter:

Most shooters are men, but only in high schools are most of the shooters teens. Few have been diagnosed as emotionally unstable; most shooters are just angry about something. Twice as many mass shooters are arrested at or near the scene of the shooting as complete suicide. When asked why they did what they did, they rarely mention a desire for media attention (p. 136).

That last note about media attention is of interest in that many believe that school shooters (as well as other mass shooters) carry out their crime so they can get their proverbial 15 minutes of fame, which has sparked discussion in media organizations of whether they can help by simply not reporting the shooter's name in an effort to keep the shooter from becoming famous/infamous.

In order to not overwhelm the reader by listing stat after stat, I am listing only the lead statistics in each area below. Among Paradice's findings, of the 343 shooting events:

There have been 420 shooting deaths at educational institutions since 1840. The majority of the shootings (61%) are classified as premeditated events (p. 141).

In 277 of the shooting events, the weapon can be identified. In 75% only a handgun was used (p. 141).

35% were because of anger and 25% were attributed to mental illness (p. 142).

Since the 1966 University of Texas shooting, there have been 40 mass events that resulted in 205 deaths. 25 took place in high schools; 16 took place in universities (p. 142).

*Since the 1966 University of Texas shooting, there have been 197 non-mass shooting events that resulted in 126 deaths. 49% (143) took place at high schools (p. 142).

*Of 328 shooting events where the gender of the shooter could be determined, 97% were male shooters (p. 143).

Paradice's research revealed the primary factors in the shootings:

61% were due to "anger, fight, or dispute" combined, where a factor could be identified. It is worth noting that, of these, 14% were related to discipline; 10% to harassment; 10% to dismissal or failure or bad grade; 8% to revenge; 4% to romance; and 2% to domestic issues (p. 143).

Many want to know what to look for in identifying and stopping the "next school shooter," and while there is no way to know for sure, we can look to what the evidence shows from past shootings. Paradice's research shows the following about the shooter:

*In 91% of shootings, the shooter has some relationship to the campus.

*70% of the shooters are students or former students.

*21% of the shooters are some adult other than a teacher or parent (p. 142).

*Of 223 student school shooters:

   *Middle school shooters—17 shooters were students.

   *School house shooters—29 were students.

   *High school shooters—135 were students.

   *University shooters—36 were students (pp. 142-143).

The statistics above are telling in that, through 2015, the vast majority of school shooters not only had a relationship to the campus but were students or former students of the school. **One of their own.** This dispels any myth that school shooters are (statistically speaking) a nameless, faceless stranger off the street. I am certainly not saying it is impossible for a stranger off the street to come into a school and commit a shooting because anything is possible (even with beefed-up security) me

What the statistics suggest, however, is that the school shooter is already inside the school. Any number of well-known school shootings come to mind. This stat also drives home the point that beefed-up security can keep the nameless, faceless stranger (as well as the ex-student) out of the school, but students who are enrolled at the school are free to enter at will (and to hold exterior doors open for each other or for strangers to sidestep security).

> ...the vast majority of school shooters not only had a relationship to the campus but were students or former students of the school. One of their own.

This statistic also means that our work is cut out for us: to work to prevent future school shootings, the work starts at home and at school with our own students/children. This statistic is both startling, knowing the most likely culprit will statistically be a student on his/her own campus, but also empowering in that our own students/children are those we have to most power to identify, observe, and to help. **This statistic makes it clear that, although it may very well feel that way, we are really not looking for a needle in the haystack.** It also means we have a chance, all of us, to make a real difference in changing the landscape of school shootings by changing the lives of school shooters before they reach the point at which they determine that murder is the solution to their problems. Everything that we have discussed in this book comes into play.

So, the facts are the facts, but the issue of school shootings is obviously complex, and most are likely left with the feeling that it could be anyone at anytime who chooses to commit a school shooting. Just as the general public expects today's schools to prevent bullying (in person or online), the general public has the same expectation of schools to prevent school shootings and (obviously) other school violence. In its simplest form, schools are scrambling to do their very best to protect their kids and employees and ensure the safety of all, but just as school counselors are not medical health care practitioners, school administrators, teachers, and counselors are not police officers. And, just as the existence of mental health hospitals does not eliminate all mental health issues, the existence of police forces and laws does not eliminate criminals and the crimes they commit, either in schools or in life in general. I say this to drive home the point that it is unrealistic to expect schools alone to "fix" the problem of school shootings. Despite these truisms, however, we must be vigilant and continue to work together to prevent school violence and strive to educate our kids in a peaceful, safe, supportive environment. That "we" involves all of us together—educators, parents, law enforcement, kids, and society and all its trappings. We all have ownership of safety in schools and in life. And the evidence tells us that we have the power to effect change by focusing our individual, purposeful efforts on our own students and children at home.

I chose to put this chapter on school shootings after all of the other topics we have discussed so far because school shootings in most cases are a combination of so many of these topics, and this book is as much a call to action for all of us as it is a book about parenting and educating in the modern world. A school shooting in today's world is often an event that involves on some level mental health, communication, social media/internet, peer and/or family relationships or the lack of, interventions taken or not taken, feelings of anger/hate/revenge/loneliness, depression, law enforcement, perceived realities and worldviews...the list goes on. While these issues have always been around (other than social media), the difference in today's world (both in schools and in the real world) is that the person dealing with the issues too often chooses a method that harms or kills innocent people—whether it is a choice possibly made as a perceived way to "solve" problems or perhaps a choice made because the shooter feels entitled to/deserving of carrying out the act in order to deal with a problem and the feelings associated with that problem.

Because school personnel are not law enforcement experts, we must look to research in the field of law enforcement to gain insight into school shootings and prevention. In terms of modern-day school shootings, Columbine seems to be the tipping point. For myself as an educator, Columbine is the event that changed everything. Before Columbine, despite the data that we are now aware of that shows that school shootings did exist, most of us—educators, students, the public—didn't really know about it (unless you lived near where the event occurred and heard about it locally) and as a result, really couldn't fathom something like that happening. Today's educators in many ways feel like sitting ducks waiting for the next event to occur, and we cannot continue to bank on "hope" alone. Even if all events cannot be prevented, we cannot continue to operate under a "business as usual" philosophy because "usual" is long gone, and schools in general seem to be in the infancy stages of creating schools and school plans that work in today's new school shooting landscape, which is evidenced by the reactive state of both school and state officials each time a school shooting (or a mass shooting in general) occurs. One example I can give you from my own experience occurred many years ago, but several years post-Columbine. I noticed that our school map was published on the school's website (as it likely had been for years), which I mentioned at the time to our administrators as a possible concern. It was an innocuous, well-intentioned decision to provide a school map online for students and parents to print out and use, but that map could also be accessed and used by anyone for much darker purposes, including harming someone at the school.

Many believe that school shootings are out-of-the-blue events in which nothing could have been done to prevent the incident from occurring, but experts suggest otherwise. Dr. J. Reid Meloy is a clinical professor of psychiatry at the University of California, San Diego, School of Medicine, and a faculty member of the San Diego Psychoanalytic Center. Meloy is also a board-certified forensic psychologist (ABPP) who consults on criminal and civil cases throughout the U.S. and Europe (Bio section). Meloy says many attacks can be thwarted when the right people intervene in time (Goral, 2016, p. 12). Meloy says school shooters exhibit some universal warning signs:

"Pathway" comes from research of school shooters that shows these individuals will plan and prepare their activity typically over weeks, if not months. The thinking used to be that these individuals somehow snapped or their acts were impulsive and completely unpredictable. But we know now that there are lots of behaviors that indicate the person is researching how to carry out the act.

"Fixation" refers to the individual constantly thinking about a particular person or group that he has a grudge against or a particular cause that he wants to advocate for. The individual will think about this continuously. They will become more isolative. They neglect their schoolwork. They begin to engage in concerning or disruptive behaviors. It may reach administrators that this particular student is troubled because he's talking a lot about violent events in schools that he's heard about before.

And that leads to the third warning behavior that we see in school shooters— "identification." The idea here is that the student will want to be like and imitate individuals who have done this at other places before him. They exhibit a curiosity that is sometimes tinged with a desire to be just like that person (p. 12).

Meloy also recommends and supports that schools use "threat assessment teams," (p. 14) which originated from the U.S. Department of Education and the U.S. Secret Service:

As part of the Safe School Initiative, the U.S. Department of Education and U.S. Secret Service authored a report in 2004 that described how schools could establish a threat assessment process "for identifying, assessing, and managing students who may pose a threat of targeted violence in schools." School-based threat assessment teams are intended to prevent and reduce school violence and are adapted from the U.S. Secret Service's threat assessment model (Hansen and Diliberti, 2018, para. 1).

The National Center for Education Statistics looked at how prevalent threat assessment teams are in public schools as of June 2018:

The School Survey on Crime and Safety (SSOCS) collected data on the prevalence of threat assessment teams in schools for the first time in 2015–16 from a nationally representative sample of 3,500 K–12 public schools. The questionnaire defined a threat assessment team as "a formalized group of persons who meet on a regular basis with the common purpose of identifying, assessing, and managing students who may pose a threat of targeted violence in schools." School-based threat assessment teams are usually composed of some combination of school administrators, teachers, counselors, sworn law enforcement officers, and mental health professionals.

While 42 percent of all public schools reported having a threat assessment team during the 2015–16 school year, the prevalence of threat assessment teams varied by school characteristics (para. 2-3).

The survey results were broken down by what types of schools were more likely to have a threat assessment team. The results showed:

*high schools (vs middle or elementary school) (52%);
*larger schools with 1000+ students (57%);
*schools that had a security member on staff (48%);
*schools where a violent incident had occurred (44%) (para. 4-5).

The last stat here is troubling to this educator. I, along with many of my fellow educators, have great concerns about policies/procedures not being put into place until after something happens, so school leaders, take note. **#prevention #proactive** I should also note that my large, urban school district has implemented the use of this type of threat assessment team district-wide (11 high schools; 29 middle schools; 82 elementary schools).

As we all know, schools are not the only place mass shootings have taken place, and school leaders are not the only professionals working to prevent future shootings. In August 2014, Meloy was the keynote speaker at the annual conference of the Association of Threat Assessment

Professionals at Disneyland attended by more than 700 law enforcement agents, psychologists, and private security experts from around the country (Follman, 2015, p. 24). *Mother Jones* journalist Mark Follman attended that conference:

> *While families splashed in the Disneyland Hotel's pools and strolled to the nearby theme park, conference attendees sat in chilly ballrooms for sessions like "20 Years of Workplace Shootings" and "Evil Thoughts, Wicked Deeds." ...it is no coincidence that Disney plays host to this conference. As gun rampages have increased, so have security efforts at public venues of all kinds, and threat assessment teams can now be found everywhere from school districts and college campuses to corporate headquarters and theme parks. Behind the scenes, the federal government has ramped up its threat assessment efforts: Behavioral Analysis Unit 2, a little-known FBI team based in Quantico, Virginia, now marshals more than a dozen specialists in security and psychology from across five federal agencies to assist local authorities who seek help in heading off would-be killers. Those calls have been flooding in: Since 2012, the FBI unit has taken on more than 400 cases (p. 24).*

In his article *Inside the Race to Stop the Next Mass Shooter,* Follman traces the chilling story of a high school student who had made a threat of killing students in his school and, as a result, received intervention through his high school's threat assessment team in Oregon beginning in 2000. During this student's time in high school, the threat assessment team put in place a "wraparound intervention" that included counseling, tutoring, help for the student in pursuing his interested in music and computers, and frequent check-ins by the school resource officer (p. 23). When the student graduated from high school in 2002, the school-based team gave his case to the local adult assessment team, which included the local police department and the county health agency. Eventually, however, the teen (now an adult) moved to another area where no one knew him (p. 24).

Eight years later, this (now ex) student committed the worst mass shooting in Portland's history: he shot two teenage girls and wounded seven people, most of them also teenagers, then shot himself outside a nightclub (p. 29).

I included this story not to discredit the idea of threat assessment teams, but rather for just the opposite. This student's story illustrates that threat assessment teams can work. In this student's case, it did work while that student was in high school. It also illustrates that the team goes beyond teachers, counselors, and school administrators. To be effective, school violence prevention must be a community effort that involves law enforcement. This story also illustrates, unfortunately, that despite the best efforts of all of us, people are going to commit crimes, and those crimes can be extremely violent. I say again, though, that we must not give up, and we must continue to work together to make our schools and our communities safe places.

It was at the Disneyland conference that Meloy commented about and gave a reason for the record number of people in the room listening to him speak: mass murder is on the rise. Meloy also discussed the three-part process of threat assessment (p. 24). While these threat assessment teams are made up of school and law enforcement personnel, I include this information in this book because parents are on the front line with their kids outside of school. Parents may see or hear something that in isolation is concerning, or that maybe the parent isn't sure whether it is alarming or not. The concept of "see something say something" comes into play here. Parents need to do the same thing here as I mentioned in previous chapters—communicate with the school (and/or law enforcement, depending on the nature of what they observe) if there is an inkling of concern. I am a big fan of overreporting because you just never know what else has happened behind the scenes that may come into play with that single detail a parent or student reports.

The three-part process of threat assessment includes: identifying, evaluating, and intervening (p. 24). Meloy says a case usually begins with a gut feeling that something is off, which is the identifying a potential problem. The person who notices something—a teacher, parent, peer—should report it so that it can be checked out by the appropriate person (administrator, counselor, police officer, depending on the type of tip), which is the evaluating step. Pending the outcome of the investigation, Meloy says, if violence seems imminent, involuntary hospitalization or arrest may be the safest approach, which is the intervention step (p. 24-25). Meloy says not all interventions are so drastic; sometimes an adult checking in on a person lets the person of concern know others have noticed, which Meloy says can itself be an effective deterrent (p. 25).

This point especially makes sense with teens who developmentally operate on a level of secrecy and hiding things from the adults around them. Once the adults are in the know, the teen's behavior could change for the better because the teen knows someone is watching and paying attention, or simply caring about what they have noticed. Anyone who has been a teen (everyone!) or who has been around a teen can verify that most (all?) teens truly believe they are smarter than all the adults around them, and this is very likely true with teen shooters. When adults take notice of and an interest in the teen and his/her behavior, that act in itself might be enough to prevent an act of violence that would have been committed by the teen.

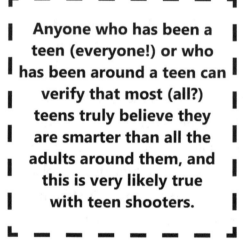

> Anyone who has been a teen (everyone!) or who has been around a teen can verify that most (all?) teens truly believe they are smarter than all the adults around them, and this is very likely true with teen shooters.

Sandy Hook Promise is a nonprofit formed by Sandy Hook Elementary School family members that seeks to prevent gun violence before it happens so that other parents do not have to experience the loss of their child (SHP Back Cover, 2016). In December 2016 Sandy Hook Promise developed a powerful PSA entitled "Evan" to educate viewers that very often warning signs are given off before a shooting, if only people would stop and take notice. You can find this video on YouTube and through the link on the Sandy Hook Promise website (cited in the Bibliography of this book). This site also contains a wealth of information on preventing future violence. The Evan PSA really drives home the point about paying attention to what is happening around us, and it is one of the most powerful videos I have seen on the topic of school shootings.

In applying the threat assessment steps to schools, Meloy brings up an additional point that is key, which is getting kids to tell what they know, rather than keeping it secret or not telling someone. Meloy says in school shootings, the majority of shooters will leak their intent to a third party before they do it. And in the vast majority of cases, at least one, if not more, students at the school know this is going to happen (Goral, 2016, p. 14). Russell Palarea, a forensic psychology and veteran of the Naval Criminal Investigative Service, believes the key is helping more people understand what threat assessment is and how it works and compares it to the "see something, say something" campaign meant to help foil terrorist attacks" (Follman, 2015, p. 29). As part of its "Know the Signs" initiative, Sandy Hook Promise lists "Say Something" as a method of intervention encouraging youth to recognize warning signs and signals, especially within social media, from those who may be a threat to themselves or others and "Say Something" before it is too late (Know the Signs, p. 2).

I should note here that all of the concepts and renditions of "see something, say something" are seemingly simplistic, filled with common sense, and easy to implement. Millions of dollars and hours of training don't seem necessary in order to get this point across, but I know that this must be a purposeful effort that needs to be part of our modern lives, and I compare it to other simplistic yet purposeful concepts from our past. It seems like common sense that we shouldn't throw trash out on the highways or other public spaces and should instead put our trash in the trash can, but it took the "Keep America Beautiful" campaign of the 1970s (the ones described as the "Crying Indian" commercials) to change—or at least draw attention to—American habits (for the most part, some people still throw their trash wherever they want). Or the "Smokey the Bear—only you can prevent forest fires" campaign that dates back to 1944 that reminds us to use what should be common sense in preventing forest fires. So although it seems like a hefty dose of common sense will remind people, especially teens, to speak up when they know something (especially something as serious as someone plotting a school shooting), it will take a continued, intentional effort on all of our parts to spread the message in an effort to ensure this happens. (Again, in part because we are fighting against something that is inherent to being a teen—secrecy, especially when it comes to telling adults, which teens can view as ratting each other out.) In other words, we can't just say it once and all move on. We must continue to teach our kids to speak up and save lives. To this end, Meloy suggests:

> Penetrating that veil of secrecy is critical, and there are ways to do it. For instance, a lot of this stuff is being posted on social media. It's on Snapchat and Instagram. It's being tweeted by students. So there needs to be a way to monitor the social media in and around the campus. There's a web service called Geofeedia where you can draw a geographical boundary around the school or around the neighborhood and it will show you everything that's being posted on open source social media within that school and across the various platforms. It's not a violation of privacy because the stuff is open source social media (Goral, 2016, p. 14).

Meloy also addressed the idea that attackers post their intentions before an attack on social media:

> Usually it's not a cry for help. There are a variety of other motivations, ranging from anxiety or even pride about what they are about to do, to anger at something and posting a retaliatory message.
>
> I should add that various kinds of depressions are common in adolescents. We need to be concerned about suicidal risks in

adolescents, as well as homicidal risks. Most kids who are depressed and then become suicidal are not going to be a risk toward other individuals.

However, a very small portion of kids who are depressed and suicidal will also then become homicidal. And those are potentially very dangerous cases. That's where you need an experienced clinician involved in working with the child as soon as possible (p. 14).

Meloy references Columbine in terms of shooters not only copying or emulating the Columbine shootings but also trying to surpass the number of deaths (p. 12). Follman also referenced the connection to Columbine:

Ever since Columbine, the FBI has been studying what drives people to commit mass shootings. Last fall it issued a report on 160 active-shooter cases, and what Simons could disclose from its continuing analysis was chilling: To a much greater degree than is generally understood, there's strong evidence of a copycat effect rippling through many cases, both among mass shooters and those aspiring to kill. Perpetrators and plotters look to past attacks for not only inspiration but operational details, in hopes of causing even greater carnage. Emerging research—including our own analysis of the "Columbine effect"—could have major implications for both threat assessment and how the media should cover mass shootings (p. 25).

Follman went even deeper regarding the connection to Columbine:

The Columbine killers authored a grimly compelling new script at the dawn of the internet age. Sixteen years later, the Columbine legacy keeps reappearing in violent plots, driven in part by online subcultures that obsess over the duo's words and images. "It's a cult following unlike anything I've ever seen before," says one longtime security specialist.

To gauge just how deep the problem goes, Mother Jones examined scores of news reports and public documents and interviewed multiple law enforcement officials. We analyzed 74 plots and attacks across 30 states whose suspects and perpetrators claimed to have been inspired by the Columbine massacre. Law enforcement stopped 53 of these plots before anyone was harmed. Twenty-one plots evolved into attacks, with a total of 89 victims killed, 126 injured, and 9 perpetrators committing suicide.

The data reveals some disturbing patterns. In at least 14 cases, the suspects aimed to attack on the anniversary of Columbine. (Twelve of these plots were thwarted; two attacks ultimately took place on different dates.) Individuals in 13 cases indicated their goal was to outdo the Columbine body count. And in at least 10 cases the suspects referred to Harris and Klebold as heroes, idols, martyrs, or God.

Copycats exist for other crimes, so Columbine isn't the only crime that has been emulated, but Columbine is significant because it occurred at the relative onset of the internet age. And it's not just America that has been impacted—in Germany alone, nine school shootings occurred in the decade after Columbine. Social media has come into play as well, evidenced by the first "social media murder" of two co-workers by a disgruntled television reporter that played out live on social media went viral within 30 minutes (p. 26-28).

Follman explained the connection between these killings and the advent of the internet:

When I asked threat assessment experts what might explain the recent rise in gun rampages, I heard the same two words over and over: social media. Although there is no definitive research yet, widespread anecdotal evidence suggests that the speed at which social media bombards us with memes and images exacerbates the copycat effect. As Dr. Meloy and his colleagues noted earlier this year in the journal Behavioral Sciences and the Law, "Cultural scripts are now spread globally...within seconds" (p. 28).

Follman's work echoes the "pathway to violence" that mass shootings typically fall under, which again supports the potential benefits of intervention when "something isn't right." Follman says:

When the next shooting happens at a school, an office building, or a movie theater, the question will again be asked: "What made him snap?" But mass murder is not an impulsive crime. Forensic investigations show that virtually every one of these attacks is a predatory crime, methodically planned and executed. Therein lies the promise of threat assessment: The weeks, months, or even years when a would-be killer is escalating toward violence are a window of opportunity in which he can be detected and thwarted (p. 25).

According to Follman's research, the vast majority of mass shooters signal their intentions in advance, though usually not directly to their intended targets (p. 25). Follman also weighs in on the million dollar question of "who will be the next shooter?":

We know that many mass shooters are young white men with acute mental health issues. The problem is, such broad traits do little to help threat assessment teams identify who will actually attack. Legions of young men love violent movies or first-person shooter games, get angry about school, jobs, or relationships, and suffer from mental health afflictions. The number who seek to commit mass murder is tiny. Decades of research have shown that the link between mental disorders and violent behavior is small and not useful for predicting violent acts. (People with severe mental disorders are in fact far more likely to be victims of violence than perpetrators).

Research shows that the belief that school shooters "just snapped" is a myth, and most school shooters show signs beforehand that may not have been noticed or that may have been ignored. "Leakage" is a term that comes up in articles about school shooters and shootings, which means that the shooter gave signs before the event happened, whether it was an obsession with violence, poor family relationships/communication skills, making threats, or even stockpiling weapons (p. 25-26).

Many have the perception that school shooters are otherwise average kids who suddenly make a rash decision to kill other kids. Experts disagree. Dr. Scott Poland is a nationally-recognized expert on school crisis, youth violence, suicide intervention, self-injury, school safety, threat assessment, parenting, and the delivery of psychological services in schools, and he is a professor in school psychology at Nova Southeastern University in Florida (NSU bio). Poland (2012) wrote that the media had referred to a recent school shooter as an "average 17-year-old kid," which he says is misleading and gives the perception that any kid could be a school shooter (p. 38). Poland cites the work of Peter Langman, a renowned expert on school shootings, who identified three categories that offer insight into the mental health of school shooters:

Psychotic school shooters are not existing in reality. This is often a consequence of schizophrenia or what Langman refers to as "schizophrenia-spectrum disorders." For this type, Langman referenced the Heath High School (Kentucky) shooter in 1997, who heard voices and thought that monsters were living in his home (p. 38).

Psychopathic school shooters often exhibit a lack of conscience, such as no moral barometer, a lack of remorse and no empathy for others. They may feel a sense of superiority and the right to hurt and/or kill people. Langman referenced the writings and tapes of one of the Columbine killers for this type (p. 38).

Traumatized school shooters have experienced significant traumatic events in their lives—such as abuse, an invalidating home environment, repeated bullying and loss of a parent to death or incarceration—which increase vulnerability to depressive symptoms and suicidal ideations. Langman referenced the shooter in the 2005 Red Lake High School

(Minnesota) shooting for this type (p. 38).

Poland's writings are in line with other research about school shooter warning signs:

School shooters often leave behind a host of warning signs preceding the attack. Sadly, such warning signs are often overlooked or even discounted. This constellation of warning signs often includes a fascination and preoccupation with other school shooters or violent historical figures; telling other students or peers that "it would be cool if something like that happened at my school"; stockpiling weapons and/or asking parents and friends to buy weapons; creating school assignments, such as presentations, papers and videos centered on violence and particularly school shootings; posting on social media sites intentions for violence; and recruiting other students (p. 38).

Poland makes recommendations for both educators and parents.

Educators need to be trained and have an open dialogue on the topic of school safety. Educators must be vigilant about watching for warning signs and reporting those to the appropriate school team. Educators should create and be a part of creating a school climate that encourages students to share information with adults—immediately when it comes to potential school violence. Schools must continue to proactively evolve when it comes to implementation of school safety plans (pp. 38-39).

Poland also addresses what parents can do when it comes to school safety:

It is important for parents to be aware of what is going on in their child's life, and this involves knowing their child's friends and their parents. Parents need to monitor online communications and postings and check their child's room when they have any concerns about their child's behavior. If a child has exhibited warning signs of violence, then parents should not deny the problem and should let their child experience logical consequences from authorities at school and in the community.

In his writings, Langman says something that I agree with: "Don't lie to protect your child and do not hesitate to get them professional help." School personnel have multiple opportunities through parent conferences and meetings to emphasize these key points to parents.

School shooters are not simply normal kids. They are kids with identifiable mental health problems who have exhibited many warning signs of potential violence. Therefore, everyone must be alert to these warning signs and to the need to increase mental health services for young people both at school and in the community (p. 39).

In closing this chapter, I want to reiterate that, like many things in life, "figuring out" school shootings and other mass violence is both simple and complicated at the same time. It can be as simple as taking an interest in another human being. The most complicated part is working together to piece together the signs before a violent event occurs, or at least figuring out that there is a potential for the event to occur. We must open our eyes and truly see and hear each other, and when there is a concern, we must take the time to reach out to someone in a position to help, whether it is a school employee, the police, a mental health care professional, or another parent, and we must follow up to ensure action has been taken.

Many times over the years as a school counselor I have received a phone call from a concerned parent who, through a variety of circumstances, came across concerning information about another child and called to report it just in case. These reports have also come to me about a student on my caseload when the concerning information was learned at another campus—the campus of a sibling or friend of my student—and the school counselor at that school called to report it to my campus. The same watchful eyes we keep on teens whom we suspect might be at risk for suicide need to also watch for teens (or adults) at risk for committing an act of violence. To help educators with this process, schools should employ the use of both suicide and violence risk assessments, and all educators should be aware of the referral process for the use of the assessments. Now more than ever, we must all work together as a team and avoid "working in silos," as we say in education, in which we work very hard but very independent of and separated from everyone else.

When we as counselors/interventionists teach students, teachers/school staff, and parents about steps to take when they are concerned that someone may be at risk for hurting him/herself or attempting suicide, a key piece we teach is the concept of telling an adult (who can help) and not keeping secrets. These same steps are critical when it comes to a suspicion that a teen might be at risk for harming others, and it applies to adults and kids. When we have a suspicion, observe something, or are directly told alarming information, we cannot keep this information to ourselves and ignore signs that might be critical. It is better to err on the side of caution and over-reporting than to ignore a sign that might be a piece of a much larger puzzle. Very often, others already have other pieces of the same puzzle, and the

> **Parents and guardians, it is critical that you are watchful of your own kids and that you do not keep secrets about your own kids, and educators and law enforcement must be equally observant and vigilant about following up on all information given to them.**

piece you provide could be the missing information that prevents an event from happening. Or, until the pieces are reported, those in the position to help may not be aware there is even a puzzle to work out.

Parents and guardians, it is critical that you are watchful of your own kids and that you do not keep secrets about your own kids, and educators and law enforcement must be equally observant and vigilant about following up on all information given to them. The lesson on the importance of reporting and acting on the information is right there in the investigative information from the Columbine shooting, according to a *60 Minutes* report from April 2001:

A year before the shooting ever took place, Eric Harris (one of the Columbine shooters) had a website in which he made threats to blow up specific classmates with pipe bombs. This website was found and read by some of the students named as targets (Kohn, 2001, para. 2).

The parents of some of the targeted students reached out to law enforcement with their concerns. Law enforcement worked on a warrant to search Harris' home but never acted on it. Law enforcement did warn the school, which did not act on the warnings because there was an open law enforcement investigation (para. 8-9).

In February 1999 (two months before the shootings), Dylan Klebold (the other shooter) turned in a violent story he had written in class about an assassin in a black trench coat who shoots down students and bombs the city. The teacher reported her concerns to Klebold's parents and to the school counselor, but no school official reportedly looked into the matter (para. 14-15).

Police interviews show that Harris' and Klebold's parents said they had no idea about the arsenal of weapons their sons were amassing in their bedrooms: knives; guns, cans full of gunpowder; coils of bomb fuse; more than 100 bombs—pipe bombs, propane bombs, homemade grenades (para. 19).

According to other Columbine students, Harris and Klebold made videos of themselves shooting their guns that they showed kids at school, and one friend was shown one of the pipe bombs while at Harris' house (para. 10-12).

Eight months before the attack, two Columbine security officials wrote a security plan that required school officials to notify and meet with parents and law enforcement officers as soon as they learned of a "threat by any student" to "commit any act of violence." They say Columbine didn't follow the plan (para. 1).

Perhaps the most telling information of all came from Harris and

Klebold themselves:

> *At night, while their parents were asleep, Harris and Klebold made*
> *video tapes in which they talked about all the weapons they had.*
> *Harris imagined his parents saying, "If only we had checked his*
> *room. If only we had asked more questions" (para. 20).*

After a school shooting or other violent event occurs, we as humans naturally want to know "why," and if we are being honest, we really prefer if it is something obvious and black and white that can be "fixed" or prevented, never to happen again. In the Columbine case, the case that seemingly set into play the modern downward spiral of violence that has played out in schools in the decades since, there were many overt warning signs. This is not meant to criticize those who were directly involved in the Columbine case, but rather for us to learn from it today.

As I mentioned earlier in the book, from this educator's standpoint, life in American education changed in an instant with Columbine. As unacceptable as it is that it occurred, I can understand to an extent the lack of urgency in the actions taken at that time by all involved in the case of Columbine. Before Columbine, as they have since the dawn of time, kids expressed anger and rebellion towards their peers and authority figures, whether school authority figures or law enforcement or their parents. Kids acted out and made wild claims that were not put into action. Leading up to Columbine, no one expected kids to actually commit the violent acts these two shooters committed. Just as the events of 9/11 changed our world in an instant, the Columbine shooting was the tipping point for school violence and more specifically, teen violence and outright murder. Whatever it was before Columbine that stopped teens from acting on their darkest thoughts was suddenly stripped away, and those dark actions instantly became glorified by many teens who felt the same way and who idolized Harris and Klebold for the actions they took. In defense of the adults directly involved in the Columbine shooting, despite the now very obvious evidence, they just did not see it coming. None of us in education would have believed something like this would ever, ever happen.

But now we know. The landscape is different for all of us, and looking the other way is just not acceptable for any of us—educators, teens, parents and guardians, law enforcement.

See something, say something. Every time.
Take action, and make sure people are listening.

Parenting and educating a teen is hard. I have said it many times throughout this book. But we cannot take the path of least resistance when it comes to our teens' decision-making and actions. We as adults are ultimately responsible for what our kids are doing, so parents, be nosy. It's ok. There is a big difference between "helicopter parenting" or other negative parenting labels and just plain knowing what your kids are up to. In today's world, someone's life might just depend on it.

Chapter 14
Putting It All Together

Chapter 14

Putting It All Together

So what does this all mean? What do resilience and grit, kids doing homework on their own, relationships, kids and parents communicating better, kids advocating for themselves, cell phone and social media usage, worldviews, parenting styles, parents and educators working together, anger, outrage, apathy, empathy, and school shootings or other violence (and on and on and on) have to do with each other? More importantly, what do they have to do with you—the parent, or your child, or you—the educator, and your students? I propose that these topics (and all of us) are all significantly intertwined, and therein lies my belief and call to action that we have in each of us the power to effect real, lasting change, and we need to work individually and as a team to make that change happen.

In some ways, just as we discussed that "grades don't happen to kids," we do have some level of power to influence whether another human chooses violence and murder as the solution to his/her problems. We may not be able to stop every event from happening, but we—each and every one of us—can certainly influence the areas we have control over in an effort to reverse the (obviously) alarming trend that we are all living with right now.

As different and wide-ranging as the topics in this book might be, they are really all connected, and we have more control over these areas than some might have acknowledged or realized before reading this book. It may be that many of the topics ring true for your situation or apply to your child. Or it may be that you have concerns or need help with only a few of these areas. Or it may be that you don't have any concerns about your child. And you may be right. This book is ultimately meant to be a catalyst for starting an open conversation in which we peel back the protective covers of complacency and status quo and try to create a movement for real change that can ultimately provide a safer school and world environment for all of us. Clearly what we have been doing doesn't always work.

As I have said throughout this book, for every situation we have talked about, 100% of students are not affected. It is not all doom and gloom. We have in our country many students who are very well-adjusted, who are able to manage their time, their friends, their social media accounts, their academics, and their relationships with effortless aplomb. Many students are respectful, kind, motivated, and very capable of dealing with life's challenges. For the parents of those students, I urge you to be a support system for your peer parents who might be struggling. I can tell you from my personal experiences as an educator, many, many families are struggling, and the range of struggle is far-reaching and does not discriminate. We cannot live on assumption alone—many families need help in any number of the areas we have discussed, and this book has hopefully been a way to help families know where to get that help or to go to work with people who will advocate for you.

I once talked with a parent who revealed that she, her child, and her family were struggling. She came from a situation that, from the outside looking in, probably looked to most to be fairly perfect and struggle-free. Through her tears she whispered that she couldn't talk to her own peers about any of it, and we discussed the difficulties of opening up to our friends when people are focused on keeping up appearances and are not willing to reveal their (perceived) "imperfections." Many families want to project the image that they "have it all together," and this closes people off from each other (much like the social media world of perfection projection by teens and adults). It is key for all of us to work together and open up to each other without judgment. It is key that we do this before something big or tragic happens in a family's life that, from the outside looking in, had looked problem-free and, to many, perfect. Many people are struggling and need support, and we are all able to give that support to each other. As adults, we need to focus on being a friend to others just as much as we want our kids to be a better friend to others. We have all seen tragic stories in the news or in our own lives in which, after the event, everyone reported that they had no idea something like this was going on or could happen. I am not blaming the neighbors/friends; I am simply pointing out the value of letting people into our lives and reaching out to offer support to others. You never know how much someone might be struggling.

We live in an angry, easily outraged world, yet we are all in disbelief when something angry and outrageous happens in which people are killed or injured. We cannot have it both ways—all disbelief but no responsibility for or ownership of the current state of affairs. The online world (and freeway driving, but I digress) often has a "Wild West" feel in which those who post anger and hate consider themselves to be judge and jury, always right, and they do not hesitate to spew hate at you to either run you off or (perceivably) put you in your place. We all have ownership in the state of anger and outrage when we add our angry two cents online, and we all need to take a step back and remember that with words come responsibility, whether you have ever met or will ever meet the other posters you are expressing your anger towards or about online. (Obviously), if you would never say it to someone's face, it probably isn't helpful to post it online. The online world isn't the only place people express their opinions via anger and aggression—do an online search for "parent brawl" or "Black Friday brawl" and you will find far too many examples of live, face-to-face acts of hate, aggression, intolerance, and violence. We just cannot operate this way and then claim shock and disbelief when the hate, aggression, intolerance, and violence enters our schools and kills students, educators, and innocent bystanders. Killing people cannot be the *modus operandi* of how people deal with their feelings.

I have said before parenting is hard, and parenting in this modern time in which people are less inclined to hold back their aggressive anger and outrage (and the assumptions that go along with these feelings) is that much more challenging than in previous generations. The level of anger, hate, and outrage we all deal with every day not only impacts our adult lives and the actions we take as adults, but it also has a trickle-down effect on how our kids choose to interact with each other as well as how they choose to work through their own problems and issues. Anger, outrage, and "me now" are the new norm for a lot of people, and teens are right in the middle of it with social media alone, never mind navigating their peers in person. Adults are definitely not immune—just take notice of how many teasers for news stories in our world lead with the descriptor "outraged." We can't go on like this and act surprised or shocked when "outraged" events take place.

Remember that kids' behaviors and coping skills are formed based on the behaviors and coping skills of the adults and other kids they are exposed to, and their worldviews are impacted by those of the adults and kids they are exposed to. When kids see adults or other kids angry and lashing out at each other, they emulate that very behavior themselves. It is the same process that toddlers use when they learn curse words. They simply imitate what they hear other people saying. Adults must be cognizant of the behaviors and coping skills they are modeling for their kids in their own lives and relationships.

When it comes to shielding kids from "bad things," old school methods rarely work in today's world. In previous generations, when parents saw someone or something as a potential "bad influence," they essentially hid "it" away from their kids by not letting the kids be exposed to it. It was much easier for parents to do this in previous generations because they could still exert some control over what their kids were exposed to. In the current 24-7 "always on" electronic world, hiding "bad influences" from kids just doesn't work. By the time adults realize there is something that needs to be hidden way from their kids, it's too late—your kids probably already know about it. JUULing/vaping/use of e-cigarettes is a prime example of this. Kids knew about JUULing and e-cigarettes way before their parents or educators did, and kids are continuing to join the wave by the thousands. We briefly discussed JUULing/smoking e-cigarettes in a previous chapter, but let's take a moment to look at some JUULing/e-cigarette information specifically.

According to data from the Centers for Disease Control and Prevention released November 16, 2018: Among high school students, current e-cigarette use increased from 1.5% (220,000 students) in 2011 to 20.8% (3.05 million students) in 2018. During 2017-2018, current e-cigarette use increased by 78% (Cullen, Ambrose, Gentzke, Apelberg, Jamal, & King, 2018, p. 1276).

How did kids learn about JUULing and e-cigarettes? According to the National Institute on Drug Abuse, as of 2016, 7 in 10 teens were exposed to ads for the products (NIH infograph, 2016). On a side note—most alarmingly, most teens do not know what is in the e-cigarette they are smoking. 66% reported that is was just flavored juice (NIH infograph, 2016. In reality, one JUUL pod lasts approximately 200 puffs and contains the amount of nicotine equal to the amount of nicotine found in a pack of cigarettes (20 cigarettes) (Truth Initiative, 2018). Truth Initiative also found that even though by law teens should not be able to legally purchase JUUL, 74% of 1000 teens (aged 12-17) they surveyed reported buying JUUL at a retail outlet, and 52% reported getting JUUL from a friend or family member. 6% reported purchasing JUUL online (Truth Initiative, 2018).

Insert wide-eyed emojis AGAIN. Not only is this e-cigarette information alarming on its own, it also drives home the point that adults can't operate on the "hiding bad things from our kids" method and hope it works (it clearly does not). While hiding things from teens in an effort to keep teens from finding out is a lost battle, it doesn't mean adults can become complacent and do nothing. Rather than working to hide things from their kids, parents must continue to work on teaching their kids about the dangers and downsides of life so that when kids are presented with those options, they are equipped to make better decisions and have the willpower to walk away or say no. Sometimes parents won't know the exact dangers, as is evidenced by the e-cigarette data, but parents must still try to instill in their kids the ability and courage to say no. Fostering a relationship with your kids in which they will talk to you first when they come across new things like e-cigarettes is an ideal antidote for situations you would never know to even warn them about.

Remember, too, that our kids only know the modern world as their "normal," and for their entire lives they have known that school shootings are happening in schools in our country. As obvious as it is that we all want school shootings to stop, because they have continued to occur year after year, we cannot become numb to it and let it be our "new normal." We cannot stop working to change the violent landscape that we find ourselves in today. Educators and parents need to work together as a team more now than ever to affect real, lasting change. We must not accept that "this is just the way it is now." Brawls at kids' sporting events or holiday sales and school shootings cannot be an acceptable way of life.

Throughout this book, I have addressed many pointers/suggestions/ observations that have either come up in conversations I have had with parents over the years, or that I have observed in my role as an educator, or that I have come across doing research for this book. Remember, not everything in this book applies to all kids, so it is important to consider your own experiences with your child. It is also important to be honest with yourself. If something you have read rings true or you have a concern about a certain area with your child, consider stepping in and addressing it, getting help, taking whatever the necessary steps may be. The key is to do something, even if it is a little uncomfortable to take those steps. There are people waiting to help you.

As I neared the end of writing this book, I continued to come across more and more evidence every day that supports so many points of this book, to the extent that I just had to stop writing and finish this current version of the information. In closing, I want to review some of the key points I hope you will take away from this book.

1. Parents and educators must work together as a proactive team.

This point cannot be made enough. In order for all of us—educators and parents—to help our kids, it is critical for parents and educators to have a good working relationship, and we must work together to put aside any adversarial components of that relationship. I recently caught a few minutes of the movie *Remember the Titans*, and a quote from Denzel Washington's Coach Boone character illustrates the teacher/parent struggle over how best to educate the child stuck in the middle:

> *You got anger, that's good. You're gonna need it, you got aggression that's even better. You're gonna need that, too. But any little two-year-old child can throw a fit! Football is about controlling that anger, harnessing that aggression into a team effort to achieve perfection! (Remember the Titans, 2000).*

It is time for parents and educators to make some changes in their sometimes adversarial relationship in educating a child. When there is anger or other heightened emotion on the side of the parent toward the school/educator, it can make it difficult for the school and parent to work together. Educators and parents must work together, whether it is teaching a student, disciplining a student, or simply holding a student to a high standard. Regardless of the scenario—discussions about discipline, grades, dress code, cheating, student behavior, cell phones, etc.—the goal is to raise teens to be responsible and accountable for their actions. Teaching students to be accountable for "smaller actions" helps students learn to be accountable when navigating much larger actions and decisions they make and will continue to make in life. This effort cannot be met with angry resistance (and/or outrage) from the adults while the student sits in the middle playing on his/her phone waiting for the adults to "sort it out."

Educators need the support of parents, and parents need the support of educators. We are better, and stronger, together. Let me be clear—I am not saying parents do not have the right to become angry and frustrated or to disagree with the school. Those are real, human emotions that we all experience. What I am saying, however, is that we can't let emotional reactions get in the way of working together as educators and parents. In the current state of outrage and social media, too, it will go a long way toward creating positive relationships between educators and parents if, when there is an issue that you disagree with, you reach out and talk to the educator about that disagreement rather than posting outrage online based on one side of the situation. Good, old-fashioned talking. Communication is key. (I urge educators to do the same when it comes to contacting parents about all types of subjects--touchy or not.) Sometimes the outcome of the conversation might be that both sides agree to disagree, but more often than not, a workable resolution can be reached. In its simplest form, having a good, old-fashioned conversation reminds us all that we are just humans helping humans. (This is true for other areas of all of our lives as well.)

What I ask of parents is to look at the *Remember the Titans* quote and picture their strong emotions, which come from the parent's protective love of the child, being redirected into a commitment to working with the school rather than against the school. Too often heightened emotion is impulsively directed at the school instead of at the action the child took and the child's responsibility in the situation. In the *Remember the Titans* example, anger is being channeled into achieving a perfect game of football; I am suggesting that any anger/frustration/other strong emotion parents feel toward educators and schools be redirected into a team effort uniting the parents with educators and the school system. We all have the same goal—to graduate a child who is ready—academically and otherwise— to successfully handle the world. Let's work together to get your child there. Essentially every topic in this book is connected. Kids must be accountable in order to become everything else we have talked about in this book—from being resilient and having grit to having the willpower to walk away from poor decisions and effectively manage stressful situations, just to name a few.

There are many reasons parents and educators must unite and truly work together as a communicative team in today's world, but fighting against violence in schools is one of the most significant, and we must focus on being proactive rather than reactive. To be able to work together to ferret out any potential school violence, educators and parents must be able to let their guards down and have open, honest discussions with each other so they can band together for a bigger cause—the safety and well-being of all kids, not to mention the end goal of all involved—for the students to become independent adults. Parents, it doesn't mean you can't disagree with the school. I am just recommending that all parties look at the whole picture and have a frank discussion about what happened rather than reacting based on emotion and turning against the school, which can break down productive communication.

In its simplest form, when educators and parents are focused on disagreeing with each other, we may be missing details of situations that need intervention. **We must instead refocus our efforts on working together to build resilient kids while staying vigilant in looking for behaviors or actions that may be a sign of potential violence so that interventions can occur *before* an act of violence occurs.**

2. Schools and parents must do a better job of building resilience within kids.

Schools expect parents to reinforce behaviors at home that build resilience—doing homework on their own, advocating for themselves by talking to their teachers, accepting a low grade if that is the grade the student earned, being accountable for their behavior and actions, etc. Parenting styles and the choices parents make when dealing with scenarios like these can go a long way toward building resilience in kids. It is important to recognize that there is a difference between parenting styles and a student's need for professional mental health services, and there is a difference between mental health issues and student habit. Students who have mental health issues need to ultimately seek the treatment and advice of a mental health professional, whether that is a therapist, a psychologist, a psychiatrist, or other type of mental health practitioner. Parents, however, can work with their kids on their kids' habits and beliefs about themselves, or their self-efficacy. There is a documented connection between parenting styles and individual students' abilities to learn to weather life's daily stresses, and there has been an increase in students' needs for intervention both at school and professionally, so anything we as educators and you as parents can do to help make our kids more resilient can only be a positive for our kids.

Many kids are capable of far more than they believe. Parents need to reinforce this concept at home and provide (and allow) opportunities for kids to figure that out for themselves. Let your child try something that he/she is genuinely interested in but that in your heart you are convinced he/she will not be successful at (and be careful when doling out all-knowing yet potentially powerful opinions—sometimes those are best kept to yourself). You might be surprised at the outcome. Let your child have the entire experience. Whether your child soars and is wildly successful or falls flat on his/her face, your child is growing and learning about what it takes to be successful at something and at the same time is building resilience. When your child fails, he/she is also learning a valuable lesson that all is not lost in the face of failure. It's a day that happened, and we move on to the next day, and everything is ok even if we didn't get everything we really wanted.

For example, let's say that your child loves singing competitions and wants to enter a competition at school or audition for the school choir or musical. And let's say that you have heard your child sing—in his/her room, in the car, in the shower—so you are fully convinced that there is no way your child could possibly be successful at this endeavor. Support your child anyway. It may be that your child comes in 15th place in the competition, or that your child earns a bit part in the musical, and you might find that your child is quite happy with that because he/she earned it. Or it may be that your child doesn't get a part in the musical at all. It's ok. One of your most important roles as a parent is to teach your child that trying and failing is ok, and that the experience itself has value. When we win at everything, the win just isn't that special and can be taken for granted or even expected, and most of us don't "win" everything we try in life.

Life's experiences are meant to be just that—experiences. Let your child experience it—whatever "it" is, whether you are a believer or not. And if your child fails, let your child experience the disappointment but remind him/her that tomorrow is a new day. *The experience of being unsuccessful at something and moving on to the next thing will teach your child that failing at something is not a final defining moment of his/her life (no matter how big or bad the failure is).* This is a learned skill that is critical for getting through life, and the feeling and confidence gained by "getting through it" will come back again and again as your child tries and succeeds or tries and fails. There will come a day, maybe when your child goes off to college, that your child will be faced with failure, and it might be a really big failure (real or perceived). What you want your child to feel and know in that moment, when he/she is alone and you are not there with him/her, and the failure is looming forefront in his/her mind, is that this is not a final defining moment of his/her life. He/she will know that, no matter WHAT the problem is, he/she can weather the consequences and get through it, and that tomorrow is a new day. Parents, this is a critical skill, and it is only learned by practice and experience. Parents must allow these experiences to happen as your kids grow up.

There are many ways parents can help their kids build resilience, but schools must do their part, too. Schools must be proactive when it comes to building resilience rather than reactive when students have no resilience. One area schools can help in building student resilience is by revisiting the current policies that are mandated to teachers regarding student grades, such as test retakes and the turning in of late work for points. This book is not an analysis of school curriculum or other technical aspects to running a school (etc.), and I am certain there is very likely research out there on the school curriculum and educational leadership side (that is school-talk for high level administrators who make big decisions about running school districts) that shows that allowing students to retake tests and turn in late work is "better" for them—perhaps by the student getting more practice on the subject, etc., which may be true when looking at education through that lens. As a long-time educator who has always worked first-hand with students, however, I can tell you the downsides to these policies are far more negative than any positive upside these policies have. I have personally witnessed the changes in student habits that have evolved along with the mandating of these policies, and virtually every student I have met with about grades or attendance tells me their struggles are directly related to their habits (and I have met with hundreds of students over the years). (Not to mention all of the conversations I have had with parents about this very topic over the years when the parents are ready to pull their hair out trying to deal with their child who has these habits because their kid's behavior is so very different from the parents' own high school experiences and expectations.)

My experience shows that these policies, while well-intentioned, reinforce very negative behaviors in students that chip away any semblance of resilience the students could be developing at school. The policy of requiring teachers to accept late work from students leads to a chronic habit of students not working as hard to "get it right the first time" because they know there will always be another chance to get additional points added to their grade. Kids who chronically turn in late work are also chronically "getting by" and "grade-chasing," working to get extra points to replace the series of 0s in the gradebook so that they can raise their grade to passing.

The same is true for mandated test retake policies. This policy leads to kids not learning to prepare for a test before the test because, in its simplest form, they do not have to (including that students never really learn solid study skills in the process because they do not have to practice these skills in high school or earlier). Students have been conditioned to know that there will always be a second shot to get enough points to get by—pass and earn the credit and graduate. This also means they never really experience what it feels like to fail a test (with the grade being final and unchangeable), which is a key place kids learn resilience in schools (while they still have the safety net of their parents' support), and which will come back on them in a very serious way in college when the retake route is suddenly unavailable to them. Because kids know they can retake a test or do test corrections to pass, they have become desensitized to a "bad" (failing) grade because it is only temporary, and it can ALWAYS be fixed. On yet another very serious level, as I explain to my students, there is a big difference between a grade and an education, and students who are constantly chasing late work and test corrections are not only missing out on a better education that they will need when they leave high school, but they are also missing out on learning those critical resiliency skills that they MUST HAVE to function effectively in the real world.

Many parents have discussed their concerns about these policies with me over the years, and I encourage you to communicate any concerns you have about these policies with your school districts. I also urge you to take note of how much your child relies on these policies, then work on and reinforce the skills that will help your child be successful without needing the policies to get by. Remind your child that when he/she relies on these policies (turning in late work for partial credit, for example), he/she is constantly behind not only with the work, but also with his/her learning, and there is a level of stress (for kids and parents) that goes with that process/

student lifestyle. Work with your child to reframe the mindset to be focused on planning, time management, goal-setting, preparation, etc. so that your child can learn to meet deadlines, successfully prepare for tests so he/she can pass the first time, and genuinely learn the material. Even if your child doesn't pass the test the first time, he/she will learn that success is possible on the next test, with a higher level of planning and preparation, and it is that process—of continuing on after failure and realizing it will be ok—that helps build resilience in kids. Again, it comes back to students practicing positive habits as they grow up so that those habits come naturally to them when they are adults/out of high school. It is also about students learning that all is not lost if they are not perfect, or immediately successful, the first time, particularly if they did not put in adequate preparation to earn that success. That is a very different feeling than one of earning a "get-by" passing grade when turning in an assignment two, three, or four weeks late and getting partial credit to "bring up the (overall) grade."

As we discussed in the chapter that covered the pressures of standardized testing and No Child Left Behind (now called the Every Student Succeeds Act), school districts are pressured to show student success through data, and all of these policies designed to "help kids" have come about based upon that pressure. When it comes to your child learning to function as an adult and how to not fall apart when he/she fails a college exam or does not get selected for a job, we have to acknowledge the connection between resilience and students' reliance on school policies such as these, and the policies themselves must be revisited. General student mental health cannot be looked at as stand-alone issue. Teachers' and counselors' hands are tied when it comes to aspects of school such as grading policies that have traditionally naturally built resiliency in kids.

Like other topics we have discussed in this book, not all kids turn in late work and rely on test corrections, but do not assume it is a "certain kind of student" who does this ("not my child" just doesn't work here for most parents). The negative habits students learn and rely on as a result of these "helping" policies are widespread. Because of how long these policies have been in place in schools, current high school students have only known an educational world in which they can turn in late work and do test corrections, and the habit is far-reaching and pervasive. The conversations I have had with the hundreds of students I have met with about grades and attendance over the years have verified that these habits are prolific in today's schools. In its simplest form, these policies can rob students of a way to learn resilience and responsibility, and without resilience, students struggle in other areas to deal with their problems. It is all connected.

3. Communication and relationships, and specifically human interaction, are critical areas that need some work when it comes to raising and educating today's kids in the modern 24-7 world. We have to put down our phones and get our kids to put down theirs.

Working on this issue is as simple as educators and parents working on the relationships they have with their kids. When people (educators, parents, strangers) take a moment to take an interest in another person, that interest could be the one thing that person needed that day. As humans, most of us need (on some level) the validation of and interaction with other humans to feel good about our day or even ourselves. It's just part of being human. As our worlds have become so hectic and filled with the "noise" of life, humans can go through the entire day "together" with numerous other humans but yet can have no meaningful interaction with any of them, which leaves each feeling ultimately alone. Students (and adults) can be left with the feeling of *Who would notice if I was gone?*

As humans we need to get back to basics and show an interest in and respect for others in an effort to rehumanize our world. It is time to get real and take ownership of our own actions and contributions to the world we live in. As I said earlier in the book, perception is reality, and many people go through their day feeling like they are the only ones feeling alone, feeling angry, feeling invisible, and assuming that everyone else's lives are perfect. In actuality, many people experience the same exact feelings, and all could benefit just from talking to each other about it. Some people are able to get human interaction via an online world such as social media, but most are not their happiest this way, whether they realize it or acknowledge it, and many teens only know this world and struggle with working through live relationships as a result.

4. We must all take responsibility for the words we put out into the world via social media and the online world, and we must teach our kids to do the same.

As we have discussed, the social media world has emboldened everyone—all age groups and demographics—to lash out at others over just about everything. The hate that is spewed online is at the root of so many of the issues people (not just teens) face today, yet I believe many people compartmentalize the opinions they put online as not being connected to other areas of life. I think this is particularly true when a person posts hateful words directed at or about a specific individual who has commented on a particular subject on social media, whether they know that person or that person is a complete stranger. Hate is spewed about any given topic, then the spewer of hate puts down the phone and turns back to whatever he/she was doing, perhaps feeling as if he/she has "won" because he/she "told that &@!%$ what he/she thought." It is easy to see that when this behavior is multiplied times everyone on social media, the connection between the online world and people's actual behavior cannot be ignored.

To put the extent of the impact of social media into persepective, use Facebook and Instagram as examples, as of October 2018, Facebook had 2.23 billion monthly active users; Instagram as of June 2018 had 1 billion users (Statista, 2019). If each user spewed only one sentence of hate or negativity each day, the amount of hate being spewed can obviously be overwhelming and world-wide. To put it simply, can't we just all get along?

We must show responsibility for our behavior and words, including the seemingly anonymous online world (even though our names and pictures are usually right there for the world to see). To effect change in other areas, we must individually take steps to contribute positive change, and this needs to happen online. **#nomorehate**

In its simplest form, just because we think it doesn't mean we have to post it.

5. *We must teach our kids to take ownership of their behavior, choices, words, and education, and we must teach kids what is means to be respectful of others.*

What I see and experience in education is that in many ways we have evolved into a "me now" time, and unless we educate kids about it, kids don't know what they don't know. As we discussed when we talked about grades, many kids struggle with taking ownership of their part in their education or seem to not care about the education at all, and this is not just my personal observation. Other educators have expressed concern about student apathy, and parents often come to me with this concern and are at their wits' end about how to handle it. I am choosing to stop short of saying "epidemic" when I describe it only because it does not apply to every single student, but it is not a good situation and it is rampant. In a worst-case example (which applies to students from all walks of life, not just to some nameless, faceless, stereotypical "bad kid" from a "bad home"—that belief is for a made-up after school special), students arrive to class carrying nothing but a phone. Nothing. Earbuds in the ears. Others bring supplies but are tethered to their phone. Earbuds in ears. Others curse their teachers and their administrators when asked to correct their behavior. And this is based on what I have seen with my own eyes. Other educators likely have their own observations to report.

It is a daily battle for teachers to get many kids to put away their phones long enough to listen to a lesson and engage in the class, never mind do their work (much less quality work in which true learning is happening), and many kids become very angry and aggressive when pressed to do so. When teachers have multiple students in their classes who subscribe to this philosophy toward education, it is truly a losing battle. As I tell my students when I meet with them about grades and attendance—education cannot be about adults forcing it down your throat, and education does not passively happen "to" students. Earning an education is an active process that students must pursue and must want for themselves. The expectation of the students taking responsibility in that process starts at home and should be continually reinforced at school. Parents, educators desperately need your help with this. Nationwide, we must continue to teach and reinforce the belief that education is important, and we have to make it important.

Students (again, not all, but too many) have also become increasingly aggressive towards their teachers and authority figures and often show little respect. Parents—if your image of a typical school day is what you experienced in 1985, you are probably way off base. Again, I am not saying every student is defiant, reluctant, and aggressive, but schools and students today are different, just as students in schools in the 1980s were different from students in schools in the 1950s. It is a natural part of progress, but I am concerned that we are at a breaking point in American education.

To give a frame of reference, in the beginning of my educational career, we would have been shocked to hear vulgar language in the halls; today it is commonplace. This language and disrespect is often directed at authority figures but also at each other. It is not uncommon for students to curse at or directly threaten teachers and/or principals, or even their own parents, at school in front of teachers and administrators. To this end, the state of Texas has passed legislation requiring students entering high school in 2018-2019 and beyond to take a class and watch a video instructing them on how to interact with a police officer as a graduation requirement, so clearly it is a state-wide concern that we teach students how to interact with authority figures (not just peace officers). For many students, learning to show respect for authority could be, at some point in their life, a life or death situation, and it must be taken seriously. Never mind what this type of behavior says about a students' respect for education in general. All of society needs to be concerned about that.

The lack of respect some students show is evident in the school buildings themselves. Sometimes even the "best students"—the ones who are engaged in their work and who appear to care very much about their educations—leave trash on the table in the cafeteria (or in classrooms or on hallway floors) and walk away, leaving it for "someone else" to clean up; chairs are very often not pushed back under the table when students leave a table. This is a phenomenon I have also witnessed at fast food restaurants—people sit at a table and eat their food, then get up and walk out the door, leaving their trash on the table even though the common practice in the fast food restaurant is to pick up your own trash and throw it away. I have personally witnessed this happen many times, and my educator husband and I just shake our heads knowing that this, in part, is why kids exhibit this same behavior at school. Again, kids don't know what they don't know, and we must be a team to teach kids that they are responsible for their actions, and to understand that to be respected begins first with showing respect for others and for their surroundings.

One simple way I can explain the difference in teen behavior today compared to yesteryear is to compare it to my own experiences as a high school student, which I have discussed many times with my peers from own generation who see the same things I do. In the 1980s, as teens, we were not perfect, and I am not in any way suggesting we were perfect and modern teens are so dramatically different. One key difference is this—in the 1980s, if we cursed or talked about something inappropriate or questionable (that we should not have been doing in the first place), we hid it from adults. We whispered it so that only our peers could hear us but the adults could not, and we showed respect to adults, whether they were authority figures or not (for the most part—remember, our brains weren't fully-formed in high school either). We also did not (at least at my high school) have school resource officers (police officers assigned to schools) at our school, so the only time we saw a police officer was out in the "real world." (And no, I am not advocating that students go back to "whispering bad things;" rather, I am illustrating the difference in behaviors between the two generations.)

Too many of today's teens are boldly unconcerned with who hears what. Walk the halls of any high school (or check social media) and see for yourself. And, as I have said earlier in this book, many teens are bold in their words and actions when speaking directly to adults, whether it is their parents or educators or other school authority figures, including school resource officers. I can guarantee that even in anger, I would NEVER have cursed at ANY adult at school or anywhere else on Earth. That I am certain of. A sign of the times? Perhaps. A slippery slope? Definitely. Acceptable? Not even.

In case you are thinking this teen behavior might be limited just to the schools where I have worked or the places I have lived, the answer is no. I have personally witnessed it in a variety of places, both in my state and beyond. You may also be thinking that I only notice it because I am looking for it, which may or may not be true. But if no one takes the time to notice and point out the obvious change in behavior, what will go next following the path of least resistance? Times have definitely changed, but that doesn't mean we have to be ok with it and just accept it. And yes, that same image of the old woman (me) lamenting about the kids with their newfangled whatsit definitely comes to mind here, but still...

6. Not all mean behavior is bullying, but it is still unacceptable behavior.

Help your kids learn to communicate with other kids and to navigate disagreements with others by focusing on resolving conflicts and working through their disagreements. Consult your school counselor for help in this area as needed. For any behavior that you are concerned about, however, call or visit the school. Educators are concerned about all negative behavior, whether it fits the definition of bullying or not. For any behavior that may just be mean behavior, you should still consult with your school counselor or administrator and let him/her know there is a problem that needs to be worked on. Behavior that currently doesn't meet the definition of bullying may, if left unchecked, become bullying as an ongoing pattern is established. What we do not want to do is get bogged down in the definition of bullying when it comes to student behavior, so communicating with your school is the best first step in helping your child.

Part of being human is dealing with other humans, and learning to deal with conflict is a skill kids learn as they grow up and experience conflict with others. Educators want to help your child learn the skills needed to navigate conflict. We all know as adults that conflict exists everywhere in the "real world," and we all need to know how to handle it so it doesn't derail our entire day or entire life. School is where kids learn to deal with and interact with others—friendly people and mean people. **Saying out loud that all mean behavior is not bullying does not mean educators support mean behavior.** We must be able to talk about the behaviors of kids and not lump all mean behavior into the very serious category of bullying.

If your child's situation does not meet the school's definition of bullying, and if your child is also an active participant in the mean behavior, parents cannot expect or demand school administrators to, as an example, remove another student from your school (or other punishment you see fit for the other child). As a school counselor I understand that parents want their kids to be happy and safe and for others to not be mean to their kids. I also understand that it is very easy for parents to lump all mean behavior into the category of bullying as they are working to protect their child. Parents and educators need to continue to put more focus on helping the kid in the situation at hand than to mince words about the definition of bullying. Parents should know that the only time the actual definition of bullying will truly come into play in the educational setting is when it comes to an administrator investigating a situation and determining disciplinary consequences. For all other educators, it really doesn't matter whether the behavior is "bullying" or "mean behavior," those educators want to help your child work through it. The administrator will work on determining everything else, and that administrator needs non-adversarial parental support in the process.

I want to note here that weeks after I had researched and written my earlier chapters addressing bullying and what it is and isn't, as well as everything I had already written about the state of outrage we all live in, I ran across a related November 22, 2018, Facebook post shared by the Georgia School Counselor Association that warrants some discussion because it illustrates many points I have tried to make in this book. The post was a shared excerpt of a story about a Michigan High School counseling department that had tried to explain to their students and parents the difference between bullying and mean behavior by putting the differences (as well as how to get help) in a pamphlet. The Georgia School Counselor Association post that was shared said:

> *School counselors: Overuse of word 'bullying' problematic: Two weeks after a controversial school flyer about bullying angered parents at a (Michigan) school, counselors in another (Michigan) district weighed in on the debate. Turns out, a lot of schools are trying to help students differentiate between bullying and plain old rude or mean behavior... (Facebook, Georgia School Counselor Association, Nov. 22, 2018).*

Curious, I clicked the link to read the original news story to get more information. The original Michigan news article about the flyer said (excerpted here):

> *"I'm absolutely flabbergasted that this idiotic piece of paper was to be handed out at a school function. Unbelievable," wrote one poster (a parent) on Facebook...*
>
> *"To me, this is making kids question whether they should even*

come forward about things," said (a parent) in an interview with (the news station). "I think at this point in time with things that have happened in (the school) and things that have happened in our entire country around bullying, the schools need to focus on making kids feel comfortable coming to them."

(The school) lost an eighth grader — a new student — to suicide in September.

(The city's) police investigated the student's death and told (the news station) it was not due to bullying.

When (the news station) reached out to (the school's) superintendent regarding the pamphlet, he immediately acknowledged it was a mistake (Wood TV, October 18, 2018).

As I read this original news story about the counselors' pamphlet, I noticed a few troubling things that are in line with the overall points I am making in this book (that I had already written well before discovering this article):

*The parents were angry *(outrage/posting anger on social media)*;

*No evidence was presented in the article that any of the parents talked to the counselors about the intent or background of the flyer before posting their outrage online *(lack of communication with the school)*;

*The parents said they felt the pamphlet would discourage students from reporting behavior they thought was bullying, even though the pamphlet listed and explained how to report (and was likely a purpose of having the pamphlet available for kids and parents) *(not all mean behavior is bullying; it doesn't mean educators don't care when they say it isn't bullying, educators want to help all kids navigate conflict)*;

*The story referenced a student's suicide that had already been determined by the police to not be a result of bullying *(perpetuates assumption that bullying and suicide are always related)*;

*The district's superintendent immediately said the pamphlet was a "mistake," which essentially undermined the professional expertise of the counselors and by association, the district) (***wanting the parents' anger and the overall conflict to stop***).

This real-life example came up after this book had essentially been completed, and it illustrates many of the concerns I have put forth in this book. Schools, including the one in the article, want to help kids navigate ALL conflict, not just behavior that meets the definition of bullying. I want to point out that I fully support a parent being able to have and share his/her opinion, but I also want to point out, as I have throughout this book, that sometimes doing so, especially in anger, on social media, is not productive. Communicating directly with the school could have helped forge relationships between the parents and the school and better serve the kids in the middle. When reading this article, I can't help but picture the scene in *Footloose* in which the community members were burning books outside the library…

The Michigan story doesn't end there. In a November 2, 2018, follow-up news story and interview with counselors from another Michigan school, two counselors expressed their own concerns when it comes to the topic of "bullying" (excerpted here):

Both counselors worry, too, that calling everything bullying desensitizes students to the real thing.

"The actual word 'bullying,' I think in society now, is an umbrella term for anything hurtful or unkind," said (one counselor). "Unfortunately, it takes away from real, true, hurtful, harmful bullying."

(The counselors) fear overuse of the word "bullying" will make it harder for students to recognize signs that someone's in real trouble and needs immediate help (Samples, Wood TV, November 2, 2018).

It turns out that these two counselors also put together information in the form of a newsletter explaining to their kids and parents about bullying and mean behavior:

…The front-page column is titled, "Managing Conflict" and subtitled

"Bullying vs. Being Mean: What's the Difference?" The column in the...newsletter listed the definitions of rude, mean and bullying. It also listed specific tips for how to handle the less serious conflicts... (Samples, Wood TV, November 2, 2018).

The flyer created by these counselors contained all good information that needs to be said, heard, and applied in helping kids learn to navigate conflict, just as was the goal of the original flyer at the original Michigan school that incited the anger in the first place.

I included the details of this particular story to illustrate that outrage cannot trump expertise in an area, even if the readers disagree with the wording of the flyer (which is essentially what seemed to anger the parents in this situation). Angry/heightened emotional reactions aimed at those who are trying to help (and who are experts in their field) can have a damaging effect on the educator/parent working relationship. Imagine instead that the pamphlet had been on smoking and the proven health dangers that can come from smoking, yet, because of anger and outrage, all pamphlets were removed as being a "mistake" because parents didn't like the wording of the pamphlet. Meanwhile, the validity of the information is ignored. People are mad (and put it on social media), therefore the pamphlets must go. It just doesn't make sense, and it is not productive or helpful for kids. Again, the *Footloose* book burning scene comes to mind…

So in the end it is simple—bullying and mean behavior are not always one and the same, and educators want to help with all behaviors, regardless of the definition. None of us as educators want bullying OR mean behavior to be present at school. We are missing the point and wasting precious energy when we engage in a debate over the wording of a pamphlet or the definition of bullying. Educators want to work with all kids and their parents to help kids navigate school and life so they can become resilient, successful adults capable of managing conflict that they will most certainly run into after they graduate from high school.

7. To have friends is to first be a friend. Encourage your child to practice kindness with others.

A little kindness can go a long way in someone's life, and there are countless ways humans can be kind to other humans. For example, talk to your child about inviting another child to sit with his/her group at lunch or offering to show the new student in his/her class around. These kind behaviors are as appropriate for high school kids as they are elementary kids. Again, the opportunities for a kid to be nice to another person are endless. Help your child be creative in including other kids.

8. If you suspect your child needs professional mental health intervention, follow through and get that help.

If you are not sure, contact the school or a doctor or a hotline for more help. Inaction cannot happen. It is important to note that if your child is at risk of needing professional mental health care in high school, he or she could also be at risk when you send him/her off to college or life after high school when you are not around. It is important to teach your child to ask for help and to follow through to get the help. This book is predominantly aimed at high school kids, but those very kids graduate and go on to college or career, where they will encounter real stress while away from your watchful eye, so it is critical they know what to do when they encounter that stress and how to reach out for help. Remember, kids' brains are not fully mature until the mid-20s. Impulsivity and bad decision-making is alive and well during the traditional college years.

9. Have high expectations for your kids and follow through with those expectations.

Set the bar high and work to get your kids to reach it. If the bar is set low, your kids will certainly reach it. Kids don't know what they don't know. It is our job as adults to teach them to expect more out of themselves as they progress through life.

10. No swooping, no matter how hard it is to resist. Life offers lessons every kid needs to experience.

We live in a world where opportunity abounds, and most parents want nothing more than for their child to "have it better" than they did. Just remember, everything we talked about in this book is connected, and life's experiences—good, bad, and ugly—deliver the most powerful lessons your child can learn. Learning to connect the dots between decisions we make as humans and the outcomes that evolve after those decisions is how we learn to live and be productive adults capable of weathering the storms that come with life.

Just before this book was published, news broke about the college cheating scandal in which, essentially and allegedly, parents with means paid/bribed/financially arranged for their kids to get into elite colleges. I won't go into what should be obvious connections between that story and all that we have discussed (hopefully it is all crystal clear by this point in reading this book), but I ran across an excellent article on the topic that drives home some of the same points this book does. Amanda Richardson, a San Francisco CEO, wrote an excellent March 2019 LinkedIn article on the topic (excerpted here):

...Failure is not something to fear. Failure is a powerful learning opportunity. Everyone fails. It's absolutely inevitable, even when someone places their thumb firmly on the scale to get you into that school or propel you into that job. At some point, you will be confronted with the brutal, inescapable fact that something you did sucked. You will disappoint a boss. You will let down a team. You will misread the market, screw up a product design, handle an important conversation poorly, or jack up that marketing campaign. Maybe an important personal relationship will fail. You might even get fired or divorced.

The earlier you fail the first time, the better, because you will get more comfortable with feeling incredibly uncomfortable. When you fail in your teens and early twenties, it teaches you so much about yourself. What you could have done differently. How to get up off the mat. What to try next time. How bad it feels to do poorly - and how good it feels to work harder and do something well. It gives you humility - and it also reinforces how capable you can become, with work and grit. There is real pride in stretching yourself, in knowing you can do it. And you will get through it faster next time (and there will be a next time because, spoiler alert, you are not perfect and this is how it works).

Most importantly, though, failure is a life experience that teaches you empathy, perspective, humility and resilience. When you enter the workforce, those qualities - which are really driven by life experience - will help you connect better with teammates, be more effective in your job, shape a product to reach different kinds of people, maneuver around project roadblocks, etc. That's true no matter your role, whether you're in product marketing, engineering, development, communications.

As a CEO whose company is hiring, I'm much more interested in the messy bits than I am in perfection. How someone comes back from a disappointment, a screw-up, a let down, is much more telling than how they operate when everything is status quo. How you handle yourself in a loss is character; winning is easy...(para. 8-11).

Well said, indeed.

A separate article from *The Chronicle of Higher Education* echoed other aspects of what we have discussed in this book. Supiano (2019) made several good points in her article *They're Already Rich. Why Were These Parents So Fixated on Elite Colleges?* I have included two of those points here:

*The Measure of a Good Parent

The admissions process is often harder on parents than it is on their children, says James W. Jump, director of college counseling at St. Christopher's School, in Richmond, Va. It may test their beliefs, he says – about parenting, about college, and about their own children. "It's easy to believe where your kids go to college is a measure of how good a parent you are," he said. "Which is ridiculous." (para. 4).

*"Curling Parents"
People used to talk about helicopter parents, said Jump, the college counselor. These days, he said, the term is "curling parents," a reference to the Olympic sport. Parenting, in other words, is no longer about hovering over one's children. It's about sweeping problems out of their way (para. 8).

Obviously, not all who may be reading this book (the writer of this book included!) are in the position to make the same arrangements for their kids as those implicated in this latest scandal, so I only included the most relevant general points from this article. One key point that this case highlights is that all parents want "better" for their kids, even those who seemingly have it "all" already. It also speaks to the section of this book in which we discuss the fact that temptation and self-control are a part of life, for kids, and for adults.

11. Kids must actively seek an education, and they have far more control over their situations than they often believe.

Continue to work with your child to remind them that an education does not happen "to them." Remind them they very much have control over many situations in their life, and the earning of grades is front and center in this belief. Remind them, too, that the point of an education is to acquire knowledge and skills, and that very knowledge that comes from actual learning vs. the "grade chasing" of turning in late work and doing test corrections to improve a grade. This includes working on and honing solid, classic, time-honored study skills.

It is critical to mention here the struggles that some students have with consistent school attendance. In order for any student to actively seek an education, that student must be consistently present at school. It seems like an obvious statement with which most would likely nod "yes" in agreement. In order for educators to help students who are struggling, those students must be consistently present at school. Again, nothing Earth-shattering here, save for the troubling fact that chronic absenteeism is actually a big problem for some schools and for the individual students and families who have fallen into this habit. Let's take a quick look at chronic absenteeism.

"Chronic" absenteeism is defined by the National Center for Children in Poverty as missing 10% of the school year, equivalent to missing 18 days out of a 180 day school year (regardless of whether the absences are excused or unexcused) (Chang & Romero, 2008, p. 3). Let's look at some fast facts regarding school attendance and chronic absenteeism from the U.S. Department of Education:

Students experience chronic absenteeism from coast to coast. Approximately 500 school districts reported that 30% or more of their students missed at least three weeks of school in 2013-2014.

More than 6 million students missed 15 or more days of school in 2013-2014. That's 14% of the student population, or about 1 in 7 students.

Chronic absenteeism spikes in high school for students of every race and ethnicity.

Females are slightly more likely to be chronically absent in high school than males.

Nearly 1 in 5 students in high school are chronically absent (U.S. Department of Education, Chronic Absenteeism in the Nation's Schools website).

When it comes to chronic absenteeism, by the time kids get to high school, a lot of damage has been done:

Chronic absenteeism may prevent children from reaching early learning milestones. Children who are chronically absent in preschool, kindergarten, and first grade are much less likely to read at grade level by the third grade. Students who cannot read at grade level by the end of third grade are four times more likely than proficient readers to drop out of high school.

Frequent absences from school can shape adulthood. Chronically absent students are more likely to drop out of high school, which is linked to poor outcomes later in life, from poverty and diminished health to involvement in the criminal justice system (U.S. Department of Education).

Finally, according to the National Center for Children in Poverty:

Schools have served our country well as gateways to more opportunity for children. What happens when children first enter school deeply affects whether this opportunity is realized. During the early elementary years, children are gaining basic social and academic skills critical to ongoing academic success. Unless students attain these essential skills by third grade, they require extra help to catch up and are at grave risk for eventually dropping out of school (Chang & Romero, 2008, p. 3).

When it comes to getting a sound education, kids must be present to win. Parents, if you are struggling with the issue of getting your kids to go to school, it is imperative to not take the path of least resistance with them. It is very difficult to "make up for" years of chronic absences when kids reach high school. It is key to make consistent school attendance an expectation for your child when he/she is young and beginning school so that it becomes a positive habit for him/her, and it is critical to continue to reinforce this habit through middle and high school. Attending school regularly is yet another key habit teens will take with them when they leave high school and go on to college and/or career. If you are struggling with getting your child to go to school, whether that child is in elementary school or high school, I urge you to reach out to your school counselor or administrator for help, and the earlier the better.

In its simplest form, even if a child does not meet the definition of being "chronically" absent, it is important to remember that every day a child is absent, he/she is missing valuable instruction, so encouraging consistent attendance can go a long way toward ensuring your child earns a solid education while in school.

12. Set limits for your kids and set up a reward system rather than a "take away" system.

Your kids may argue and fight you every step of the way, but most kids actually do want those limits, whether it is a curfew or not being allowed to attend that crazy party at the "cool parents' house" they have heard about. Many parents struggle getting their kids to live up to their responsibilities and try to manage their child's behaviors by taking away things the child wants, which for many kids is namely their phone and any related media that goes with the phone. Rather than giving your kids everything to start with, create your own reward system at home in which your child earns something AFTER he/she meets other expectations, whether it is grades earned or chores completed, etc., and stick to it. The "sticking to it" part is the hardest in everything we do, from parenting, to teaching, to working out or eating right. But it will be worth it in the end. If everything was easy, there would be no issues for all of us to contend with, now would there? Review the chapter on motivation and relationships when working with your child to set up a reward system at home. What the adult thinks is not necessarily what the teen thinks.

13. The habits your kids have now will be the exact same habits they have when they leave high school.

No magic happens the night of high school graduation. Kids wake up the next day with the EXACT SAME habits they had in high school. The same kids who struggle to go to class and study in high school will (without change) struggle in college or in their job with applying themselves. Teach your kids good, old-fashioned study skills. Many kids today really do not understand that they must memorize information to learn it—they are just getting by, and when the majority of kids operate on that level, it can water down education in general. We owe it to our kids and all of our futures to help kids work on forming positive habits. Get your kids to put down the phone and pick up a planner, then follow through and use it. Kids can definitely use their phones as a planner, but they must work on their habit of self-control and putting responsibilities first over fun. They must be able to put the phone away and not get distracted by a rabbit-hole app right next to the calendar on their phone. You get the picture.

And if you know in your heart your teen's grades are too good to be true (i.e. you NEVER see him/her studying at home), do some checking. One problem might be that everyone in your child's class is seemingly brilliant, as evidenced by everyone receiving fantastic grades with minimal effort. Learning takes effort, and effort takes time out of each day. Don't let the report card fool you, and don't have selective vision. If your child has NO study habits and you are (rightfully) concerned or suspicious, take ten minutes and quiz him/her on information from the class, or have him/her write a couple of pages on a given topic in the class from memory. You will have all the information you need.

14. Eating right and getting physical activity are needed in life. Kids today have access to just about everything they want, and that includes eating poorly.

Many kids prefer electronics and sitting over any type of physical activity, and it shows in their reported anxiety and depressive qualities. Physical activity helps fight symptoms of depression as well as obesity and promotes positive health. Other than physical education classes, educators' hands are tied when it comes to promoting physical activity in that they are all in classrooms, so I encourage you as a family to promote and reinforce physical activity at home. Put down the phone and go outside. Do something simple like take a walk as a family. No phones, even for the adults. This allows for physical activity, family conversations, and human interaction.

Encourage your child to join a sport or other group activity at school or outside of school that gets him/her moving and talking to other people. Being a part of a team has many benefits for kids (and for adults who belong to adult leagues, etc.). Not only will your kids get the physical benefits from being physically active, but they will benefit from the camaraderie of being on a team, whether that is basketball, football, volleyball, cheerleading, drill team, dance, band, or any of the numerous opportunities out there. According to the University of Missouri Health Care Children's Hospital, physical exercise is good for the mind, body and spirit. Team sports help teach adolescents accountability, dedication, leadership and other skills (para. 1). MU Health Care goes on to list benefits of being a part of a team:

Many athletes do better academically. Playing a sport requires a lot of time and energy, which doesn't actually distract students from schoolwork. Sports require memorization, repetition and learning, which support students' school work. The determination and goal-setting skills a sport require provide a benefit to kids in and out of school (para. 2). This is true for participating in any type of similar group, whether it is a dance team, a marching band, a cheerleading squad, etc.

Sports teach teamwork and problem-solving skills. Working towards a common goal with a group of teammates and coaches teaches kids how to work with people (teamwork) and how to communicate effectively to solve problems (para. 3). These are all skills that we have talked about in this book and that carry over into adult life.

Physical health benefits of sports. In addition to helping teens work on goals of being fit and maintaining a healthy weight, being a part of a sport or other team can also encourage and establish healthy decision-making habits that last throughout life (para. 4).

Sports boost self-esteem. Experiencing your own hard work combined with working hard alongside others to achieve the same goal develops self-confidence. Achieving a sport or fitness goal encourages teens to achieve other goals, which in itself is a rewarding and exciting learning process (para. 5). This is true whether the end result is a win or loss. Weathering a loss together as a team teaches teens that losing is a natural part of life, that there will be a new day after the loss, and that the experience (win or lose) is valuable.

Reduce pressure and stress with sports. (All points are important, but this is a biggy.) Exercising is a natural way to loosen up and let go of stress. Kids (and adults!) can make new friends who can be there for them as a support system. When kids feel under pressure or stressed, they can talk to their teammates (or coaches) and/or play it out (para. 6).

There are many similar lists of the benefits of participating in team sports and activities, and I encourage you to do your own research. There are documented benefits to being in sports as well as music groups that go well beyond the immediate goal of that particular group or team "winning" or "doing well." When you combine the human interaction with teammates working together, the work put in as an individual, the work put in toward achieving a common goal, and the fact that phones (etc.) are out of teens' hands during the process, it's a win-win for all involved. Remember, the physical activity, camaraderie, etc. doesn't just take place in the game. Practices, whether alone or in a team setting, working out, eating well, and all the work that goes in behind the scenes also build quality skills that benefit teens (and adults) in life.

Just a reminder, however, to keep emotions in check when it comes to hot topics like winning, coaching decisions, your child's "playing time" (time on the court/field/etc.), how your child actually played/performed, missed calls by the referees/judges/etc. The experience of being on a team, win or lose, is more valuable than the outcome. Parent brawls and outrage aimed at coaches/referees/other players/other parents/etc. destroy the experience and the benefits of the experience. Watching your child participate on a team is a great activity you can share with your child, but you can also volunteer to help in order to be a part of the activity, whether that is being a "team mom/dad" or being a part of the team booster club or other supporting organization. Or you can simply support your child as he/she lives the experience.

Just as humans benefit from physical activity, it is obvious that all humans need to eat well to be their healthiest. Teens are not exempt from that fact. According to Costa (2016):

Teens are faced with myriad physical changes and academic demands, all while being bombarded by what their peers are doing – from what not to wear, to what to say and when to say it, to how to get the attention of you know who. And in the midst of all this, the body's most critical organ – the brain – is still developing, says Dr. Neville Golden, a member of the American Academy of Pediatrics' Committee on Nutrition and chief of adolescent medicine at Stanford University School of Medicine in California.

"If [teens] don't eat right, they can become irritable, depressed [and] develop problems such as obesity and eating disorders – and those have a whole host of psychological morbidities," Golden says, adding that proper nutrition can help prevent and manage these conditions.

During adolescence, the brain is undergoing serious renovations…This brain remodeling phase in a teen's life is known as "pruning," says Jeanette Johnstone, a postdoctoral fellow in the department of neurology at the Oregon Health & Science University in Portland, where she's also a child and adolescent psychologist resident. And without proper nutrition, the brain's ability to learn new tasks or skills decreases – certainly not good news for students.

"It's a huge time of growth and development in a person's life. Therefore, the brain needs adequate sleep, hydration and good food," Johnstone says. "What you eat impacts your brain, because your gut and brain are connected" (para. 3-7).

As far as specifics about what exactly your kids should be eating to achieve a "balanced diet," do some research and/or ask your child's doctor.

The key is to work with your teen on understanding that eating appropriately, along with getting adequate sleep and physical activity, is part of a healthy lifestyle. As with everything else, it's all connected.

15. *Temptation and self-control are a part of life.*

Becoming an adult means that teens themselves must take control of their own behaviors and actions, rather than expecting an adult to force them to do the right thing. At school (and out) there will ALWAYS be a temptation to do something other than what the teen is supposed to be doing. Part of growing up is learning to say no to the temptation and to make better choices for oneself so that as adults we can be independent of our parents or other adults. (See #10 about not swooping. I know it comes from love, but proceed with caution.)

16. *See something, say something, and make sure people are listening.*

This cannot be said enough. As humans we have a responsibility and obligation to help other humans. Teens are naturally secretive developmentally, which is what makes this one a challenge. We must instill in our kids a level of empathy for other people as well as teach our kids to tell someone when they suspect or are directly aware of a problem, whether that is a friend who might be suicidal, or a friend who is threatening or planning to hurt someone. Remind your child that no one will ever know that your child is the one who reported it (whatever "it" is). There are eyes and ears everywhere, and that report could come from anyone. It is critical that your child report what he or she knows about. It could be a life or death situation.

17. *Step up and step in.*

Parents, parenting is hard, but it is also very simple, and the same is true for educators and educating. We as adults must all step up and step in to do the right thing as adults when it comes to parenting and educating our kids, even if it is not the easy or convenient thing to do.

18. We cannot take the path of least resistance and avoid getting involved.

We must dig deep for our sense of community and find a way to "get real" about issues that we may tend to ignore because it is just easier to ignore them. As I said in the beginning of this book, so many of the "big issues" we are all concerned about, namely school shootings and other violence, seem insurmountable when it is one educator or one parent at home thinking about it. But there are things we can all do to create that ripple effect that we need for real change. What I know for certain is that if we do nothing, nothing will change. We must break down any walls keeping us from working together to improve not only our schools but our world in general. We are all sitting on a train that is barreling toward something, and only together can we have some control over where that train is headed. We must get involved and take action.

19. In the social media world, everyone believes he/she is right.

On social media, people believe in their "rightness" first because they put their opinion out there, but they confirm their "rightness" by the people who have jumped in to support and cheer on the person's opinion, either through "likes" or through other people's comments. One caveat to social media reasoning that many do not acknowledge is this: Most people's social media accounts are already filled with like-minded people who will readily agree with and support everything each person says, all the while insulating themselves from others with equally "right" but differing opinions, which in turn drives all involved to believe even more vehemently in their "rightness" and other people's "wrongness." (Or the social media account will become filled with like-minded people as those who post a differing opinion are deleted or unfollowed.) The truth of the matter is this: just because someone posts something online, whether it gets one, 1,000 or one million "likes," it doesn't mean that person's opinion is "right." It just means that that person's feed is full of people who are like-minded. Opinion is not fact, and fact is not opinion, and because most issues are grey, both sides could be equally "right."

If we are all truly concerned about making the world, and specifically schools, a safer place, it is critical as we move forward that we as adults remember this about our own social media presence but that we also truly educate our kids about what truth is. In the adult world, an untrue hate-filled social media post can lead to violent behavior and certainly to intolerance of others who think differently, even in one's own family. In the teen world, a world filled with impulsive, sensitive teens whose minds are nowhere near fully developed or able to reason or think through the here and now, a hateful untrue social media post can be that teen's downfall, whether impulsive and immediate or a slow burn of depression and serious mental health concerns. In many ways with social media we have lost our way and made it into something that is ugly and self-righteous, and a lack of personal responsibility for words that are put out there is a central reason for that. We all have a hand in this, and we must all do better to forge a positive change.

20. Building relationships goes a long way toward solving many issues we are all facing.

I mentioned relationships earlier in this list but must say it again. Relationships can improve a very wide range of issues. Relationships can help:

families get along and be more functional
classroom teachers be more effective
students be more active, productive learners
teens feel included rather than alone and isolated
people take an interest in each other, humanizing each other and making

it more difficult to be aggressive or violent to each other

*lines of communication be more productive

*social media feeds be less narcissistic and self-righteous by humanizing the other people right there with you

*motivation in teens' and adults improve

*humans get back to being human

*humans remember that we are all imperfect, no matter what we say, do, or what image we put out there on social media

Relationships are a very powerful means to solve, or at least help solve, all types of issues, and we all have the power within us to make a positive change in all relationships that we are a part of. Like many other areas, relationships take work, and that investment can pay off immensely.

21. Be nice to each other.

Watch in amazement how people respond to kindness, both online and in person. When it comes to mean, hurtful opinions, just because you think it doesn't mean you have to say it or post it. And just because you are angry (at the driver who cut you off, at the person who shared a comment online that is just plain %$@!*&#!…), it doesn't mean you have to act on that anger. Let that driver get in in front of you even though he should have waited like everyone else. Scroll past the comments that set you off. You can do it. We all have choices, and we have this one life. Do we really want to spend our lives bowing up to everyone who makes us mad? I am not suggesting being a doormat. *Au contraire.* I am simply suggesting that we focus on kindness and make meaningful decisions when it comes to our actions and reactions. Focus instead on opening a door for a stranger or helping the elderly person in front of you in the grocery store get her items on the checkout counter. Compliment someone. Send a note to someone you haven't talked to in a while just to say hello. Be an agent for positive change.

There are several versions of a saying/quote that comes to mind here: **Everyone you meet is fighting a battle you know nothing about. Be** kind. **Always** (Pinterest). Spreading kindness is the ultimate drop in the water/ripple effect. It may seem overly simple to some, but if we focused on spreading as much kindness as compared to the amount of hate and outrage that is spread, positive change is inevitable. In-person kindness toward people we know as well as toward perfect strangers can go a long way toward improving our collective experience on Earth.

Kindness is clearly important online as well. We cannot live our lives one way (hateful/angry/critical etc. commentary) online and believe that is has no impact on the live, human world offline. Reminder, as I mentioned previously when talking about the spreading of hate—as of October 2018, Facebook had 2.23 billion monthly active users; Instagram as of June 2018 had 1 billion users (Statista, 2019). If each user showed kindness (vs. hate) toward someone else each day while online, the amount of kindness being spread (vs. hate being spewed) can obviously be impactful world-wide.

22. School shootings are not a "school problem" any more than a workplace shooting is a "workplace problem" or a movie theater shooting is a "movie theater problem."

School shootings cannot be reduced to be thought of as "a problem in today's schools," which puts the blame and responsibility solely on schools to "fix" the problem. As I said at the beginning of this book, dealing with school shootings is complicated, and we are all part of the problem AND finding a solution. **School shootings are a human act and a human problem, and we must focus our efforts on helping all humans (teens or otherwise).** Some who read this book may try to oversimplify the message of the book by reducing it to a negative sound bite such as "bad parenting causes or equals school shootings." I can assure you that is **NOT** the message of this book, either overtly or covertly. To reduce this book to a negative message such as this is an example of the very root of our problems as a modern society.

The truth of the matter is that we all have a hand in the current state of affairs, and we all have to work together to make it right. That is why everything else we have talked about in this book matters, and we all need to work together to care for and improve every area in this book that we interact with, experience, or have influence over. Change can happen. Just as we have evolved to the current state of our world, we can evolve to a better state of our world, but it will not happen by magic or accident. We must all actively pursue positive change.

~

So it comes down to this. Everything we have talked about in this book is connected, and we are all connected. My hope is that what we have talked about in this book will make a light bulb go off for some and inspire others to rally for change. As a school counselor, I have been through several situations involving the death of a teen, most of which were by suicide. The death of a student is by far one of the most difficult situations any educator encounters, and it is obviously something no parent should ever have to face. I have sat in a hospital with parents whose child lay in another room on life support. I have looked into the hollow eyes of parents who are faced with the death of their child they just sent off to college. I have seen the tears and the anguished faces of the teachers who are being told *we have lost another student*. I have shed those same tears for a student. I have been fortunate enough to not have experienced a school shooting firsthand, but someone I know lost a family member in a recent school shooting in my state. This is real life. This is not a fictional television series about something dramatic that "happens to someone else."

Will all teens attempt suicide? No. Will all troubled teens become school shooters? No. But picture in your mind a group photo of all students in a school. Can you pick out the one who will commit suicide, now or when they are away at college? Can you pick out the one who will become a school shooter or commit a violent act at school or in the workplace ten years from now? Probably not. Can you pick the ones who will seek out a parent's worst nightmare (whatever that is) online? Unlikely. I can tell you from my own personal experiences as an educator that you never know when it comes to some things. But when you hear or see something that sets off an alarm in your mind, I urge you to act on it by reaching out to someone to report it because we can't help if we don't know about your concerns. And we must continue to teach our kids to do the same. Silence can indeed be deadly.

Regarding school (and other) shootings specifically, while our current world is focused, out of necessity, on active shooter drills and increasing school security, we must continue to insist on getting to the root of the problem, focusing our efforts on the human side of the problem, and working for real, lasting change in an effort to make these shootings stop. We must continue to focus on raising (both at home and at school) strong, resilient humans who are capable of dealing with stress and emotion in a healthy, non-violent way both in high school and beyond as an adult. We all have the power to teach those skills to our kids. We have the power to begin to reverse the trend of violence and murder as the answer to conflict and emotional situations.

The issue of mental health and school shootings will continue to need to be addressed, and humans with mental health issues will continue to need support and professional help. We must all continue to stay vigilant and to *notice* when someone or something is not right, and we must continue to reach out to get the help that is needed and appropriate for that situation. ***See something, say something. Every time. Take action, and make sure people are listening.***

Everything we have talked about in this book is, on some level, connected. From seemingly unmotivated teens to perfectionist teens and all of those in between, with all of their habits, wants, needs, beliefs, relationships and worldviews, all are together walking the halls of their high schools, at times united and at times divided. Whether you are a parent or an educator, and no matter where you individually stand on any of the topics we have discussed, the time is now for all of us to roll up our sleeves and put some work in—into the teens themselves but also into the educational world and society as a whole to make it a better place. We all have a level of power, control and influence within us to reach out, foster and create change through and for other human beings, starting with ourselves, and with our own children and students, who will be the next generation of adults. We are indeed at a crossroads, and where we choose to go from here is paramount.

Every situation, issue, and scenario we have discussed in this book has exceptions to it, and we cannot say "all teens will…" and be 100% accurate. Still, we are all active participants in this world, and we must do our part to make it a better place not just for our teens, but for all—those who are here now as well as the generations that will follow behind us who will only know their present situation as their reality. We have a responsibility to make it a better world.

I am closing this book with an admittedly cheesy method I use sometimes with kids and parents when I am meeting with them about a topic that is frequently heavy and overwhelming, much like the topics we have discussed in this book. I very often use this very simple and corny (yet visual) way to explain how we are all going to get through it together. I have them picture a giant dinosaur sitting out in front of the school, and I ask them how they would eat that dinosaur. Sometimes, they will sit and ponder a moment wondering what I am getting at, and eventually I will ask them if they would eat it in one giant bite, and, of course they say no. They will usually come up with the old "one bite at a time" answer.

That philosophy will work with just about anything we are dealing with, no matter how big and unsurmountable the problem seems—we can only take one bite at a time, and we can only get through one day at a time. The issues we have discussed in this book are some of the "dinosaurs" we are all dealing with in life today, and I urge you as parents and fellow educators to look at the issues the same way. As a whole, the problem might seem giant and insurmountable, but when we take one step at a time, we can effect change. When we form a strong team in the process, together we can effect even greater change in areas that are bigger than all of us individually. And change is what we all need when it comes to bettering the lives of our kids and bettering our world for all who live in it.

It all starts with an open, honest conversation.

Chapter 15

Don't Just Take It from Me

Chapter 15

Don't Just Take It from Me

There is no shortage of resources and opinions, expert and otherwise, on all topics addressed in this book. Rather than continue to quote into infinity, I have including an extensive bibliography of resources I referenced in this book as well as others that I have read or come across throughout the writing of this book. I encourage you to read each of these (or watch the video as the case may be) in order to continue to broaden the information you have on all subjects. I also encourage you to do your own research. An internet search on any topic in this book will produce more than enough results for you to read, and read, and read (and watch).

I began this book immediately after the Santa Fe High School (Texas) shooting in May 2018 because I had just had enough, and I was not seeing anything significant from lawmakers or the field of education in the immediate reaction to it other than discussions of arming teachers, adding more school security, and a lack of focus on the human aspect of school shooters themselves other than general references to mental health. I mention this here simply to give you the time period during which I researched and wrote the book. As a side note, as I wrote this final chapter and continued through the editing process, shootings continued to occur. I mention this to drive home the point that we don't seem to be nearing an end to these types of events, which is what makes all of our actions moving forward critical for creating positive change.

Many of the opinion pieces that are referenced in the bibliography of this book were written by educators. Many were written out of frustration and an outcry for making "things" better, whether that is classrooms, student behavior or motivation or responsibility, or people's lives, just to name a few. It is educators' (and my own) opinions that I want to support again because I believe that those who work in education, particularly public education, have a unique, broad "real world" perspective on everything mentioned in this book but also on "real life" in general. Educators have chosen to be in their field, and as the joke goes, it's not for the pay. Most educators are "helpers" by nature and desperately want much-needed improvements in the field of education to improve students' educations and lives and so that good educators will enter the profession and stay, to give just two reasons. In its simplest form, educators have a realistic perspective on "what's really going on" in our world. Educators see it all: raw, unfiltered, unpoliticized real life. We see the real lives students and their families are living, we know the obstacles students and their families face every day, and we ultimately want one thing—to help those people. I mention again, too, that this is not a political book even if it discusses topics that may be considered political. This is a book about change—positive, proactive change that is much-needed.

As you investigate the resources I have included, I urge you to read/listen with an open mind, free of any preconceived opinions or beliefs. It might or might not change your own worldview, but my hope is that it sparks change in our world. Start the conversation now.

Afterword

Below is a list of the deadliest single day mass shootings in U.S. history from 1949 to the present compiled by CNN (school and other mass shootings). If the shooter was killed or committed suicide during the incident, that death is not included in the total (CNN Library, December 15, 2018). This list illustrates that gun violence can touch anyone anywhere, and we must all be unrelenting in working together to stop future violence. Please note this list only includes mass shootings. This list does not include other mass acts of violence committed with weapons other than guns, such as bombs or motor vehicles driven into crowds, which are obviously equally concerning.

Mass Shooting Events:

58 killed - October 1, 2017; Nevada, concert.

49 killed - June 12, 2016; Florida, nightclub.

32 killed - April 16, 2007; Virginia, Virginia Tech University.

27 killed - December 14, 2012; Connecticut, Sandy Hook Elementary School.

25 and an unborn child killed - November 5, 2017; Texas, church.

23 killed - October 16, 1991; Texas, restaurant.

21 killed - July 18, 1984; California, restaurant.

18 killed - August 1, 1966; Texas, University of Texas.

17 killed - February 14, 2018; Florida, Marjory Stoneman Douglas High School.

14 killed - December 2, 2015; California, workplace.

14 killed - August 20, 1986; Oklahoma, workplace.

13 and an unborn child killed - November 5, 2009; Texas, military base.

13 killed - April 3, 2009; New York, community center.

13 killed - April 20, 1999; Colorado, Columbine High School.

13 killed - February 18, 1983; Washington, gambling and social club.

13 killed - September 25, 1982; Pennsylvania, residence.

13 killed - September 5, 1949; New Jersey, city street.

12 killed - November 7, 2018; California, bar.

12 killed - September 16, 2013; Washington, Navy yard.

12 killed - July 20, 2012; Colorado, movie theater.

12 killed - July 29, 1999; Atlanta, residence.

11 killed - October 27, 2018; Pennsylvania, synagogue.

10 Killed - May 18, 2018; Texas, Santa Fe High School.

10 killed - March 10, 2009; Alabama, residence and place of business.

9 killed - October 1, 2015; Oregon, Umpqua Community College.

9 killed - June 17, 2015; South Carolina, church.

9 killed - March 21, 2005; Minnesota, Red Lake High School.

9 killed - August 10, 1991; Arizona, Buddhist temple.

9 killed - June 18, 1990; Florida, workplace.

8 killed - October 12, 2011; California, salon.

8 killed - August 3, 2010; Connecticut, place of business.

8 killed - January 19, 2010; Virginia, residence.

8 killed - March 29, 2009; North Carolina, nursing home.

8 killed - December 5, 2007; Nebraska, mall.

8 killed - July 1, 1993; San Francisco, law office.

8 killed - September 14, 1989; Kentucky, workplace.

8 killed - August 20, 1982; Florida, workplace.

*Note: not included in the CNN list (but local to me):

*7 killed - September 15, 1999; Texas, church.

As this book is about to be published, new laws addressing school shootings and other violence are being considered in our state, including the addition of more school counselors. As I have said before, this book is not about laws or guns. It is about humans and the decisions they make as they view and assess their lives and problems through their own lens or "filter," their worldview.

In its simplest form, every mass shooting listed above (which does not include every shooting--just the worst of them based on number of deaths) was carried out by a *human* who made a *decision* based on how he/she felt in the moment and viewed the world. It is this aspect of humanity that we must purposefully address. We cannot shrug our shoulders in defeat and wonder "why?" when we review the number of deaths that have occurred at the hands of another human. Yes, many of these murders were carried out by someone with (diagnosed/determined prior to the event) mental health issues. A diagnosis of a mental health issue does not mean that a person cannot be helped or that a mass shooting carried out by that person is inevitable. We must still be vigilant and continue to provide support for *all* people in an effort to stop the violence.

The most recent mass shooting took place just days before this book was published. While it was not a school shooting, and while it was not in the United States, it, like all mass shootings, is relevant. 50 killed in a mosque in New Zealand. Hate posted online prior to the attack. We must begin now to make active changes where we have the most power to make that change—with ourselves, and with our kids. Kids grow into teens, and teens grow into adults. Humans who make decisions. We cannot view any shooting as "something that happens somewhere else to someone else."

And in the days just before this book was published, a teen survivor of the Parkland shooting died by suicide. The teen had reported feeling survivor's guilt and had recently been diagnosed with post-traumatic stress disorder (Rosenberg, para. 5). Soon after, another Parkland student died by "apparent suicide." It was unconfirmed if it was related to the shooting (Hartung, para. 5). And then news came of the "apparent suicide" of the father of one of the Sandy Hook shooting victims (Yan, para. 1). We must do everything in our power to intervene in this cycle. School shootings and other violent acts have both immediate and residual, ongoing effects. We may not be able to prevent every destructive decision, behavior, or action being taken, but we—all of us—must do *something*. Prevention. Intervention. Noticing. Stepping in. Reaching out. Taking action.

My home growing up was very small, and very quiet, and we had a clock on the wall that had a swinging pendulum. Every hour, or perhaps it was half-hour, the clock's low, slow chime sounded to let us know another increment of time had passed. Those sounds were a specific part of life in our house. Tick...tock, tick...tock. Time passing. Decisions, behaviors, actions. Choices being made. Defining moments of and for people's lives. Time passing.

We—all of us—have the power to help. A ripple effect. A call to action. If not us, then who? If not now, then when? The time is now.

Regardless of changes to laws, personnel, school security or safety planning and response, the fact remains that shootings and violence as a means of solving problems are a reflection of how *people* have changed and of the *decisions* they make. Laws and safety procedures alone will not be enough if we continue along the same path as people and as a society. We must be purposeful and deliberate in addressing *all* of the issues that could be contributing to the level of violence, anger, and outrage in schools and in our world, and it begins well before a student ever enters high school.

We each possess the power to create change. The key is to follow through and do it.

Bibliography

6 important facts about JUUL. (2018, August). *Truth Initiative.* Retrieved from https://truthinitiative.org/news/6-important-facts-about-juul

9 things teachers need if the United States ever wants another globally competitive generation (2018, November 6). *We Are Teachers. (*Web log post.) Retrieved from https://www.weareteachers.com/what-teachers-need/

10 apps teens are using that parents should know about. (2018, April). *ABC.* Retrieved from https://abc13.com/society/10-apps-every-parent-of-a-teen-should-know about-/3309450/

10 benefits of reading aloud to children (infograph). (2017, September 2017). *What Do We Do All Day?* (Web log post.) Retrieved from https://www.facebook.com/whatdowedoallday/posts/1469386156449638

10 facts about school attendance. (N.D.). *Attendance Works.* Retrieved from https://www.attendanceworks.org/chronic-absence/the-problem/10-facts-about-school-attendance/

10 girls. 14 days without any social media. Here's how they fared. (2018). *Good Morning America.* Retrieved from https://www.goodmorningamerica.com/living/story/10-teen-girls-give-social-media-weeks-fared-58967114

10 things parents can do to prevent suicide. (2018). *Healthychildren.org.* Retrieved from https://www.healthychildren.org/English/health-issues/conditions/emotional-problems/Pages/Ten-Things-Parents-Can-Do-to-Prevent-Suicide.aspx

24-7. (N.D.) *Merriam-Webster.* https://www.merriam-webster.com/time-traveler/1985

A brief history of tobacco. (N.D.). *CNN.* Retrieved from http://edition.cnn.com/US/9705/tobacco/history/

Firearm access is a risk factor for suicide. (N.D.). *Harvard T.H. Chan School of Public Health.* Retrieved from https://www.hsph.harvard.edu/means-matter/means-matter/risk/

Aizenman, N. (2018). Deaths from gun violence: How the U.S. compares with the rest of the world. *National Public Radio.* Retrieved from https://www.npr.org/sections/goatsandsoda/2018/11/09/666209430/deaths-from-gun-violence-how-the-u-s-compares-with-the-rest-of-the-world

Akin, A., Arslan, S., Arslan, N., Uysal, R., & Sahranc, U. (2015). Self-control management and internet addiction. *International Online Journal of Educational Sciences, 7*(3), 95-100.

Alia-Klein, N., Wang, G., Preston-Campbell, R.N., Moeller, S.J., Parvaz, M.A., Zhu, W., Jayne, M.C., Wong, C., Tomasi, D., Goldstein, R.Z., Fowler, J.S., & Volkow, N.D. (2014). Reactions to media violence: It's in the brain of the beholder. *PLoS ONE, 9*(9): e107260. doi:10.1371/journal.pone.0107260

All about resilience. (N.D.) *Psychology Today.* Retrieved from https://www.psychologytoday.com/us/basics/resilience

Alter, A. (2017). Why our screens make us less happy. *Ted Talk* video. Retrieved from https://www.ted.com/talks/adam_alter_why_our_screens_make_us_less_happy

Anderson, C.A. (2010). Violent video games and other media violence (Part I). *Pediatrics for Parents, 26*(1&2), 28-30.

Anderson, M., & Jinjing, J. (2018). Teens, social media & technology 2018. (*A Pew Research Center Study.*) Retrieved from http://www.pewinternet.org/2018/05/31/teens-social-media-technology-2018/

Appropriate and inappropriate activities for school counselors. (N.D.) *American School Counselor Association*. Retrieved from: https://www.schoolcounselor.org/asca/media/asca/home/appropriate-activities-of-school-counselors.pdf

Awake, online and sleep-deprived—the rise of the teenage "vamper." (2014). *The Conversation*. Retrieved from https://theconversation.com/awake-online-and-sleep-deprived-the-rise-of-the-teenage-vamper-34853

Arain, M., Haque, M., Johal, L., Mathur, P., Nel, W., Rais, A., Sandhu, R., & Sharma, S. (2013). Maturation of the adolescent brain. *Neuropsychiatric Disease and Treatment, 9*, 449-461.

Bale, C. (2011). Raunch or romance? Framing and interpreting the relationship between sexualized culture and young people's sexual health. *Sex Education, 11*(3), 303-313.

Baron, M. (2014, November 4). Natural consequences: What are they and how can I get my teen to face them? *Psychology Today*. (Web log post.) Retrieved from https://www.psychologytoday.com/us/blog/the-verge/201411/natural-consequences

Bayless, K. (N.D.) What is helicopter parenting? *Parents*. Retrieved from https://www.parents.com/parenting/better-parenting/what-is-helicopter-parenting/

Bell, B. (2018). Not all unkindness is bullying. Here's why we need to teach kids to differentiate. *The Washington Post*. Retrieved from https://www.washingtonpost.com/news/parenting/wp/2018/08/16/not-all-unkindness-is-bullying-heres-why-we-need-to-teach-kids-to-differentiate

Bell, W. (2004). Who is really evil? *The Futurist*, 54-59.

Benefits of sports for adolescents. (2019). *University of Missouri Health*

Care Children's Hospital. Retrieved from https://www.muhealth.org/ conditions-treatments/pediatrics/adolescent-medicine/benefits-of- sports

Bergland, C. (2016, September 6). Deconstructing the neurobiology of resilience. *Psychology Today.* (Web log post.) Retrieved from https:// www.psychologytoday.com/us/blog/the-athletes-way/201609/ deconstructing-the-neurobiology-resilience

Bergland, C. (2018, July 5). Growth mindset advice: Take your passion and make it happen! *Psychology Today.* (Web log post.) Retrieved from https://www.psychologytoday.com/us/blog/the-athletes- way/201807/growth-mindset-advice-take-your-passion-and-make-it- happen

Berry, N.B., Dollar, J.M., Calkins, S.D., Keane, S.P., & Shanahan, L. (2018.) Childhood self-regulation as a mechanism through which early overcontrolling parenting is associated with adjustment in preadolescence. *Developmental Psychology, 54*(8), 1542-1554. http:// dx.doi.org/10.1037/dev0000536

Bhardwaj, P. (2017). Yes, colleges check applicants' social media posts. *Consumer Reports.* Retrieved from https://www.consumerreports. org/social-media/colleges-check-applicants-social-media-posts/

Birk, S. (2012). Playing violent video games alters men's brain function: From the annual meeting of the radiological society of north America. *Clinical Psychiatry News, 40*(1), 16. Retrieved June 2018 from Gale Academic One File.

Blachino, A., & Przepiorka, A. (2016). Dysfunction of self-regulation and self-control in Facebook addiction. *Psychiatric Quarterly, 87*, 493-500. doi:10.1007/s11126-015-9403-1

Blad, E. (2014.) In Washington school tragedy, gunman defies 'typical' profile. *Education Week, 34*(11), 6.

Blad, E. (2018). 'Juuling' and teenagers: 3 things principals and teachers need to know. *Education Week.* Retrieved from https://www.

edweek.org/ew/articles/2018/07/18/juuling-and-teenagers-3-things-principals-and.html

Blad, E. (2014). Psychologist: 'He just snapped' a myth in school shootings. *Education Week,* 11.

Bodford, J.E., Kwan, V.S.Y., & Sobota, D.S. (2017). Fatal attractions: Attachment to smartphones predicts anthromorphic beliefs and dangerous behaviors. *Cyberpsychology, Behavior, and Social Networking, 20*(5), 320-326. doi:10.1089/cyber.2016.0500

Bond, B.J. (2016). Following your "friend": Social media and the strength of adolescents' social relationships and media personae. *Cyberpsychology, Behavior, and Social Networking, 19,* 656-660. doi:10.1089/cyber.2016.0355

Boschert, S. (2013). Teen smartphone addiction linked to psychopathology. *Family Practice News, 43*(11), 3. Retrieved September 2018 from Gale Academic One File.

Bowes, L., Maughan, B., Avshalom, C., Moffitt, T.E., & Arseneault, L. (2010). Families promote emotional and behavioural resilience to bullying: Evidence of an environmental effect. *The Journal of Child Psychology and Psychiatry, 51*(7), 809-817.

Bowler, L., Knobel, C., & Mattern, E. (2015). From cyberbullying to well-being: A narrative-based participatory approach to values-oriented design for social media. *Journal of the Association for Information Science and Technology, 66*(6), 1274-1293. doi:10.1002/asi

Brandt, A. (2014, Oct 1). Is your reaction to conflict destroying your relationship? *Psychology Today. (*Web log post.) Retrieved from https://www.psychologytoday.com/us/blog/mindful-anger/201410/is-your-reaction-conflict-destroying-your-relationship

Brown, S.L. (2017). IPad generation's fingers not ready to write, teachers say. *ABC News Australia.* Retrieved from https://www.abc.net.au/news/2017-11-14/ipad-generations-fingers-not-ready-to-write/9143880

Bumgarner, D. (N.D.) *Motivating Your Intelligent But Unmotivated Teenager*. Retrieved from: https://behavior-coach.com/ EbookMotivatingVer3.pdf

Butrymowicz, S. (2017). Most colleges enroll students who aren't prepared for higher education. *PBS*. Retrieved from https://www.pbs.org/ newshour/education/colleges-enroll-students-arent-prepared-higher-education

Carey, M.P., & Forsyth, A.D. (N.D.). Teaching tip sheet: Self-efficacy. *American Psychological Association*. Retrieved from https://www.apa. org/pi/aids/resources/education/self-efficacy.aspx

Carll, E. (2007). Violent video games: Rehearsing aggression. *The Chronicle of Higher Education, 53*(45). Retrieved June 2018 from Gale Academic One File.

Cassidy, S. (2015). Resilience building in students: The role of academic self-efficacy. *Frontiers in Psychology, 6*:1781. doi: 10.3389/ fpsyg.2015.01781

Cassidy, W., Brown, K., & Jackson, M. (2012). "Making kind cool": Parents' suggestions for preventing cyberbullying and fostering cyber kindness. *Journal of Educational Computing Research, 46*(4), 415-436. doi:http://dx.doi.org/10.2190/EC.46.4.fhttp://baywood.com

Chandler, C. (2018, October 14). Helping students hone key communication skills. *Middle Web*. (Web log post.) Retrieved from https://www.middleweb.com/38881/helping-students-hone-key-communication-skills/

Chandra, A. (2016). Social networking sites and digital identity: The utility of provider-adolescent communication. *The Brown University Child and Adolescent Behavior Letter, 32*(3), 5-7. doi:10.1002/cbl

Chang, H.N., & Romero, M. (2008). Present, engaged, and accounted for: The critical impact of addressing chronic absence in the early grades? *National Center for Children in Poverty*. Retrieved from http://www. nccp.org/publications/pub_837.html

Children's mental health facts. (2014.) *National Alliance on Mental Illness.* Retrieved from https://www.nami.org/getattachment/Learn-More/Mental-health-by-the-numbers/childrenmhfacts.pdf

Chronic absenteeism in the nation's schools. (N.D.). *U.S. Department of Education.* Retrieved from https://www2.ed.gov/datastory/chronicabsenteeism.html#intro

Comaford, C. (2018). What stress, change, and isolation do to your brain. *Forbes.* Retrieved from https://www.forbes.com/sites/christinecomaford/2018/10/20/what-stress-change-and-isolation-do-to-your-brain/#5832a3ba1940

Compas, B.E., Hinden, B.R., & Gerhardt, C.A. (1995). Adolescent development: Pathways and processes of risk and resilience. Annual *Review of Psychology, 46,* 265+. Retrieved June 2018 from Gale Academic One File.

Conlan, B. (2018, November 14). Middle school misfortunes then and now, one teacher's take. *Wait Until 8th.* (Web log post.) Retrieved from https://www.waituntil8th.org/blog/2018/11/12/middle-school-misfortunes-then-and-now-one-teachers-take

Cooper, A. (2018). Groundbreaking study examines effects of screen time on kids. *CBS News 60 Minutes.* Retrieved from https://www.cbsnews.com/news/groundbreaking-study-examines-effects-of-screen-time-on-kids-60-minutes/

Costa, D. (2017). Fast forward: Are smartphones hurting our kids? *PC Magazine Digital Edition.* Retrieved from: https://www.pcmag.com/article/356050/are-smartphones-hurting-our-kids

Costa, S. (2016, January 5). Teens, your brain needs real food. *U.S. News & World Report.* Retrieved from https://health.usnews.com/health-news/health-wellness/articles/2016-01-05/teens-your-brain-needs-real-food

Counselor's pamphlet to kids: Are you really being bullied. (2018). *NBC WoodTV.* Retrieved from https://www.woodtv.com/news/kalamazoo-

and-battle-creek/counselor-s-pamphlet-to-kids-are-you-really-being-bullied-/1534331082

Cross, D., & Barnes, A. (2014). Using systems theory to understand and respond to family influences on children's bullying behavior: Friendly schools friendly families program. *Theory Into Practice, 53,* 293-299. doi:10.1080/00405841.2014.947223

Cukier, A. (2017). How to handle your child's perfectionism. *Today's Parent.* Retrieved from https://www.todaysparent.com/family/family-health/nobodys-perfect-how-to-handle-your-childs-perfectionism/

Cullen, K.A., Ambrose, B.K., Gentzke, A.S., Apelberg, B.J., Jamal, A., & King, B.A. (2018). Use of electronic cigarettes and any tobacco product among middle and high school students—United States, 2011-2018. *Morbidity and Morality Weekly Report, 67*(45), 1276-1277.

Curran, T., & Hill, A.P. (2017). Perfectionism is increasing over time: A meta-analysis of cohort differences from 1989 to 2016. *Psychological Bulletin.* Advance online publication. http://dx.doi.org/10.1037/bul0000138

Cyr, B., Berman, S.L., & Smith, M.L. (2015). The role of communication technology in adolescent relationships and identity development. *Child Youth Care Forum, 44,* 79-92. doi:10.1007/s10566-014-9271-0

David, S. (2017) The gift and power of emotional courage. *Ted Talk* video. Retrieved from https://www.ted.com/talks/susan_david_the_gift_and_power_of_emotional_courage

Deadliest mass shootings in modern U.S. history: Fast facts. (2018, November). *CNN.* Retrieved from https://www.cnn.com/2013/09/16/us/20-deadliest-mass-shootings-in-u-s-history-fast-facts/index.html

Deadly lessons: School shooters tell why. (2000). *Chicago Sun-Times.* (Compilation of newspaper articles.) Retrieved from ERIC September 29, 2018.

Degraff, J. (2017, July 20). Your worldview is your greatest strength. *Psychology Today.* (Web log post.) Retrieved from https://www.

psychologytoday.com/us/blog/innovation-you/201707/your-worldview-is-your-greatest-strength

Diaz, A. (2018). Parents of Parkland victims are outraged about a new video game that would let players shoot up a school. *CNN*. Retrieved from https://www.cnn.com/2018/05/28/us/active-shooter-video-game-steam-valve-trnd

Divecha, D. (2017, November 30). Teenagers might have a problem with respect but it's not one you think. *Developmental Science*. (Web log post.) Retrieved from http://www.developmentalscience.com/blog/2017/11/29/teenagers-might-have-a-problem-with-respect-but-its-not-the-one-you-think

Dr. Reid Meloy. (N.D.) *Dr. Reid Meloy*. Retrieved from http://drreidmeloy.com/bio/

Drash, W. (2018). What parents should know about the 'huge epidemic' of vaping. *CNN*. Retrieved from https://www.cnn.com/2018/11/17/health/vaping-ecigarette-fda-parenting/index.html

Duckworth, A. (2016). *Grit: The Power of Passion and Perseverance*. New York: Scribner.

Duckworth, A. (2016). *Q & A. Grit: The Power of Passion and Perseverance*. Retrieved from https://angeladuckworth.com/qa/

Dutta, R. & Truax, J. (2018). How pervasive are procrastination and delay behaviors in young adults and what is the role of perceived parenting? *North American Journal of Psychology, 20*(2), 355. Retrieved June 2018 from Gale Academic One File.

Dweck, C.S. (2006). *Mindset: The New Psychology of Success*. New York: Penguin Random House.

Dweck, C.S., Walton, G.M., & Cohen, G.L. (2014). Academic tenacity: Mindsets and skills that promote long-term learning. *Bill & Melinda Gates Foundation*. Retrieved from https://ed.stanford.edu/sites/default/files/manual/dweck-walton-cohen-2014.pdf

Dwyer, C. (2018). U.S. life expectancy drops amid 'disturbing' rise in overdoses and suicides. *National Public Radio.* Retrieved from https://www.npr.org/2018/11/29/671844884/u-s-life-expectancy-drops-amid-disturbing-rise-in-overdoses-and-suicides

Education rankings. (N.D.). *U.S. News & World Report.* Retrieved from https://www.usnews.com/news/best-states/rankings/education

Ehmke, R. (N.D.) How using social media affects teenagers. *Child Mind Institute.* Retrieved from: https://childmind.org/article/how-using-social-media-affects-teenagers/

Emanuel, R., Bell, R., Cotton, C., Craig, J., Drummond, D., Gibson, S., Harris, A., Harris, M., Hatcher-Vance, C., Jones, S., Lewis, J., Longmire, T., Nash, B., Ryans, T., Tyre, E., Walters, D., & Williams, A. (2015.) The truth about smartphone addiction. *College Student Journal, 49*(2), 291-299.

Estroff Marano, H. (2014, January 31). Helicopter parenting—It's worse than you think. *Psychology Today.* (Web log post.) Retrieved from https://www.psychologytoday.com/us/blog/nation-wimps/201401/helicopter-parenting-its-worse-you-think

Everybody Loves Raymond. (1996-2005). CBS; Worldwide Pants.

Facts for families: Teen brain: Behavior, problem solving, and decision making. (2016). *American Academy of Child & Adolescent Psychiatry.* Retrieved from http://www.aacap.org/aacap/fffprint/article_print.aspx?dn=The-Teen-Brain-Behavior-Problem-Solving-and-Decision-Making-095

Fairfield Stokes, E. (2014). College professor warns: How not to be a lawnmower parent. *Grown and Flown.* (Web log post.) Retrieved from https://grownandflown.com/college-professor-warns-lawnmower-parent/

Faller, G. (2001). Positive psychology: A paradigm shift. *Journal of Pastoral Counseling, 36*(7): 7-20.

Fancher, K. (N.D.). College professor warns: How not to be a lawnmower parent. *Grown and Flown.* (Web log post.) Retrieved from https://

grownandflown.com/college-professor-warns-lawnmower-parent/

Fink, J. (2018). Teacher claims she was fired for violating 'no zero' policy by not giving credit to students who didn't turn in project. *Newsweek*. Retrieved from https://www.newsweek.com/teacher-claims-she-was-fired-violating-no-zero-policy-not-giving-students-who-1137573

Fink, J.L.W. (2013). True Grit: 10 tips for promoting strength, resilience, and perseverance among your students. *Scholastic Instructor*, 26-31.

Flett, G. (2012). The price of perfectionism. *Association for Psychological Science*. Retrieved from https://www.psychologicalscience.org/observer/the-price-of-perfectionism

Follman, M. (2015). Trigger warnings: Inside the race to identify and stop the next mass shooter. *Mother Jones*, 23-29.

Footloose. (1984). Paramount Pictures; Phoenix Pictures; IndieProd Company Productions.

Free, C. (2017). Florida high school students start lunch club so no one eats alone: 'Relationships are build from across the table'. *People*. Retrieved from https://people.com/human-interest/florida-high-school-students-start-lunch-club-no-one-eats-alone/

Frisen, A., Jonsson, A., & Persson, C. (2007). Adolescents' perception of bullying: Who is the victim? Who is the bully? What can be done to stop bullying? *Adolescence, 42*(168), 749-761.

Fritz, G.K. (Ed.) (2015). Cyberbullying linked to mental health problems in teens; protective factor seen in family dinners. *The Brown University Child and Adolescent Behavior Letter*, 4-5.

Fritz, G.K. (Ed.) (2009). Psychiatric symptoms may predict internet addiction in teens. *The Brown University Child and Adolescent Behavior Letter*, 3-4.

Fritz, G.K. (Ed.) (2012). Teaching your child not to be a bully. *The Brown University Child and Adolescent Behavior Letter*, 11-12.

Fuller, T. (N.D.) Stop relying on teachers to teach our kids to be good people! *Bored Teachers*. (Web log post.) Retrieved from https://www.

boredteachers.com/inspiring/stop-relying-on-teachers-to-teach-our-kids-to-be-good-people

Gao, X., Weng, L., Zhou, Y., & Yu, H. (2017). The influence of empathy and morality of violent video game characters on gamers' aggression. *Frontiers in Psychology, 8*:1863. doi: 10.3389/fpsyg.2017.01863

GenZ: Leaders of the mobile social movement. (2017.) (*AwesomenessTV* survey.) Retrieved from: https://awesomenesstv.com/genz/

Genzale, T.J. (2008). Beyond the bully. *Scholastic Parent & Child,* 68.

Giesler, R. (N.D.) Parents' guide to teens and cell phones. *Children's Hospital Los Angeles.* (Web log post.) Retrieved from https://www.chla.org/blog/rn-remedies/parents-guide-teens-and-cell-phones

Godlasky, A., & Dastagir, A.E. (2018). Suicide rate up 33% in less than 20 years, yet funding lags behind other top killers. *WFAA.* Retrieved from https://www.wfaa.com/article/news/nation-world/suicide-rate-up-33-in-less-than-20-years-yet-funding-lags-behind-other-top-killers/618827777

Goldsmith, B. (2011, Nov 11). 9 communication tips to help improve your life. *Psychology Today.* (Web log post.) Retrieved from https://www.psychologytoday.com/us/blog/emotional-fitness/201111/9-communication-tips-help-improve-your-life

Gonzalez, Tiphanie. (2010). *Why kids kill: Inside the minds of school shooters.* (Book review of *Why Kids Kill: Inside the Minds of School Shooters,* by P. Langman). *Professional School Counseling, 13*(5). Retrieved from Education Research Complete.

Goral, T. (2016). Spotting the danger signs in schools: Interview of J. Reid Meloy. *District Administration,* 12-14.

Gorman, G. (2017). It's good for kids to climb trees. *News.com.au.* Retrieved from https://www.news.com.au/lifestyle/parenting/kids/its-good-for-kids-to-climb-trees/news-story/9e8c775123e39530eb66c6846141b4bd

Goudarzi, S. (2006). Why teens don't care. *Live Science.* Retrieved from https://www.livescience.com/7151-study-teens-care.html

Gray, P. (2015, September 22). Declining student resilience: A serious problem for colleges. *Psychology Today.* (Web log post.) Retrieved from https://www.psychologytoday.com/us/blog/freedom-learn/201509/declining-student-resilience-serious-problem-colleges

Grover, S. (2016, April 24). The 3 types of children who bully their parents. *Psychology Today.* (Web log post.) Retrieved from https://www.psychologytoday.com/us/blog/when-kids-call-the-shots/201604/the-3-types-children-who-bully-their-parents

Gun violence archive 2018. (2018) (List of current statistics.) *Gun Violence Archive.* Retrieved from: https://www.gunviolencearchive.org/

Hae-Jung Song, E., Anderson, J. (2001). How violent video games may violate children's health. *Contemporary Pediatrics, 18*(5), 102-120.

Haller, S. (2018). Helicopter parenting actually makes life harder for your kids, not easier. *USA Today.* Retrieved from https://www.usatoday.com/story/life/allthemoms/2018/06/25/helicopter-parenting-study-linked-negative-effects-kids/731026002/

Haller, S. (2018). Meet the 'lawnmower parent' the new helicopter parents of 2018. *USA Today.* Retrieved from https://www.usatoday.com/story/life/allthemoms/2018/09/19/meet-lawnmower-parent-new-helicopter-parents-types-parents-tiger-attachment/1347358002/

Handby Hudgens, L. (2018). How to fix the apathy problem in schools. *The News & Observer.* Retrieved from https://www.newsobserver.com/opinion/op-ed/article81668307.html

Hansen, R., & Diliberti, M. (2018). What are threat assessment teams and how prevalent are they in public schools? *National Center for Education Statistics* blog. Retrieved from https://nces.ed.gov/blogs/nces/post/what-are-threat-assessment-teams-and-how-prevalent-are-they-in-public-schools

Hartung, K., Cullinane, S, & Yan, H. (2019). Parkland mourns 2 student suicides a year after Stoneman Douglas shooting. Now parents are

urged to be alert. *CNN.* Retrieved from https://www.cnn.
com/2019/03/25/us/parkland-shooting-support/index.html

Harter, S., Low, S.M., Whitesell, N.R. (2003). What we have learned from Columbine: The impact of the self-system on suicidal and violent ideation among adolescents. *Journal of School Violence, 2*(3), 3-26.

Herge, W.M., LaGreca, A.M., & Chan, S.F. (2016). Adolescent peer victimization and physical health problems. *Journal of Pediatric Psychology, 41*(1), 15-27. doi:10.1093/jpepsy/jsv050

Hinduja, S., & Patchin, J. (2018.) Teen sexting: A brief guide for educators and parents. *Cyberbullying Research Center.* Retrieved from: https:// cyberbullying.org/sexting-a-brief-guide-for-educators-and-parents

Hoffman, J. (2018). The price of cool: A teenager, a JUUL and nicotine addiction. *The New York Times.* Retrieved from https://www.nytimes. com/2018/11/16/health/vaping-juul-teens-addiction-nicotine.html

Holt, M.K., Kantor, G.K., Finkhelhor, D. (2009). Parent/child concordance about bullying involvement and family characteristics related to bullying and peer victimization. *Journal of School Violence, 8*, 42-63. doi:10.1080/15388220802067813

Hwang, Y.G. (1995). Student apathy, lack of self-responsibility and false self-esteem are failing American schools. *Education, 115*(4), 484-489.

Ihm, J. (2018). Social implications of children's smartphone addiction: The role of support networks and social engagement. *Journal of Behavioral Addictions, 7*(2), 473-481. doi:10.1556/2006.7.2018.48

Irimia, C. (2010). Empathy as a source of attitude change. *Contemporary Readings in Law and Social Justice, 2*(2), 319-324.

Ives, E.A. (2012). *iGeneration: The social cognitive effects of digital technology on teenagers.* (Master's thesis). Retrieved from https:// scholar.dominican.edu/masters-theses/92

Jiang, J. (2018). How teens and parents navigate screen time and device distracations. (*A Pew Research Center Report.*) Retrieved from http:// www.pewinternet.org/2018/08/22/how-teens-and-parents-navigate-screen-time-and-device-distractions/

Jimenez, D.E., Bartels, S.J., Cardenas, V., Daliwal, S.S., & Alegria, M. (2012). Cultural beliefs and mental health treatment preferences of ethnically diverse older adult consumers in primary care. *The American Journal of Geriatric Psychiatry, 20*(6), 533-542. https://doi.org/10.1097/JGP.0b013e318227f876

Jimenez, L., Sargrad, S., Morales, J., & Thompson, M. (2016). Remedial education: The cost of catching up. *Center for American Progress.* Retrieved from https://www.americanprogress.org/issues/education-k-12/reports/2016/09/28/144000/remedial-education/

Jolly, J. (2018). Facebook adds tools to curb screen addiction: I tried it with my teen. *WFAA.* Retrieved from https://www.wfaa.com/article/news/nation-now/facebook-adds-tools-to-curb-screen-addiction-i-tried-it-with-my-teen/465-91db2a26-8192-49ba-bbd9-02b4d5817f9e

Kamenetz, A. (2018). The 'overparenting' crisis in school and at home. *National Public Radio.* Retrieved https://www.npr.org/sections/ed/2018/07/24/628042168/the-over-parenting-crisis-in-school-and-at-home

Keaten, J., & Cheng, M. (2018). Compulsive video-game playing now new mental health problem, says WHO. *WFAA.* Retrieved from https://www.wfaa.com/article/news/nation-world/compulsive-video-game-playing-now-new-mental-health-problem-says-who/565245304

Kennedy-Paine, C., & Crepeau-Hobson, F. (2015). FBI study of active shooter incidents: Implications for school psychologists. *Communique, 43*(7), 1-23.

Khazan, O. (2018). 'Find your passion' is awful advice. *The Atlantic.* Retrieved from https://www.theatlantic.com/science/archive/2018/07/find-your-passion-is-terrible-advice/564932/

Kids competing with mobile phones for parents' attention. (2015, June). *AVG Technologies* online survey. Retrieved from https://now.avg.com/digital-diaries-kids-competing-with-mobile-phones-for-parents-attention

Klein, A. (2015). No child left behind: An overview. *Education Week*. Retrieved from https://www.edweek.org/ew/section/multimedia/no-child-left-behind-overview-definition-summary.html

Know the signs. (2016). Sandy Hook Promise. Retrieved from https://www.sandyhookpromise.org/preventionprograms?lightbox=0#say-something

Kohn, D. (2001). Columbine: Were there warning signs? *CBS News*. Retrieved from https://www.cbsnews.com/news/columbine-were-there-warning-signs/

Kolbert, J.B., Schultz, D., Crothers, L.M. (2014). Bullying prevention and the parent involvement model. *Journal of School Counseling, 12*(7), 1-20.

Kraayenbrink, A., Skaar, N., & Clopton, K. (2018). Using mindfulness to promote resilience. *Communique, 46*(8), 1-33.

Lamia, M.C.. (2010, October 30). Do bullies actually lack empathy? *Psychology Today*. (Web log post.) Retrieved from https://www.psychologytoday.com/us/blog/intense-emotions-and-strong-feelings/201010/do-bullies-actually-lack-empathy

LaMotte, S. (2018). E-cigarette warnings to arrive in high school bathrooms nationwide. *CNN*. Retrieved from https://www.cnn.com/2018/09/18/health/e-cigarette-fda-prevention-campaign/index.html

LaMotte, S. (2018). Limit screen time to protect your child's heart, American Heart Association says. *CNN*. Retrieved from https://www.cnn.com/2018/08/07/health/screen-time-children-heart-health/index.html

Landrum, S. (2017). Why millennials are struggling with mental health at work. *Forbes*. Retrieved from https://www.forbes.com/sites/sarahlandrum/2017/01/17/why-millennials-are-struggling-with-mental-health-at-work/#7f71da3e4a9b

Lange, N.L. (2018, August 15). Natalie Lacy Lange, Brenham ISD School Board. *Facebook.* (Web log post.) Retrieved from https://www.facebook.com/NatalieLangeForBrenhamSchoolBoard/posts/1886115798138897?__tn__=K-R

Lawmakers shouldn't ignore sensible gun restrictions when adopting school safety plans. (2018, August 7). *Star Telegram.* Retrieved from https://www.star-telegram.com/opinion/editorials/article216254960.html

Lawnmower parents are setting their kids up for failure. (N.D.). *Bored Teachers.* (Web log post.) Retrieved from https://www.boredteachers.com/trending/lawnmower-parents

Lawnmower parents are the new helicopter parents & we are not here for it. (2018, August 30). *We are Teachers.* (Web log post.) Retrieved from https://www.weareteachers.com/lawnmower-parents/

Lenhart, A., Ling, R., Campbell, S., & Purcell, K. (2010). Chapter two: How phones are used with friends—What they can do and how teens use them. (*A Pew Research Center Report.*) Retrieved from http://www.pewinternet.org/2010/04/20/chapter-two-how-phones-are-used-with-friends-what-they-can-do-and-how-teens-use-them/

Lenhart, A., Smith, A., Anderson, M., Duggan, M., & Perrin, A. (2015). Teens, technology & friendships: Video games, social media and mobile phones play an integral role in how teens meet and interact with friends. (*A Pew Research Center Report.*) Retrieved from http://www.pewinternet.org/2015/08/06/teens-technology-and-friendships/

Levermore, M.A. (2004). Violent media and video games, and their role in creating violent youth. *The Forensic Examiner,* 38-41.

Little House on the Prairie. (1974-1983). NBC; Ed Friendly Productions.

Lopez, R. (2018). Texas Congressional leaders say more needs to be done on gun violence. *WFAA.* Retrieved from https://www.wfaa.com/article/news/texas-congressional-leaders-say-more-needs-to-be-done-on-gun-violence/612800028

Lukianoff, G. (2018) Are we setting up a generation for failure? *CNN* video. Retrieved from https://www.cnn.com/videos/tv/2018/10/31/exp-social-challenges-facing-igeneration.cnn

Lythcott-Haims, J. (2015) How to raise successful kids—without over-parenting. *Ted Talk* video. Retrieved from https://www.ted.com/talks/julie_lythcott_haims_how_to_raise_successful_kids_without_over_parenting

McAlister, A. (2018). The ABCs of Gen X, Y(P), Z: Teen girls and the pressure of perfection. *American Music Teacher, 68*(1), 40-42.

McAlone, N. (2017). Young people spend about twice as much time watching Netflix as live TV, and even more time on YouTube. *Business Insider.* Retrieved from https://www.businessinsider.com/teens-watching-netflix-youtube-more-than-tv-2017-5

McDaniels, A.K. (2016). Pediatric researchers suggest potential dangers for children from cellphone exposure. *The Baltimore Sun.* Retrieved from https://www.baltimoresun.com/health/blog/bal-cell-phones-child-brain-story.html

McLean, L., & Griffiths, M.D. (2013). Violent video games and attitudes towards victims of crime: An empirical study among youth. International *Journal of Cyber Behavior, Psychology and Learning, 2*(3), 1-16.

Maciag, M. (2018). Chronic absenteeism a major problem in U.S. schools. *Governing.* Retrieved http://www.governing.com/topics/education/gov-chronic-absenteeism-schools.html

Mandel, B. (2018). Rewarding failure has become an American epidemic. *New York Post.* Retrieved from https://nypost.com/2018/06/02/rewarding-failure-has-become-an-american-epidemic/

Massari, L. (2011). Teaching emotional intelligence. *Leadership, 40*(5), 8-12.

Matthews, D. (2017, November 23). Turn off that smartphone, Mom and Dad! *Psychology Today.* (Web log post.) Retrieved from https://www.

psychologytoday.com/us/blog/going-beyond-intelligence/201711/
turn-smartphone-mom-and-dad

Miller, S., & McCoy, K. (2018). Thousand Oaks makes 307 mass shootings
in 311 days. *WFAA*. Retrieved from https://www.wfaa.com/article/
news/nation-world/thousand-oaks-makes-307-mass-shootings-in-
311-days/612764844

Moran, T.M. (2018). Concerning bullies. *The Humanist,* 40-41.

Morehouse, R. (2016). *Grit: The Power of Passion and Perseverance.*
(Review of the book *Grit: The Power of Passion and Perseverance*, by
A. Duckworth.) *Canadian Journal of Education, 39*(4): 1-4.

Morsunbui, U. (2015). The effect of identity development self-esteem,
low self-control and gender on aggression in adolescence and
emerging adulthood. *Eurasian Journal of Educational Research, 61,*
99-116. http://dx.doi.org/10.14689/ejer.2015.61.6

Most famous social network sites worldwide as of October 2018, ranked
by number of active users (in millions). *Statista.* Retrieved January 1,
2019 from https://www.statista.com/statistics/272014/global-social-
networks-ranked-by-number-of-users/

Mulvahill, E. (2018, January 4). Why good teachers quit teaching. (Web
log post.) *We Are Teachers.* Retrieved from https://www.
weareteachers.com/why-teachers-quit/

Myruski, S., Gulyayeva, O., Birk, S., Perez-Edgar, K., Buss, K.A., & Dennis-
Tiwary, T.A. (2018). Digital disruption? Maternal mobile device use is
related to infant social-emotional functioning. *Developmental Science.*
doi: 10.1111/desc.12610. Epub 2017 Sep 24

Narayanan, A., & Betts, L. (2014). Bullying behaviors and victimization
experiences among adolescent students: The role of resilience.
The Journal of Genetic Psychology, 175(2), 134-146. doi:
10.1080/00221325.2013.834290

Natanson, H. (2018). Yes, teens are texting and using social media instead
of reading books, researchers say. *The Washington Post.* Retrieved

from https://www.washingtonpost.com/news/inspired-life/
wp/2018/08/20/for-american-teens-texting-and-social-media-are-
replacing-books/?utm_term=.922a66e8bfc8

Neighmond, P. (2014). For the children's sake, put down that smartphone.
National Public Radio. Retrieved from https://www.npr.org/sections/
health-shots/2014/04/21/304196338/for-the-childrens-sake-put-
down-that-smartphone

Nicolaus, P. (2018). When teens bully themselves. *Psychology Today,
51*(2), 16.

Niz, E.S. (N.D.). Kids feel unimportant to cell phone-addicted parents.
Parenting. *Parenting.* Retrieved from https://www.parenting.com/
news-break/kids-feel-unimportant-to-cell-phone-addicted-parents

Papatraianou, L.H., Levine, D., & West, D. (2014). Resilience in the face of
cyberbullying: An ecological perspective on young people's
experiences of online adversity. *Pastoral Care in Education, 32*(4),
264-283. http://dx.doi.org/10.1080/02643944.2014.974661

Paradice, D. (2017). An analysis of U.S. school shooting data (1840-2015).
Education, 138(20), 135-144.

Park, A. (2016). Cell-phone distracted parenting can have long-term
consequences: Study. *Time.* Retrieved from http://time.com/4168688/
cell-phone-distracted-parenting-can-have-long-term-consequences-
study/

Patchin, J.W. (2017). New teen sexting data. Cyberbullying Research
Center. *Cyberbullying.* Retrieved from https://cyberbullying.org/new-
teen-sexting-data

Paul, K. (2018.) This is what happens when you take phones away from
teenagers. *MarketWatch.* Retrieved from https://www.marketwatch.
com/story/this-is-what-happens-when-you-take-phones-away-from-
teenagers-2018-08-22

Perkins-Gough, D. (2013). The significance of grit: A conversation with
Angela Lee Duckworth. *Educational Leadership,* 14-20.

Pickhardt, C.E. (2012, May 28). Adolescent apathy and what loss of caring can mean. *Psychology Today.* (Web log post.) Retrieved from https://www.psychologytoday.com/us/blog/surviving-your-childs-adolescence/201205/adolescent-apathy-and-what-loss-caring-can-mean

Phorn, B. (2018) Teen accused of killing mom and burying her in a fire pit after an argument over his D grade. *ABCNews.* Retrieved from https://abcnews.go.com/US/teen-accused-killing-mom-burying-fire-pit-argument/story?id=58941450

Poland, S. (2012). What we know about school shooters. *District Administration,* 38-39.

Popcorn lung: A dangerous risk of flavored e-cigarettes. (2016). *American Lung Association.* Retrieved from https://www.lung.org/about-us/blog/2016/07/popcorn-lung-risk-ecigs.html

Porter, G., Starcevic, V., Berle, D., & Fenech, P. (2010). Recognizing problem video game use. *Australian and New Zealand Journal of Psychiatry, 44,* 120-128.

Prooday, V. (N.D.) The silent tragedy affecting today's children. *FaithIt.* Retrieved from https://faithit.com/silent-tragedy-affecting-todays-children-victoria-prooday/

Quast, L. (2017). Why grit is more important than IQ when you're trying to become successful. *Forbes.* Retrieved from https://www.forbes.com/sites/lisaquast/2017/03/06/why-grit-is-more-important-than-iq-when-youre-trying-to-become-successful/#205a3af67e45

Quigley, R. (2014). Empowering our children to succeed. *Reclaiming Children and Youth, 23*(1), 24-27.

Rausch, J.L., Lovett, C.R., & Walker, C.O. (2003). Indicators of resiliency among elementary school students at-risk. *The Qualitative Report, 8*(4), 570-590.

Remember the Titans. (2000). Jerry Bruckheimer Films; Run It Up Productions Inc.; Technical Black; Walt Disney Pictures.

Richardson, A. (2019, March 13). Message to students and parents: As a CEO, I'm 10x more interested in your failures than your perfection. *LinkedIn*. Retrieved from https://www.linkedin.com/pulse/message-students-parents-ceo-im-10x-more-interested-your-richardson/

Rickwood, B.R., & Pilgrim, D. (2011). Promoting youth mental health through early intervention. *Advances in Mental Health, 10*(1); 3-5.

Rideout, V.J., Foehr, U.G., & Roberts, D.F. (2010). Generation M2: Media in the lives of 8- to 18-year-olds. (*A Kaiser Family Foundation Study.*) Retrieved from https://www.kff.org/other/event/generation-m2-media-in-the-lives-of/

Rieff, C., Camodeca, M. Empathy in adolescence: Relations with emotion awareness and social roles. *British Journal of Developmental Psychology, 34,* 340-353.

Riutzel, K. (2018). Cellphones in classrooms contribute to failing grades: Study. *ABC News*. Retrieved from https://abcnews.go.com/Health/cellphones-classrooms-contribute-failing-grades-study/story?id=56837614

Robinson, C. (2017). Growth mindset in the classroom. *Science Scope,* 18-21.

Rosenberg, E. (2019). A 19-year-old dies by suicide one year after surviving the Parkland school shooting. *The Washington Post*. Retrieved from https://www.washingtonpost.com/education/2019/03/22/year-old-takes-her-own-life-year-after-surviving-parkland-shooting/?noredirect=on&utm_term=.af2c406db6ba

Sagiv Riebling, R. (N.D.) Discipline your kids with natural consequences. *Parents*. Retrieved from https://www.parents.com/parenting/better-parenting/positive/disciplining-with-natural-consequences/

Sales, N.J. (2016). American girls: How social media is disrupting the lives of teenagers. *Time*. Retrieved from http://time.com/americangirls/

Sales of JUUL e-cigarettes skyrocket, posing danger to youth. (2018).

Centers for Disease Control and Prevention. Retrieved from https://
www.cdc.gov/media/releases/2018/p1002-e-Cigarettes-sales-danger-
youth.html

Samples, Susan. (2018). School counselors: Overuse of word 'bullying'
problematic. *NBC WoodTV*. Retrieved from https://www.woodtv.
com/news/kent-county/school-counselors-overuse-of-word-bullying-
problematic/1569729905

Sandy Hook Promise--Evan. (2016). *Sandy Hook Promise*. (YouTube
video). Retrieved from https://www.youtube.com/
watch?v=A8syQeFtBKc

Saturday Night Live. (1975-). NBC; NBC Productions.

Savoca Gibson, J. (2018). I am 18. I belong to the massacre generation.
Chicago Tribune. Retrieved from https://www.chicagotribune.
com/news/opinion/commentary/ct-perspec-generation-massacre-
parkland-lockdown-drills-active-shooter-tree-of-life-1102-story.html

Schachter, R. (2011). Can kindness be taught? *Instructor, 120*(4), 58-63.

Scheff, S. (2017, December 13). Teens tell us how they are stopping
cyberbullying. *Psychology Today*. (Web log post.) Retrieved from
https://www.psychologytoday.com/us/blog/shame-nation/201712/
teens-tell-us-how-they-are-stopping-cyberbullying

Schiffrin, H.H., & Liss, M. (2017). The effects of helicopter parenting on
academic motivation. *Journal of Child & Family Studies, 26*, 1472-
1480. doi:10.1007/s10826-017-0658-z

Schnarch, D. (2011, May 23). People who can't control themselves try to
control others. *Psychology Today*. (Web log post.) Retrieved
from https://www.psychologytoday.com/us/blog/intimacy-and-
desire/201105/people-who-cant-control-themselves-try-control-
others

Schweizer, A., Berchtold, A., Barrense-Dias, Y., Akre, C., & Suris, J. (2017).
Adolescents with a smartphone sleep less than their peers. *European
Journal of Pediatrics, 176*, 131-136. doi:10.1007/s00431-016-2823-6

Scutti, S. (2018). JUUL to eliminate social media accounts, stop retail sales of flavors. *CNN*. Retrieved from https://www.cnn.com/2018/11/13/health/juul-flavor-social-media-fda-bn/index.html

Scutti, S. (2018). Males may be more likely to become addicted to gaming, say researchers. *CNN*. Retrieved from https://www.cnn.com/2018/11/28/health/male-brain-internet-gaming-disorder

Seaman, M. (2012). Beyond anti-bullying programs. *The Education Digest, 78*(1), 24-28.

Shafer, L. (2017). Social media and teen anxiety. *Harvard Graduate School of Education*. Retrieved from https://www.gse.harvard.edu/news/uk/17/12/social-media-and-teen-anxiety

Simmons, R. (2018). Perfectionism among teens is rampant (and we're not helping). *The Washington Post*. Retrieved from https://www.washingtonpost.com/news/parenting/wp/2018/01/25/lets-stop-telling-stressed-out-kids-theyre-putting-too-much-pressure-on-themselves-its-making-things-worse/?utm_term=.d620c7aca990

Smoking & tobacco use fast facts. (N.D.) *Centers for Disease Control and Prevention*. Retrieved from https://www.cdc.gov/tobacco/data_statistics/fact_sheets/fast_facts/index.htm

Smyth, C. (2018, November 5). Connect the dots to ACES. *Facebook*. (Web log post.) Retrieved from https://www.facebook.com/cherylleahsmyth/posts/294267894517207?__tn__=K-R

Stallings, J. (2018). Teacher to parent—A child must be a willing participant in his own education. *Moultrie News*. Retrieved from https://www.moultrienews.com/opinion/teacher-to-parent---a-child-must-be-a/article_d6f11c06-698a-11e8-b017-53c8296979a0.html

Stixrud, W. (2018). It's time to tell your kids it doesn't matter where they go to college. *Time*. Retrieved from http://time.com/5210848/prestigious-college-doesnt-matter/

Stixrud, W., & Johnson, N. (2018). When a college student comes home to stay. *The New York Times*. Retrieved from https://www.nytimes.

com/2018/11/19/well/family/when-a-college-student-comes-home-to-stay.html

Status of mind: Social media and young people's mental health and wellbeing. (N.D.) (*A Royal Society for Public Health Report.*) Retrieved from https://www.rsph.org.uk/our-work/campaigns/status-of-mind.html

Steiner-Adair, C., & Barker, T. (2013). *The Big Disconnect: Protecting Childhood and Family Relationships in the Digital Age.* New York: Harper Collins Publishers.

Supiano, B. (2019, March 13). They're already rich. Why were these parents so fixated on elite colleges? *The Chronicle of Higher Education.* Retrieved from https://www.chronicle.com/article/They-re-Already-Rich-Why/245889?

Sweet, K. (N.D.) Examples of SMART goals in education. *Classroom.* Retrieved from: https://classroom.synonym.com/examples-smart-goals-education-6388837.html

Sutter, J.D. (2012). Survey: 70% of teens hide online behavior from parents. *CNN.* Retrieved from https://www.cnn.com/2012/06/25/tech/web/mcafee-teen-online-survey/index.html

Tamborini, R., Eastin, M.S., Skalski, P., Lachlan, K., Fediuk, T.A., & Brady, R. (2004). Violent virtual video games and hostile thoughts. *Journal of Broadcasting & Electronic Media, 48*(3), 335-357.

Tamborini, R.W., Bowman, N.D., Eden, A., & Skalski, P. (2013). Violence is a many-splintered thing: The importance of realism, justification, and graphicness in understanding perceptions of and preferences for violent films and video games. *Projections, 7*(1), 100-118. doi: 10.3167/proj.2013.010108

Tamburro, C. (2017). Teens & tech: Remaining aware & responsible in the social media age. *Exceptional Parent,* 23-25. Retrieved from https://www.eparent.com/eparent-connect/teens-tech/

Taylor, J. (N.D.) 9 effective communication skills. *Habits for Wellbeing.*

Retrieved from https://www.habitsforwellbeing.com/9-effective-communication-skills/

Technology & teen dating abuse survey. (2007.) (Teenage Research Unlimited study.) *Break the Cycle*. Retrieved from http://www.breakthecycle.org/dating-violence-research/technology-teen-dating-abuse-survey

Teenagers (15-17 years of age). (N.D.) *Centers for Disease Control and Prevention*. Retrieved from https://www.cdc.gov/ncbddd/childdevelopment/positiveparenting/adolescence2.html

Teens and e-cigarettes. (2016). *National Institute on Drug Abuse*. Retrieved from https://www.drugabuse.gov/related-topics/trends-statistics/infographics/teens-e-cigarettes

The iPad is a far bigger threat to our children than anyone realizes. (2017). *Eco News Media*. Retrieved from http://econewsmedia.info/2017/12/29/ipad-far-bigger-threat-children-anyone-realizes/

The Love Boat. (1977-1987). ABC; Aaron Spelling Productions; Douglas S. Cramer Company; The Love Boat Company.

The role of the school counselor. (N.D.) *American School Counselor Association*. Retrieved from https://www.schoolcounselor.org/asca/media/asca/Careers-Roles/RoleStatement.pdf

The role of the school counselor. (N.D.) *American School Counselor Association*. Retrieved from https://www.schoolcounselor.org/administrators/role-of-the-school-counselor

The school counselor and group counseling. (2014.) *American School Counselor Association*. Retrieved from https://www.schoolcounselor.org/asca/media/asca/PositionStatements/PS_Group-Counseling.pdf

Title I. (2018.) *US Department of Education*. Retrieved from https://www2.ed.gov/programs/titleiparta/index.html

Tornio, S. (2018, October 9). We need to do more for teachers who are exhausted, stressed, and burned out. *We Are Teachers*. (Web log post.) Retrieved from https://www.weareteachers.com/teacher-mental-health/

Turner, C. (2018). Empowering kids in an anxious world. *National Public Radio.* Retrieved https://www.npr.org/sections/ed/2018/07/18/620074926/empowering-kids-in-an-anxious-world

Twenge, J. (2017). Analysis: Teens are sleeping less. Why? Smartphones. *PBS.* Retrieved from https://www.pbs.org/newshour/science/analysis-teens-are-sleeping-less-why-smartphones

Twenge, J.M. (2017). Has the smartphone destroyed a generation? *The Atlantic.* Retrieved from https://www.theatlantic.com/magazine/archive/2017/09/has-the-smartphone-destroyed-a-generation/534198/

Twenge, J.M., Joiner, T.E., Rogers, M.L., & Martin, G.N. (2018). Increases in depressive symptoms, suicide-related outcomes, and suicide rates among U.S. adolescents after 2010 and links to increased new media screen time. *Clinical Psychology Science, 6*(1), 3-17. doi:10.1177/2167702617723376

Twenge, J.M., Martin, G.N., & Spitzberg, B.H. (2018). Trends in U.S. adolescents' media use, 1976-2016: The rise of digital media, the decline of TV, and the (near) demise of print. *Psychology of Popular Media Culture. Advance* online publication. http://dx.doi.org/10.1037/ppm0000203

Van Noorden, T.H.J., Cillessen, A.H.N., Haselager, G.J.T., Lansu, T.A.M., & Bukowski, W.M. (2017). Bullying involvement and empathy: Child and target characteristics. *Social Development, 26*(2), 248-262. doi: 10.1111/sode.12197

Vasich, T. (Ed.) (2016). Put the cellphone away! Fragmented baby care can affect brain development. (*University of California Irvine* study.) Retrieved from https://news.uci.edu/2016/01/05/put-the-cellphone-away-fragmented-baby-care-can-affect-brain-development/

Vessey, J.A., & Lee, J.E. (2000). Violent video games affecting our children. *Pediatric Nursing, 26* (6), 607-632.

Walton, A.G. (2017). 6 ways social media affects our mental health. *Forbes*. Retrieved from https://www.forbes.com/sites/alicegwalton/2017/06/30/a-run-down-of-social-medias-effects-on-our-mental-health/#12b6877d2e5a

Walton, A.G. (2016). Taking a break from Facebook may boost mental health, study finds. *Forbes*. Retrieved from https://www.forbes.com/sites/alicegwalton/2016/12/23/want-mental-health-for-the-holidays-take-a-break-from-facebook-study-says/#71a9ca1d5ce6

Warnick, B.R., Kim, S.H., Robinson, S. (2015). Gun violence and the meaning of American schools. *Educational Theory, 65*(4), 371-386.

Warning signs for bullying. (N.D.). *Stopbullying.gov*. Retrieved from https://www.stopbullying.gov/at-risk/warning-signs/index.html

Webb, S. (2018). Spike in mental health issues, suicidal thoughts alarms Texas school counselors. *Houston Chronicle*. Retrieved from https://www.houstonchronicle.com/news/houston-texas/houston/article/Spike-in-mental-health-issues-suicidal-thoughts-13360931.php

What I can't control. What I can control (infograph). (2018, October 14). Children's Advocacy Center for Denton County. *Facebook*. (Web log post.) Retrieved from https://www.facebook.com/CACDC/posts/10157985057908986

What is bullying? (N.D.). *Stopbullying.gov*. Retrieved from https://www.stopbullying.gov/what-is-bullying/index.html

What is cyberbullying? (N.D.). *Stopbullying.gov*. Retrieved from https://www.stopbullying.gov/cyberbullying/what-is-it/index.html

Wiederhold, B.K. (2016). Low self-esteem and teens' internet addiction: What have we learned in the last 20 years? *Cyberpsychology, Behavior, and Social Networking, 19*, 359. doi:10.1089/cyber.2016.29037.bkw

Willis, J. (2013, May 25). What to do about your teenager's "eye-roll." *Psychology Today*. (Web log post.) Retrieved from https://www.psychologytoday.com/us/blog/radical-teaching/201305/what-do-about-your-teenager-s-eye-roll

Wood, A.H. (2018, February 27). Ten reasons middle schoolers don't need social media. *Today.* (Web log post.) Retrieved from http://community.today.com/parentingteam/post/ten-reasons-middle-schoolers-dont-need-social-media

Woodard, T. (2018). Mother of Columbine shooter speaks in Dallas: 'I hated what he did, but I never hated him'. *WFAA.* Retrieved from https://www.wfaa.com/article/news/mother-of-columbine-shooter-speaks-in-dallas-i-hated-what-he-did-but-i-never-hated-him/287-610449882

Woodruff, S. (2018). A new prescription for depression: Join a team and get sweaty. *National Public Radio.* Retrieved from https://www.npr.org/sections/health-shots/2018/10/22/656594050/a-new-prescription-for-depression-join-a-team-and-get-sweaty

Worley, B. (2018). Can't get your kids off their devices? These automatic kill switches can help. *Good Morning America.* Retrieved from https://www.goodmorningamerica.com/family/story/kids-off-devices-automatic-kill-switches-58977043

Worley, B. (2018). Why you should get your kid a flip phone instead of a smartphone in 2018. *Good Morning America.* Retrieved from https://www.goodmorningamerica.com/family/story/kid-flip-phone-smartphone-2018-58997293

Yan, H. (2019). The father of a Sandy Hook victim dies from an apparent suicide. *CNN.* Retrieved from https://www.cnn.com/2019/03/25/us/sandy-hook-victim-father-jeremy-richman-suicide/index.html

Yeager, D.S., & Dweck, C.S. (2012). Mindsets that promote resilience: When students believe that personal characteristics can be developed. *Educational Psychologist, 47*(4), 302-314. doi:10.1080/00461520.2012.722805

Yilmaz, S.H., Bilgic, A., & Isik, U. (2015). Internet addiction is related to attention deficit but not hyperactivity in a sample of high school students. *International Journal of Psychiatry in Clinical Practice, 19,*

18-23. doi:10.3109/13651501.2014.979834

Young Teens (12-14 years of age). (N.D.) *Centers for Disease Control and Prevention.* Retrieved from https://www.cdc.gov/ncbddd/childdevelopment/positiveparenting/adolescence.html

Index

$\mathcal{D}$

104, 132, 134, 163, 200, 216, 241, 245, 250, 257, 264

grit, 42, 46-47, 59, 92, 104, 233, 241, 259

growth mindset, 42, 46-47, 59, 92, 131

guidance, 6, 14, 64, 68, 73, 89, 105, 120, 131, 158-159, 195, 198, 201

guns, 31-37, 207-209, 216, 218, 222, 228, 281, 283

H

habit, 3, 25-27, 54, 77, 85, 91-92, 97, 104, 119, 130, 132, 150, 152-154, 171-172, 176, 178, 186, 198, 202, 220, 242, 244, 246, 261, 263-264, 266, 275

hate, 1, 2, 4, 21-22, 28, 31, 36, 111, 132, 212, 235-236, 247-248, 270-272, 283

hopelessness /hope, 1, 4, 6, 23, 31, 38, 59, 72, 84, 112, 121, 137, 156, 177, 197, 202, 209, 213, 221, 234, 237, 239, 258, 273, 280

I

insecurity, 122, 147, 163, 165

Instagram, 5, 114, 143, 146, 162, 166, 220, 248, 272

internet, 1, 2, 5, 27, 53, 74, 100, 111, 118, 141-143, 145, 148, 150-151, 157-158, 161-162, 167, 171, 175, 177, 198, 212, 221-222, 279

intervention, 62, 102, 117, 122-123, 183-186, 188-189, 194, 212-213, 216-219, 223-224, 227, 241-242, 257, 286

intolerance/tolerance, 1, 22, 28, 73, 123, 236, 270

J

JUUL/JUULing, 176-178, 237

K

kindness,2, 132, 137, 234, 256-257, 271-272

L

limits, 75, 93-94, 145, 160, 172, 175, 263

lonely/loneliness, 93, 146-147, 155, 166, 212

M

N

O

P

R

S

T

About the Author

Lisa Wright is a Texas public high school counselor whose career in education began almost three decades ago and includes twenty years as a middle school/junior high and high school teacher. Wright has observed the changes in students and the educational system brought about by the advent of technology and cell phones, by education mandates designed to help kids, and by evolving parenting styles, all of which were well-intentioned but have at times resulted in unintended negative consequences. Wright has witnessed the evolution of schools and the educational system as school shootings have happened again and again. Wright's experience over three decades of a changing educational landscape and her research bring a unique perspective to her discussion of modern student and school issues. She addresses those issues head-on while including ways both parents and educators can help their kids/students. Wright promotes open discussion so that educators and parents can unite to work together to make our schools and our world safer places and our kids more resilient future adults.

Find Me Online

Let's talk.
I would love to hear from you—
your stories and experiences.
Thoughts, comments, ideas—
all are welcome.

www.lisawrightauthor.com
@thelisawauthor